FRAUD AND MISCONDUCT IN
MEDICAL RESEARCH

FRAUD AND MISCONDUCT IN MEDICAL RESEARCH

Edited by

STEPHEN LOCK
*Research associate, section of the
history of twentieth century clinical science,
Wellcome Institute, and editor,
British Medical Journal 1975–91*

and

FRANK WELLS
*Medical director, the Association
of the British Pharmaceutical Industry*

Published by the BMJ Publishing Group
Tavistock Square, London WC1H 9JR

© BMJ Publishing Group 1993
All rights reserved. No part of this publication may be reproduced, stored in a retrieval system, or transmitted, in any form or by any means, electronic, mechanical, photocopying, recording and/or otherwise, without the prior written permission of the publishers.

First published 1993
Second impression 1993

British Library Cataloguing-in-Publication Data.
A catalogue record for this book is available from the British Library.

ISBN 0 7279 0757 3

Printed and bound in Great Britain by
Latimer Trend & Company Ltd., Plymouth

Contents

	Page
Preface	vii
Acknowledgments	ix
Introduction JOHN HOWIE, *professor of general practice, University of Edinburgh*	1
Research misconduct: a résumé of recent events STEPHEN LOCK, *research associate, section of the history of twentieth century clinical science, Wellcome Institute, London, and editor of the British Medical Journal 1975–91*	5
A pharmaceutical company's approach to the threat of research fraud PETER BROCK, *medical director, Lederle Ltd, Gosport, Hampshire*	25
Fraud in general practice research: intention to cheat JAMES HOSIE, *general practitioner, Glasgow*	42
The pharmaceutical industry and contract research organisations MALCOLM VANDENBURG, MARK DAVIS, HAROLD NEAL, *MCRC Group Ltd, Romford, Essex*	51
Statistical aspects of the detection of fraud STEPHEN EVANS, *professor of medical statistics, the Royal London Hospital Medical College, London*	61
The British pharmaceutical industry's response FRANK WELLS, *medical director, the Association of the British Pharmaceutical Industry, London*	75

CONTENTS

Investigating, reporting, and pursuing fraud in clinical research: legal aspects and options in England and Wales
CHRISTOPHER HODGES, *partner, McKenna & Co, Solictors, London, and vice chairman of the district ethical committee, Harrow Health District* — 91

Fraud in clinical research from sample preparation to publication: the French scene
D LAGARDE, *chef du corps des pharmaciens inspecteurs, Ministère de la Santé et de l'Action Humanitaire, Paris,*
H MAISONNEUVE, *président des Laboratoires Belmac SA, Sophia-Antipolis, Valbonne, France* — 108

Fraud in medical research: the Danish scene
POVL RIIS, *professor of internal medicine, University of Copenhagen, and chairman of the Central Research-Ethics Committee of Denmark* — 116

Data audits in investigational drug trials and their implications for detection of misconduct in science
MARTIN F SHAPIRO, *associate professor of medicine, UCLA School of Medicine, Los Angeles, USA* — 128

Baron Munchausen at the lab bench?
NORMAN SWAN, *general manager, Radio National, Australian Broadcasting Corporation, Sydney, Australia* — 142

Fraud and the editor
STEPHEN LOCK — 158

A head of department's view
IAIN E GILLESPIE, *professor of surgery, University of Manchester* — 173

Appendices — 183

Index — 197

Preface

All studies of deviance are plagued by problems of prevalence. We still have little idea of how frequent fraud is in scientific research, though most doctors now accept that there is a small amount—and probably always has been. The revelations of the past 15 years, however, might imply that the problem is now more common; are we even in the middle of a mini epidemic?

For several reasons we can never answer this question. Since the second world war research activity has risen exponentially with time, so that, with a fixed proportion of cases being fraudulent, the total number of cases would have risen anyway. Coincidentally, there has been the increased emphasis on the public exposure of all kinds of fraud (helped in the United States by the Freedom of Information Act). And, given that today we know how to suspect and deal with probable instances, suspicions are less likely to remain hidden than they were. Various official bodies, in the United States, United Kingdom, Australia, and Denmark have all shown the way for both prevention and management of suspected cases, while the International Committee of Medical Journal Editors and the US National Library of Medicine have emphasised the need to retract published fraudulent work.

Nevertheless, not all countries with active research programmes—including Canada, New Zealand, and many in the European Community—have come to grips with the problem, though almost certainly it is present. Moreover, while some of the recent reports have concerned research done in prestigious departments headed by world famous bosses, it has become clear that there is another focus for fraud: in general practice, where family doctors have invented data for multicentre clinical trials. This book aims at covering both these aspects.

Fraud and Misconduct in Medical Research, then, has several thrusts. The first is to take a historical approach, and to review events worldwide since 1975, when William Summerlin was found to have faked a successful black skin graft in a white mouse by using a felt-tip pen. The second is to summarise the official recommendations, including the interesting document from Denmark; this was produced in a vacuum and distilled from experience elsewhere in response to a hypothetical future case, given that no true case had ever been reported in Denmark. Thirdly, several chapters take varying perspectives—of the family doctor, head of an academic unit, contract research company director, statistician, and editor. And, lastly,

PREFACE

there is practical advice on how individuals or pharmaceutical companies can report well grounded suspicions to a disciplinary body, such as the General Medical Council in the United Kingdom, to ensure that justice is done. For so far the United Kingdom is the only country to have imposed really effective sanctions for fraud; elsewhere fraudsters may not be employed in contract research again, but they are allowed to continue practising medicine.

Hence our approach is somewhat different from that of other books. Mostly this was by design. We have deliberately not considered issues that are currently undecided: the question of a qui-tam suit, whereby a whistleblower can claim for a payment of up to three times the research grant involved; and the threat on the horizon that those journals refusing to publish bona fide retractions of fraudulent work will be removed from the *Index Medicus*.

A final, and trivial, point: nomenclature. We have not imposed any uniformity on the terms used by our contributors. Even in official reports from the United States "misconduct" has meant several things: restricted in one case to the extreme of piracy, plagiarism, and forgery, extended in another to the whole spectrum from bias and self delusion through gift authorship, to piracy, and so on. Similarly "fraud" may mean piracy, plagiarism, and forgery, or just the last of these. In our title we have used misconduct to imply every abuse up to these extremes, which are all subsumed under fraud. Eventually, no doubt, there will be an international agreement on terminology.

In the meantime this is the least important aspect of solving an important problem. We hope the commitment that we have reflected, in our choice of contributors, to dealing appropriately with fraud and misconduct, will encourage others to tackle this problem seriously. For tackle it we must, within our own profession; otherwise, outsiders will impose a situation on us.

STEPHEN LOCK
FRANK WELLS

Acknowledgments

We thank all the many people who have been concerned in this book: our contributors; Professor Marcel LaFollette, of the Center for International Science and Technology Policy at the George Washington University, who advised SL on his overview; Jane Smith, deputy editor of the *British Medical Journal* for commenting on the manuscripts; Ruth Holland, our creative and unflappable technical editor; Lesley Hines, who typed or copied many of the manuscripts; Margaret Cooter, the indefatigable indexer; and Mary Banks, the books editor of the *BMJ* Publishing Group, for her patience and encouragement.

To Shirley and Janet

Introduction

JOHN HOWIE

Fraud is a stark, angry, and aggressive word. In many ways it is antithetical to the term "medical research" and putting them together must inevitably provoke discomfort for the listener or reader. This anthology does just that. Events of recent years have left it beyond doubt that unacceptable practices occur. The profession—and indeed the public, who are at risk too—may express collective dismay when researchers of ability, but flawed commitment, find it necessary to make false claims to win acclaim for non-existent discovery; and it is even easier to make a scapegoat of the (stereotypical) general practitioner who invents clinical trial data primarily for personal gain. But is the problem large enough to merit a publication, or are the authors and editors making more than is necessary of a problem that will now be contained having been recognised? The material in the body of this text seems worrying enough to justify development. What constitutes fraud—and is that the best collective description for the various forms of misconduct it encompasses? Can we identify the aetiology of the disorder? And can we suggest solutions?

The problem

Various documents (the Royal College of Physicians' report on *Fraud and Misconduct in Medical Research* is helpful reading) have sketched the range of practices from the manifestly criminal (the false creation and dissemination of misinformation) to the misguided (minor levels of plagiarism—sometimes unwitting) and the careless, which most researchers have probably been guilty of at some time in their lives. The worrying message which comes through repeatedly in this text is that the level of deception towards the more serious end is more substantial than widely recognised and seems to be a worldwide phenomenon. This does not need further comment in the introduction.

There are, however other issues as well as those in the predominantly bioscientific aspects of research generally covered in this collection. Increasingly much medical research concerned with applied science overlaps with social science aspects which (and this is to be welcomed) are becomingly increasingly interwoven into topics such as the cultural determinants of illness behaviour and the ability of traditional medicine to recognise and meet health needs. This partnership is an increasingly prominent part of the researches of general practice, academic departments of which now contain as many social science researchers as medically qualified researchers. Here new conflicts arise. The research data available depend on the methods used to collect them. Researching beliefs and values quickly becomes politicised as can the way "results" are organised, interpreted, and diffused. In the best possible faith, people with different ideologies can read different meanings into the same data, which in turn may (often innocently) have been collected as if to prove a point rather than to elicit whatever truth may be. Social science researchers, and medical researchers with social science interests, are as powerful people as the more easily typecast molecular biologists and as apt to want to use research to enable their philosophies to gain influence. Over enthusiasm? misconduct? fraud?—not always an easy line to draw, but a problem that needs to be diligently watched.

The aetiology

I have already alluded to the obvious causes of fraud and misconduct, principally inappropriate personal ambition and greed, and to the more subtle problems of conviction and political drive. This is, however, a good time and a good place to raise two other, possibly related, issues. The first is the advent of accountability and its runaway twin the performance indicator. There is no sadder sight in academic life than that of university groups drawing up league tables of research income and output divided by full time equivalent staff, and then allocating value and resources on that basis. Nothing more certainly devalues the quality of research than this, and it directly promotes at least the more minor forms of misconduct incurred in multiple publication and multiauthorship. That the university system (in the United Kingdom) has now apparently accepted this kind of discipline as a way of living is difficult to believe but seems to be the case. Fortunately the official party line is that quality and not quantity is under review—although the data required for recurrent audits cast at least some doubt on this.

The second issue is the poor career structure for research staff. Not only are the levels of reward in academic research generally low, but the prospects of gaining tenure and security are poor too. A researcher approaching mid-career becomes expensive to fund and dependent on seeming to continue to be both productive and innovative. The temptations are obvious, and the relative independence which senior researchers usually enjoy is an added hazard.

A different problem can affect those in general practice, where time is income and income is almost entirely structured to pay for clinical work. Partnerships are generally unsupportive of partners who wish for time out of routine clinical work to undertake non-remunerative activity. Research is generally unremunerated, certainly at the stage of developing ideas and methods, but undertaking clinical trials work for pharmaceutical companies either often or usually carries a financial reward. There is little evidence to suggest that there is much overlap between general practitioner researchers with a wish to innovate and those who enjoy being part of a clinical trials organisation, but the difference in reward between the two may again provide temptation.

The solution

Various codes of practice (the Royal College of Physicians' report; the Harvard Medical School's *Guidelines for Investigators in Scientific Research*) are helpful, particularly in the more biomedical aspects of research. Vigilance amongst editors and referees must help too, and promising approaches to detecting fraudulent data are included in this monograph. However, not many referees have the necessary statistical skill or the time to study new data that would be required if higher levels of suspicion began to increase the frequency with which papers were to be scrutinised in that kind of depth.

The fundamental change needed seems to be to move the research "climate" firmly back from quantity towards quality. That itself is a political decision but one which the university and research communities generally could bring about with a concerted effort. Such a move would need to be linked to a proper reward system and career structure, both of which are overdue—and apparently overdue throughout the world. Funding-protected research time for general practitioners is part of that agenda, and within reach in the United Kingdom as the "Peckham initiative" focuses on priorities across the whole research field. If, more generally, appointments committees developed the growing practice of looking at limited lists of chosen publications only, the pressure to publish inappropriately (already strongly criticised by editors) would surely fall, with obvious benefits in parallel.

Two further issues remain. The first is the adequacy of research training. Failure to follow the time honoured sequence of formulating ideas, reading up on the background, testing methods, and collecting and validating data, leads inexorably to inconclusive research which has to be patched up by using opportunist strategies of varying levels of credibility and acceptability. Lower academic staffing levels have had a major effect on the standard of training and supervision. New techniques of statistical analysis have reduced the perceived need to identify hypotheses, or even aims, before collecting data, and computers have distanced researchers from handling their own data input and analyses in a way that compounds the risk of misinterpretating data, innocently as well as misguidedly.

Second, there has been an over simplification of what is meant by significance and thus truth. Research is sometimes about fact, but in medicine it is as often about ideas or beliefs or feelings as well. The standards of proof that apply in an attempt to analyse a gene are different (but not better or worse) from those that apply to a study of the implications of being found to have malignant disease. But we attempt to define the rules of disseminating research as if the models of medical and social science research were identical. The discipline of thinking *is* the same; the level of certainty which follows is not.

As well as talking about research fraud, we must also talk about research integrity. In that more positive approach, the onus returns rightly to the researcher. That remains, as with clinical practice, the best safeguard for the future.

Research misconduct: a résumé of recent events

STEPHEN LOCK

"Sexual intercourse began/In nineteen sixty-three," wrote Philip Larkin in "Annus Mirabilis." Much the same attitude could be taken towards misconduct in scientific research (piracy, plagiarism, and forgery): that it all started in 1974 with the publicity surrounding William Summerlin and his use of a felt-tip pen to fake a successful skin transplant from a black mouse to a white one. There were, of course, earlier cases but most of these shared certain characteristics. To start with, a few of the features were in doubt: did, for example Sir Cyril Burt really invent all his cases as well as his coauthors? And was Piltdown man primarily a joke or a fraud with a serious intent? The arguments about these and other cases, as well as detailed descriptions of the classic instances, are to be found in major books on the subject,[1-4] so here I will choose 1974 as the watershed. Not only is it a convenient starting point for summarising the events that have gone on since (several of which are too recent to have been recorded in the books), but in retrospect it seems to have heralded a mini epidemic, which, though still with us, has led to important actions on prevention and management of suspected cases.

Here I will give the salient details of as many cases as I have been able to find in the literature, though only briefly if they are described elsewhere in this book. The list is not comprehensive, and some descriptions are much longer than others—not because they are better documented but because they have become the "classic" cases, often cited to illustrate particular aspects of the problem. I will then discuss some of the major themes to have emerged—such as settings, motives, and disciplines particularly at risk— and end with detailing measures introduced by the scientific community. And, given that the thrust of the book is biomedical, I will confine my treatment to this discipline (even though a few of the most interesting cases fall outside it, such as the fossils that Viswa Gupta claimed he had found in the Himalayas but that in reality had come from many other parts of the world).[5]

Case histories

I have classified case histories by country, listing them by year of detection. Self evidently these deal only with reported misconduct, and the true prevalence is larger—how large it is impossible to say. But in a confidential, small, and non-systematic survey in 1988, with a response rate of 100% of the 80 people questioned,* I found that over half knew of some instance: 42 in Britain, 7 in the United States, 4 in Australia, 7 in other countries, and 13 in unspecified countries.[6] Over half the dubious results had been published, but in only 6 cases had retractions appeared subsequently in the journals, all too vague to indicate what had gone on. In some cases the fraudster had retained his job; in others he had moved anyway by the time misconduct was discovered so he was allowed to stay in his new post; and in yet others he had been allowed to resign. Apart from Dr Siddiqui, the Durham psychiatrist whose case is discussed in detail in the chapter by Wells, in only one instance (not in the United Kingdom) had the perpetrator been dismissed.

Since the publication of these findings, my coeditor Frank Wells has been responsible for reporting no fewer than 26 cases involving 16 doctors to the General Medical Council (GMC) all except two concerning family doctors. (Those cases which are not listed below are either pending, or the doctors have been disciplined by the GMC, which usually then does not publish their names.) I have been told of at least 10 further unreported cases, all but one of them in hospital/academia, in at least one of which (I was told), though the facts were established by an internal "three wise men" inquiry, the perpetrator was allowed to resign and to pursue his career, successfully, at another hospital. (To be fair, however, four episodes occurred before or at the beginning of the period I am considering, when no guidelines for management were available.)

Another type of audit was done by Shapiro and Charrow (see p 128). Using the Freedom of Information Act they reviewed the results of the Food and Drug Administration's routine data audits, and also the for-cause audits between June 1977 and April 1988—finding that the rates of substantial violations had not gone down over this period, and that about 16% of for-cause audits had led to disciplinary action. Nevertheless, for various reasons they did not advocate generalising this audit approach to other forms of research.[7]

KNOWN OR SUSPECTED MISCONDUCT IN AUSTRALIA

1981 **Michael Briggs**, professor of endocrinology at Deakin University, Geelong, who forged data on oral contraceptives (see p 142).

* The discrepancy between these findings and that in my 1988 article[6] arises because the 80th respondent telephoned me after publication—thus making the response rate 100% and adding a definite case (intermediate status) in surgery, originating outside the United Kingdom.

1985 **Ronald Wild**, professor and dean of social science at La Trobe University, Victoria. His fifth book contained large-scale plagiarisms from 10 different sources. He resigned after difficulties with the initial inquiry.[8]

1987 **Ashoka Prasad**, consultant psychiatrist at the Victoria Mental Health Institute, Melbourne, fabricated data on 8000 patients with schizophrenia (see p 150). Such was the concern about the possible legal implications of publishing this conclusion—another theme that was subsequently, but erroneously, to be used as an excuse for doing nothing—that the findings were released under privilege in the Victoria State Parliament.

1988 **William McBride**, director of Foundation 41 in Sydney, New South Wales, who forged data on the action of hyoscine in fetal rabbits. An important case for not only does it concern a world famous figure, who was powerful enough to raise a major threat to an important drug, Debendox, but it also illustrates the difficulty of instigating an inquiry at a private foundation when such a procedure is resisted by the head of the unit (see p 146).

KNOWN OR SUSPECTED MISCONDUCT IN THE UNITED KINGDOM

1975 **J P Sedgwick**, a High Wycombe family doctor, who had agreed with a pharmaceutical company to coordinate and take part in a trial of an antihypertensive drug. He returned 101 completed clinical trial forms, many of which contained forged signatures of the seven other participating doctors, and results which showed that the active drug was having a uniform and consistent effect that was appreciably different from test results from other sources. Reported by the company to the GMC, Dr Sedgwick had his name removed from the medical register.[9]

1977 **Robert Gullis**, biochemist at Birmingham University. Faked results in research done in both the United Kingdom and Germany into messenger chemicals in the brain (cyclic guanosine monophosphate and cyclic adenosine monophosphate), forming the basis of his PhD thesis and 11 articles, all of which were retracted by the departments concerned.[1,2]

1980 **E A K Alsabti**, who was a major plagiarist. Though he worked largely in the United States, he is included in the United Kingdom section since he probably also worked here at some time (giving at least two addresses in the United Kingdom), while his misconduct was featured prominently in three British journals (*Nature*, the *Lancet* and the *British Medical Journal*). An Iraqi immunologist, Alsabti worked at various research centres in the United States in 1977–8, and then qualified from the American University of the Caribbean in May 1980, going on to practise at various medical centres until 1982 and privately until 1989. In September 1990 he was reported to have been killed in a car crash in South Africa, but as of April 1991 no death certificate had been forthcoming in response to inquiries.[3]

In his earlier posts Alsabti had fallen foul of his superiors; the Temple University authorities speaking of his "irresponsible and non-professional behaviour," the microbiologist Professor E F Wheelock at Jefferson Medical College finding "very strong" evidence of fraud, and the M D Anderson Hospital asking him to leave because a manuscript he had submitted for review was an obvious plagiarism of Wheelock's work.

It was Wheelock who some months after this last episode was to bring charges of plagiarism into the open—a case subsequently reinforced when Daniel Wierda, a postdoctoral student, found that his article in the *European Journal of Cancer* had been published in an almost identical version in the *Japanese Journal of Medical Science and Biology* under the names of Alsabti and two fictitious coauthors. The European journal had refereed Wierda's paper to Dr Jeffrey Gottlieb, who had worked at the M D Anderson Hospital but had been dead for four years. Alsabti had picked it up, made minor alterations, and submitted it to the Japanese journal, which had published it before the bona fide article had appeared.

This article was formally retracted by the editor of the Japanese journal, while comments about the case appeared in various scientific journals, one of which led to Alsabti's resignation from an internal medical residency programme of the University of Virginia and subsequently from at least two training programmes elsewhere. In all, it seems likely that Alsabti plagiarised some 60 articles, most of them in obscure journals.[10]

1981 **Michael Purves**, reader in physiology at the University of Bristol, who faked data to show that the uptake of radioactivity labelled 5-deoxyglucose (a marker for glucose itself) was greater in the brain cells of active, awake sheep embryos than of sleeping ones. These findings were presented at the 1981 International Congress of the Physiological Sciences, and published in its proceedings. Nevertheless, colleagues could not replicate the work and a university investigation was held. Purves resigned his post and retracted his findings in a letter to *Nature*.[1,2]

1986 **Art Conolly**, medical student at Oxford, who plagiarised an anonymous *British Medical Journal* editorial on the differential diagnosis of dementia[11] and published it under his own name in another journal. Both journals published statements about what had happened.

1988 **V A Siddiqui**, Durham psychiatrist who faked data in a trial of an antidepressant. Reported by the pharmaceutical company to the Association of the British Pharmaceutical Industry (ABPI) and thence to the GMC, which removed his name from the medical register (see p 81).

1990 **Kollunnar Francis**, Coventry family doctor who faked dates of birth in some of his patients entered in a comparative trial of antibiotics. Reported by the contract research organisation to the ABPI and thence to the GMC, which suspended his registration for six months (see p 85).

1990 **Sheo Kumar**, Hornchurch family doctor who faked data in a trial of drugs used for hypertension. He submitted to the pharmaceutical company record forms and related documents that were misleading and failed to conduct the study trial in accordance with the study protocol. Reported by the company to the ABPI and thence to the GMC, which found him guilty of serious professional misconduct and admonished him.[11]

1991 **Lakshmi Pandit**, Wimbledon family doctor who faked data in a trial of drugs used in obstructive airways disease. Reported by the contract research organisation to the ABPI, and thence to the GMC, which removed his name from the medical register (see p 82).

1991 **R B Gonsai**, London family doctor who faked data in a comparative trial of two inhalation techniques. Reported by the contract research organisation to the ABPI, and thence to the GMC, which removed his name from the medical register (see p 86).

1991 **David Latta**, Glasgow family doctor who faked data in a comparative trial of two antihypertensive drugs. Reported by pharmaceutical company to ABPI, and thence to the GMC, which removed his name from the medical register (see pp 45 and 88).

KNOWN OR SUSPECTED MISCONDUCT IN THE UNITED STATES

1974 **William Summerlin**, immunologist at the Sloan-Kettering Institute, New York, who faked transplantation results, darkening transplanted skin patches in white mice with a black felt-tip pen, and alleging that human corneas had been successfully transplanted into rabbits. Sir Peter Medawar, who was present at the latter demonstration, has given a good and amusing account of prevailing attitudes at the time, which led fellow scientists to keep quiet about results they just did not believe. Admitting that he had been a moral coward on this occasion, Medawar said that he believed that the whole demonstration was either a confidence trick or a hoax.[13] Subsequently Summerlin's boss, the celebrated immunologist Robert Good, resigned from the directorship of the Institute.

1978 **Marc J Straus**, head of a cancer research team at Boston University, working on a clinical trial drug treatment in cancer, in which 15% of data were found to be false. Straus resigned, but stated that, although data had been faked, he had not had any role in the faking.[1,2]

1979 **Vijay Soman**, an assistant professor of medicine at the Yale School of Medicine, who plagiarised parts of a manuscript sent in 1978 by the *New England Journal of Medicine* for peer review to his boss, Philip Felig, who passed the job on to him. Subsequently Soman and Felig published an article on the same topic, insulin binding in anorexia nervosa, in the *American Journal of Medicine*. Accused of plagiarism and conflict of interest, Felig seemed to settle the difficulties by stating that the work had been completed before they had received the paper for review; but its author, Dr Helena Wachslicht-Rodbard, a young researcher at the National Institutes of Health (NIH), who during this episode was to switch to hospital practice, persisted with her complaints—which in an inquiry by Dr Jeffrey Flier, a Boston diabetologist, in February 1980 were shown to be justified. Not only had Soman copied her manuscript, but most of the data in his own joint study had been faked. A subsequent investigation soon afer found that, of 14 articles, only two could be approved, and the data were either missing or fraudulent in the remaining 12 (10 of them with Felig as coauthor). All these articles were retracted by Felig.

This case is important as it features peer review and conflict of interest, as well as the hesitancy in those early days of instigating a full and proper inquiry into an accusation made against a senior figure, and only Wachslicht-Rodbard's persistence brought about the disclosures. It was also a personal tragedy for Felig, who resigned a prestigious post at Columbia University, to which he had been appointed while the episode was unfolding.

1980 **Joseph Cort**, physician who while working at Mount Sinai Hospital, New York, faked data on vasopressin analogues that would stimulate the production of factor VIII without hypertensive and diuretic side effects.[1,2]

1980 **John Long**, pathologist at Massachusetts General Hospital, who faked data on four allegedly separate cells lines derived from Hodgkin's disease tissue, only one of which was human (though not Hodgkin's cells) and the remainder were derived from contamination by cells from a northern Colombian brown-footed monkey. He resigned, and the work was retracted in the *Journal of the National Cancer Institute*.[1,2]

1981 **Mark Spector**, a Cornell University graduate student, who faked data on a theory of cancer causation—in which a tumour virus infects a cell, causing it to produce the viral src protein. This, a kinase, then sets up a cascade of other cellular kinases, which finally results in phosphorylation of the cell membrane ATP-ase. The result is a diminished activity of the ATP-ase characteristically found in tumour cells but not in normal cells. Given the potential importance of these findings, others tried rapidly to replicate them, but could not and it was then found that Spector had used radioactive iodine to label his gels rather than radioactive phosphorus— thus vitiating the findings. Not all of these were faked, however, but which were true remains uncertain. Spector's coauthors retracted the article in *Cell* in the same year as its publication.

1981 **John Darsee**, Harvard research worker in cardiology, who was seen to falsify data during a laboratory study; his overall head of department, the distinguished cardiologist Eugene Braunwald, decided that this was a single bizarre act and allowed him to continue to work under close supervision, but terminated his NIH fellowship. Six months later, however, it became clear that Darsee's data in a multicentre study of treatments to protect the ischaemic myocardium were different from those at the three other units taking part (see p 69). Harvard Medical School set up a committee of investigation, as did the NIH and Emory University, where Darsee had also worked. It emerged that Darsee had committed an extensive series of frauds, originating during his undergraduate days at Notre Dame University and continuing at Emory and Harvard. These included non-existent patients or collaborators, and invented data, as in the multicentre trial. There were also procedures and results that on reflection were virtually impossible: drawing blood from the tail veins of 200 rats weekly for all of their 90-week lifespan, and obtaining venous blood specimens in all 43 members of a family on two consecutive days after an overnight fast twice a year as well as complete sets of 24-hour urine specimens (including a 2 year old child). In all, during his career Darsee published over 100 papers and abstracts, many of them in prestigious journals and with distinguished coauthors; many of these had to be retracted.[1-4]

Possibly, until recently, more ink has been shed on Darsee's case than on any other. In part this was because it was the first major publicised case that was not an isolated blemish on the face of science (not mad—rather, bad); in part because it concerned prestigious institutions, coauthors, and journals; in part because of the charismatic personality of one of the central figures; in part because it started the whole debate about the rights and wrongs of authorship, data retention, supervision of juniors, and the management of suspected cases of fraud; and, finally, in part because it shifted the whole climate of feeling of trust to thinking the unthinkable—the possibility that things might not be as they seemed. These ramifications are ably explored in Marcel LaFollette's new book,[4] and a particularly cogent account of why Darsee was trusted in the conditions prevailing at the time is provided by his former mentor, Eugene Braunwald.[3]

1983 William Aronow, a cardiologist at Long Beach, California, who after the Food and Drug Administration had found irregularities in five studies involving four different drugs between 1974 and 1978—with "all discrepancies noted being on the side of favouring drug efficacy"—agreed not to participate in further drug trials without FDA approval. Dr Alan Lisook, chief of the FDA's clinical investigation branch, stated that the agency had reached similar agreements in seven other cases—while after an official procedure 50 researchers had been disqualified.[1,2] (See also the chapter by Shapiro.)

1985 Robert Slutsky, a resident in cardiological radiology at the University of California, San Diego, who between 1978 and 1985 was the author or coauthor of 137 articles. The possibility of fraud was raised by an astute referee who queried apparently identical statistical results for two different sets of data in consecutive articles he had to read when Slutsky applied for promotion.[14] An inquiry found experiments and measurements that had never been done, incorrect procedures, and reports of statistical analyses that had never been performed. A committee of investigation was set up and, after interviewing coworkers, looking at lab notebooks, and reading the articles, classified these as valid (77), questionable (48), or fraudulent (12). Some of these last were retracted, and a few statements of validity were also published.

This is yet another important case, illustrating several other features about medical misconduct. Firstly, there was Slutsky's high productivity—at one stage he was producing one paper every 10 days—which occasioned little but admiration from his colleagues. Secondly, several of the latter were happy to accept "gift" authorship on papers reporting work with which they had had nothing to do—and indeed couldn't have had, given that the work hadn't been done. Thirdly, there was the way in which this junior worker had successfully managed to escape any supervision of his research by his seniors. And, lastly, there was the curious behaviour of several journals, which either declined to insert any retraction or statement of validation (sometimes but not always on legal grounds) or, if they did so tended to do this in such terms as to make the retractions non-retrievable on electronic databases.[14]

1986 **Charles Glueck**, professor of internal medicine at the University of Cincinnati, published in 1986 an article in *Pediatrics* concluding that a low cholesterol diet, supplemented with drug treatment, lowered blood cholesterol concentrations in children but did not interfere with their growth and development, or sexual maturation.[15] A committee of inquiry found that he had committed serious scientific misconduct by misrepresenting the study findings. It had not been a prospective study, as stated, the data were internally inconsistent, and the charts of some of the patients did not contain data to substantiate the findings cited. An NIH review concluded that, given the diversity of opinion about the term prospective, this finding was not substantiated, but the second and third findings were. The committee recommended that Glueck should be debarred from receiving federal funds for two years and serving on any peer review or advisory committee for five years. Glueck resigned from his post (moving immediately to become director of the Cholesterol Center at the Jewish Hospital of Cincinnati), and the article was retracted.

1986 **Claudio Milanese**, an Italian immunological worker at Harvard's Dana-Farber Cancer Institute, who, as coauthor of articles in *Science* and the *Journal of Experimental Medicine*, reported that IL-4A, a lymphokine, induced interleukin-2 receptors. Failure to replicate the works after Milanese had returned to Italy (Turin) led to an investigation and the finding that IL-4A did not exist.[16] The articles were retracted by Milanese's colleagues and two unpublished manuscripts were withdrawn.

1986 **Theresa Imanishi-Kari**, a Tufts University biologist who fabricated key data in transgenic mice experiments. The work, published in *Cell*, showed that genetic changes could be triggered by the transplanted genes, and had as coauthors five colleagues, including the Nobel laureate, David Baltimore. In response to suggestions by Margot O'Toole, a postdoctoral worker, that some of the work had never been done, an ad hoc committee of inquiry was convened by Tufts, which concluded that there had been only scientific disagreement, and a review of the case by Herman Eisen, professor at the Massachusetts Institute of Technology, found minor errors but no fraud.

From this point onwards there was a long chain of events, starting when a colleague of O'Toole's contacted the well known "fraudbusters" Walter Stewart and Ned Feder of NIH (who had had a prominent role in the Darsee story); after examining the 17 pages from Imanishi-Kari's notebooks, they said that they suspected misconduct. In May 1988 the Congressional Committee on Energy and Commerce's Subcommittee on Oversight and Investigations, chaired by Representative John Dingell, held its first hearing, focusing on this case, subsequently turning over the notebook pages to the secret service. At its fourth hearing, in May 1990, the latter was to show that the records and reported experiments were "not contemporaneous with respect to time." In March 1991 a draft report of the Office of Scientific Integrity (OSI) found serious scientific misconduct, while two months later, Baltimore—who had previously defended the article very vigorously and attacked Stewart, Feder, and Dingell's staff for unwarranted meddling—accepted the findings and apologised for his failure to act rigorously in investigating Margot O'Toole's doubts.[17] Baltimore, who had initially made minor corrections to the article in *Cell*, then retracted it. Again, the sequel was a personal tragedy for Baltimore, who resigned his post as president of Rockefeller University, to which he had been appointed only 18 months beforehand. Very recently, however, given that the US Attorney has decided not to prosecute Imanishi-Kari, Baltimore has apparently "unretracted" the article.

1987 **Stephen Breuning**, a psychologist at the University of Pittsburgh who faked data purporting to show that in retarded children stimulant drugs were more effective and had fewer side effects than the standard treatment with tranquillisers. This is said to have led to changes in therapeutic policy, notably in the state of Connecticut. Breuning was dismissed and the case referred to the US Attorney's office; in the autumn of 1988, after pleading guilty to two charges of making false statements on federal grant applications, he was sentenced to serve 60 days in a halfway house, 250 hours of community service, and five years of probation. He was also required to return to the university $11 352 (his salary from the grants) and to stay out of psychology for the five-year period. Apparently, not all of the articles were fraudulent, but four were retracted.[3] This case is important as it is possibly the first where there was demonstrably an actual or potential serious implication for patients, and where criminal prosecution was instigated.

1987 **C David Bridges**, an ophthalmologist at Baylor University who was alleged to have used in an article of his own information in a paper sent to him for peer review by the *Proceedings of the National Academy of Sciences* (see p 166).

1987 **Shervert Frazier**, a professor of psychiatry at Harvard Medical School and former director of the National Institute of Mental Health, who resigned his professorship after admitting that he had plagiarised large sections of four review articles published between 1960 and 1975.[18] He was, however, allowed to continue practising on the staff of McLean Hospital, which is operated by a group that includes Harvard.

1988 **Philip A Berger**, Stanford professor of psychiatry who was found guilty of "deviation from accepted practices in the conduct and reporting of science." Some participants in a drug trial had been identified as not taking drugs but were in fact receiving medication, and some allegedly normal controls were found to have been suffering from mild senile dementia. After scrutiny of the investigation's report by the Office of Scientific Integrity Review, Berger was debarred from Health and Human Services grants or contracts for three years.[19]

This case is important as Stanford spread the blame among all the coauthors of the articles, suggesting that every author is responsible for the data in these. And the university also issued an official statement on its standards for promotions, reminding the faculty that the total number of publications is not as important as quality, while "the least publishable unit" or repetitive publication would be detrimental to a candidate's record. The university also stated that it was drawing up a set of guidelines for multidisciplinary research.

1988 **Stephen Stahl**, a Stanford psychiatrist who was a colleague of Berger's, was faulted in the same inquiry for using inappropriate controls and inaccurately describing patients in two studies. Like Berger, he was banned from serving on Public Health Services committees for five years, and grant applications in which the two collaborated over the following five years were required to include certification of their reliability from the institutions applying for them.[20]

1989 **Douglas Nelson**, a physiologist at Northwestern University, Evanston, Illinois, who "misrepresented the publication status of his papers in manuscripts and grant applications submitted to NIH." He was excluded from sitting on NIH advisory panels and was required to submit his federally funded research to supervision.[21]

1989 **Lonnie Mitchell**, a psychologist of Coppin State University, Baltimore, Maryland, who had used plagiarised material in a grant application. He was prevented from serving on Public Health Services advisory committees for five years and required to provide "certification as to the integrity, honesty, and reliability" of any Public Health Services application made in the following five years.[21]

1990 **Arnold Rincover**, associate professor of psychology, University of North Carolina at Greensboro, was found by a university investigation to have committed plagiarism. He resigned.

1990 **Martin Bak**, research fellow in surgery at Harvard University Medical School, was found by a university investigation to have fabricated data for a draft manuscript and published abstracts. He resigned and was banned from receiving federal grants and contracts for three years.

1990 **David H Van Thiel**, professor of medicine, surgery, and psychiatry at the University of Pittsburgh Medical School, was found by a university investigation to have plagiarised review articles in a book chapter he wrote. His tenure was revoked and he was barred from serving on Public Health Services committees for three years.

1990 **L Cass Terry**, professor of neurology at the University of Michigan, was found by a university investigation to have plagiarised articles sent to him to review as well as using plagiarised material in portions of his doctoral thesis, grant applications, and a book chapter. He was banned from serving on Public Health Services committees for five years.

1991 **Hiroaki Shimokawa**, advanced research fellow in internal medicine at the University of Iowa Medical School, was found by a university investigation to have altered data. He had returned to Japan by the time of the investigations, but was banned from receiving federal research and training support for three years.

1991 **Paul P Demedluk**, adjunct professor of neurology at the University of California, San Francisco, was found by a university investigation to have fabricated data in two published articles and an unpublished paper and book chapter. He resigned and was banned from receiving federal grants and contracts for three years.

1991 **Herbert K Naito**, head of the Cleveland Clinic Foundation's section of lipids, nutrition, and metabolic diseases, was found by a foundation committee to have committed plagiarism in three articles. He was asked to resign and banned from serving on Public Health Services committees for three years.

RÉSUMÉ OF RECENT EVENTS

1991 **George E Eagan**, senior histology technician in the New York State Department of Public Health's Wadsworth Center for Laboratories and Research, Albany, New York, confessed to having altered experimental results by adding snake venom to tissue samples. He resigned and was banned from receiving federal grants and contracts for three years.

1991 **Rakesh Singhal**, research associate in neuroscience at Tufts University Medical School, was found by a university investigation to have altered and fabricated data. He committed suicide.

1991 **Russell P Santo**, assistant scientist in the division of neurosciences at Oregon Regional Primate Center, Beaverton, Oregon, was found by a centre investigation to have used the same photograph of cells to represent different sets of data in published articles. He resigned and was banned from serving on Public Health Services committees for three years.

1992 **Mitchell Rosner**, a graduate student in embryology at the NIH who faked data showing that embryonic cell division requires Oct-3, a protein that switches on genes, and that the protein may even regulate DNA replication in early development. The 1991 article in *Cell* was retracted by his three coauthors in May 1992, and Rosner withdrew his candidacy for a doctorate at Georgetown University Medical School.[22]

OTHER COUNTRIES

1992 **Isidro Ballart**, a South American PhD student at the University of Zurich who faked data to show that he had produced functioning measles viruses in cell cultures from cloned complementary DNA. His coauthors failed to replicate this finding, and Ballart committed suicide; the coauthors retracted the article in *EMBO Journal* (1990) in 1991.[23]

At the time of writing several other cases under investigation had received some publicity but had not been concluded, and hence I have not included them here. (I have also not included any case in which, though widely publicised, the findings remain equivocal.)

Major themes

From these cases, and the ones described in my survey and the study by Shapiro and Charrow (p 128), can we draw up an identikit of the typical research fraudster? Though I suspect that the true answer is no, it is tempting to try. Any speculation will lead to a bimodal pattern. On the one hand are those without a research background who tend to work in isolation: some family doctors in the United Kingdom and some hospital physicians in the United States, usually not practising in the most prestigious or research oriented milieu. Their research is mainly part of a multicentre drug trial, and the motive greed: even in 1986, Dr Siddiqui was being offered £700 for every patient taking part in the antidepressant trial.

The picture on the other hand is strikingly different. Here we have energetic middle grade researchers, often medically qualified and usually male, who are working more than full time in a prestigious research institution with a distinguished, if often remote, boss. The yearly number of publications (articles and conference abstracts) is high, and the peer pressure to produce positive results intense. Thus the research tends to be into "hot" topics—molecular biology, cancer, cardiology—with the rewards not money but prestige, promotion, and prizes; did not the 24 year old Spector's associates predict that his work would soon earn him the Nobel prize? And shading into all this are other needs. A few more patients are needed to make the results statistically significant, so why not invent them? On first principles, clearly drug A is teratogenic in humans, so why put any more fetuses at risk? Why not invent the results of the relevant studies in animals? In a few cases, moreover, there is possibly an element of mental illness underlying such Messianic complexes. At least one of the cases reported by Wells to the GMC falls into this category.

Against such speculations, however, are several features on the other side of the balance. Plenty of single-handed GPs take part in multicentre drug trials with utterly scrupulous standards. Plenty of postdoctoral students work in busy research laboratories and are totally honest. (In any case, as Rennie has asked,[24] is the stress of pressure from a high powered team wanting positive results for publication any greater than that suffered by a coalminer?) To be sure, there is a spectrum of wrong practices (p 161), and anybody might be tempted to go down the slippery slope—but there is also a spectrum of human probity, and, significantly, there is some evidence that a few fraudsters had always been less than honest: the unconfirmed report that one fraudster cheated in his undergraduate exams; the previous conviction of another (Spector) for bouncing cheques (together with his inventing his degree); and yet another's (Darsee's) long trail of faked work at three universities. As a working hypothesis, then, we could do worse than go along with Peter Medawar's idea that every group contains its quota of crooks and there is no reason why medicine should be any different.

Response of the scientific community

Initially the academic community responded to the disclosures with disbelief, shock, and horror—attitudes, which, it has to be said, have still not entirely gone. Those in authority did not want to hear unpleasant things, assuming that the fraudster must be ill (Summerlin, for example, was given a year's sick leave on full pay). The overriding priority was to hush things up, a theme Marcel LaFollette develops by discussing some counterparts in fiction.[4] A "piece of scientific fraud is of course unthinkable," C P Snow's Master reflects, but "any unnecessary publicity about it ... is [also] as near unforgivable as makes no matter." It would achieve nothing "except harm for the College."

WHISTLEBLOWERS

Like Snow's character who brings out the whole story, the real life whistleblowers (as they came to be known) have not fared very well, even in some cases ending worse off than the fraudster. Many suffered obloquy, were threatened with libel suits, or even lost their jobs, despite the fact that by 1988 over half the states in the USA had passed laws to protect them.[25] The difficulties in such cases were well brought out by Harold Green, a law professor at the George Washington University.[26] Engaged by Dr Jerome G Jacobstein, a nuclear medicine specialist at Cornell University Medical College, Green had as his objective to obtain a fair inquiry into some complaints about Dr Jeffrey S Borer, a cardiologist, not to convict him. The case was referred to the NIH, which set up an inquiry, reporting after five and a half years that there had been significant departures from accepted standards of record keeping, of collecting and recording data, and of reporting research results. Nevertheless, the inquiry found no evidence of intentional misconduct, though subsequently the NIH did impose fairly stiff sanctions against Borer. In the initial few months Green was paid several thousand dollars, but he then undertook to represent Jacobstein for the public good. When Green took the matter to the NIH he was threatened by an attorney in the Cornell office that he and Jacobstein would be held accountable for any damage that might result to the university and its personnel because of the allegations. As Green comments, a less dedicated scientist without financial resources would have retreated from the cause, discredited and with a tarnished reputation.

Even some years later, in 1991, when guidelines had appeared and their recommendations been put into effect, the prominent whistleblower in the Imanishi-Kari case, Margot O'Toole, was to write a commentary on her experiences, several passages in which show that attitudes are slow to change. "The [OSI's] report states that I lost my job as a result of raising questions. This is essentially true, but the facts are a little complicated. . . . It surprises me that the principle which guided my actions is not a universally accepted one among scientists. . . . I therefore sadly conclude that the attitude that scientific careers are more important than science has become common among scientists." To be fair, however, her account was challenged by David Baltimore, a coauthor of the article, and Professor Eisen, who conducted the 1986 inquiry.

RÉSUMÉ OF RECENT EVENTS

COAUTHORS

Less contentious are the facts about the behaviour of the coauthors in many cases. Most of them did nothing about seeking retractions of the relevant articles (neither did many of the editors behave any more positively—see p 169—despite public statements that there was little to fear from legal action). When the fraudsters had put the names of authors on to the paper without their knowledge, this inertia is understandable—but many of them had accepted "gift" or "honorary" coauthorship, as in the Slutsky case. "Our experience with Slutsky's coauthors," Paul Friedman of the University of California, San Diego, wrote, "is that they were uninterested in taking any initiative to reproduce research results or correct the literature. Two coauthors disagreed with the committee's judgment about articles in which they were involved; the other 58 coauthors remained passive with regard to the committee's conclusions. It will take considerable education to persuade coauthors to review their work when a question arises."[14]

GUIDELINES

The first report to deal with scientific misconduct (1975) was largely tangential to the main issue. Set up by the American Association for the Advancement of Science partly to deal with allegations by two early whistleblowers that standards of safety in the United States Atomic Energy Commission were lax, this "Edsall report" concluded that not only did scientists have the right and the duty to blow the whistle but that "the responsibilities are primary."[27] Such a conclusion was echoed by the Association of American Medical Colleges in its 1982 report.[28] "From the outset," this emphasised, "institutions should protect rights and reputations for all parties involved including the individual(s) who report perceived misconduct in good faith." The report went on to consider in detail the institutional responses of alleged research fraud, outlining the three-stage procedure since adopted in several other recommendations; initial complaint and review, investigation, and subsequent action. Throughout, the procedure was to ensure "due process"—protecting the rights of all concerned—but at the same time being "responsive to the special responsibility that science and faculty have to society."

Much the same framework was to be presented by the Association of American Universities seven years later.[29] An additional stipulation was that people chosen to help in the inquiry should have no real or apparent conflict of interest bearing on the case, yet any committee must have sufficient expertise. Other requirements were both confidentiality and expeditiousness (with deadlines, respectively, of 30 and 120 days for the inquiry and the investigation). A further possibility raised in this report was an additional appeals process and even a final review by the institution's chief executive.

Subsequent guidelines (the Australian Vice-Chancellors/National Health and Medical Research Council—1990 (see p 187); the Royal College of Physicians—1991;[30] the Danish national commission—1992 (see p 116); and the ABPI—1992 (see p 89) have mostly leant heavily on these earlier documents, as well as that produced by Harvard Medical School.[31] This last was concerned particularly with prevention, by promoting high standards of research practice. Trainees must be carefully supervised; the gathering, storage, and retention of data must be scrupulous; and units should develop a policy on authorship, deploring honorary authorship and limiting the number of publications candidates for promotion could submit.

Thus the Royal College of Physicians derived a lot from these major reports (reproducing both the Harvard guidelines and the statement on authorship by the International Committee of Medical Journal Editors as appendices). It too recommended that all the authorities concerned should adopt a twofold approach: promoting high standards of research and developing a mechanism for the management of complaints of research fraud—publicising the name of the screener and setting up the threefold process of receipt, inquiry, and investigation. "Two features are essential to this," the Royal College of Physicians report concluded. "First, to avoid accusations of defamation, the details must be kept confidential and every part of the procedure strictly followed; second, the procedure should accord with natural justice."

PUBLIC ARENA

From this review it might be concluded that these issues have mostly been thrashed out in the pages of *Science* and *Nature* and in the academic corridors of power. So they have, but I doubt whether we would have got nearly so far without another participant coming on the scene: the United States Congress. For since the early 1980s a whole series of public hearings has been held, latterly and notably under the chairmanship of Representative John Dingell. Not only chairman of the house's Energy and Commerce Committee, but also of the subcommittee on oversight and investigations, Dingell has a large, skilled staff, whose power is backed by the ability to subpoena. "Dingell," says Daniel Greenberg, the *Lancet's* correspondent, "is widely regarded as a political vulture, circling for prey. Indeed he is. But if there were no prey, he would uncomplainingly go away."[32]

At these hearings not only has it been possible for many facts to be disclosed under conditions of privilege (it was at a hearing that Stewart and Feder reported that publication of their Darsee analysis was held up on legal grounds), but Dingell has also persisted in pursuing important cases (such as Imanishi-Kari) against all opposition. And it was a result of the continuing shilly-shallying responses to Congressional criticisms by those who should have put matters right that the authorities finally lost patience. For by 1989 virtually nobody was satisfied with the procedures for investigating scientific misconduct. Investigations had taken much longer than expected, there had been squabbles over who should do them, and Congress had felt that the NIH lacked the will to tackle matters vigorously. The Institute of Medicine report, published in February 1989, urged the NIH to establish a new office not only to encourage proper research conduct but also to require that by 1992 all federally funded institutions should have set up mechanisms for investigating misconduct.[33]

In fact, the NIH—which had taken part in the Institute of Medicine's discussions—had already been discussing creating such an office; by April that year not one, but two offices had come into being: an Office of Scientific Integrity (OSI), reporting to the director of the NIH and an Office of Scientific Integrity Review (OSIR), reporting to the assistant secretary for health in the Department of Health and Human Services. The OSI was to oversee misconduct investigations done elsewhere, recommend punishments, and promote high standards of research conduct; it could also initiate investigations of its own. The OSIR was to oversee OSI and to help develop policy.

In 1990, over a year after OSI was started, its director, Jules Hallum (who had been appointed only in April 1990), and his deputy, Suzanne Hadley, published a review of its workings.[34] It had resolved, they stated, over 60 cases of possible misconduct in its first 15 months, and had been successful because it relied not on the traditional "direct confrontation" of Anglo-Saxon law but on a "scientific dialogue" model similar to that used in editorial peer review. The professional staff of OSI were trained scientists, who could examine and evaluate data provided by the respondents to substantiate their claims. If no evidence was found suggesting that there had been scientific misconduct, the inquiry was closed; if such evidence was found, then the process proceeded to an investigation.

Interestingly, in view of subsequent complaints that the OSI procedure did not sufficiently protect the rights of the respondent, Hallum and Hadley dealt with the issue in their article, listing several safeguards. All persons interviewed could be accompanied by counsel, and could introduce evidence at any time as well as suggesting witnesses—who would be interviewed, as well as the respondent; the latter would be sent a transcript of the interviews for comment. To be sure, to protect the whistleblower, there would be no direct confrontation or cross examination of witnesses— but there would be confrontation of the *scientific* issues (their italics). And if the findings of an investigation pointed to misconduct, further rights included a review of the reports for thoroughness, fairness, and objectivity, not only by the respondent but by three bodies: the agency director, OSIR, and the assistant secretary for health. If the recommendation was for debarment, there was an additional right for a formal hearing, using direct confrontation.

Despite these objectives, so far OSI has had a stormy first three years. There have been claims that it was slow and secretive, had succumbed to unwarranted political influence, leaked documents before they had been released, and had confused investigation with adjudication. And most of its findings of misconduct had been based on the findings of reports from universities rather than its own investigations.

The principal complaint, however, centred on a lack of due process for those it had investigated. This claim was brought to a head with the case of James Abbs, a professor of neurology at the University of Wisconsin, whom a graduate student accused of misrepresenting curves in an article published in *Neurology* in 1987. In January 1990 Abbs was told by OSI that he was under investigation, and he then found that he had also been listed on its computerised database of scientists under scrutiny. In a federal district court in Wisconsin, Abbs and the university argued that before OSI could arrive at a verdict it must allow him due process. In a judgment delivered at the end of the year, however, Judge Barbara Crabb went even further, ruling that the OSI policies and procedures were illegal because it had not followed the obligatory requirement to publish proposed regulations and invite public comment.[35] Things became even more complicated in May 1992 when at a federal court in Chicago an appeal against this decision by both sides (by Abbs concerning the alleged violation of due process) ruled against Abbs on both counts.[36]

Subsequently it was to be claimed that a rival set of procedures set up by a sister body, the National Science Foundation, had worked better, given that this used lawyers at every stage of the investigation.[37] Against that, however, were differences in the case load (which consisted mainly of accusations of plagiarism and intellectual theft at the National Science Foundation) and in its relative insulation from political pressures. At the time of writing (September 1992) the future of both the OSI and the OSIR was in the air.[38] A new plan by the Public Health Services proposed renaming the OSI the Office of Research Integrity Assurance—assigning this to the assistant secretary for health's office—and transferring the staff of the OSIR to service a new Research Integrity Policy Board, which would hold hearings on request by a respondent. (This might not necessarily be in his or her interests, however, given that the hearing might be in public). Despite all the talk, no public notice of changes to the present set-up has yet been given.

It is all too easy to criticise these organisations for their composition and workings. What impresses an outsider, however, is the speedy way in which the problem has been tackled in the United States, and the vigorous debate that has gone on at all levels of society, notably aided by accounts in the major journals, such as *Science, Nature,* and the *Lancet*. And however messy in practice such arrangements may be, at least the problem is recognised as something that cannot be allowed to go on unchecked. Whistleblowers have somewhere to go to, universities are reminded that they can no longer turn a blind eye to suspicions of misconduct, and eventually the debates will ensure that the respondent's right to due process is built in to any procedure. Although a few other countries— Australia, Denmark, the United Kingdom—have all taken steps in the same direction, many have not. Where are the recommendations for dealing with possible misconduct for other Nordic countries, The Netherlands, Germany, Italy, and France, all of which carry on a sizable amount of scientific research? (And instances of fraud certainly exist: I have documentation of at least one fraudster who, I suspect, is still at his tricks, besides having heard a mass of anecdotes, and the chapter by Lagarde and Maisonneuve confirms that the problem exists in France). Perhaps this is a topic that the European Commission should be seen to be tackling on a multination basis. Should it do so, it will find the lessons learnt in the United States, and to a lesser extent elsewhere, an excellent guide.

1 Broad W. Wade N. *Betrayers of the truth.* New York: Simon and Schuster, 1982.
2 Kohn A. *False prophets.* Oxford: Blackwell, 1986.
3 Miller DJ, Hersen M (eds). *Research fraud in the behavioral and biomedical sciences.* New York: Wiley, 1992.
4 LaFollette MC. *Stealing into print.* Berkeley: University of California Press, 1992.
5 Talent JA. The peripatetic fossils: part 5. *Nature* 1990; 343: 405–6.
6 Lock S. Misconduct in medical research. *BMJ* 1988; 297: 1531–5.
7 Shapiro M, Charrow R. The role of data audits in detecting scientific misconduct. *JAMA* 1989; 261: 2505–11.
8 McAdam A. Professor resigns after barrage of plagiarism charges. *The Bulletin* 1 July 1986: 30.
9 Anonymous. Erasures from register. *BMJ* 1975; 2: 392.
10 Anonymous. Must plagiarism thrive? *BMJ* 1980; 281: 41–2.
11 Anonymous. Differential diagnosis of dementia. *BMJ* 1987; 294: 1236.
12 Lock S. Research fraud. *BMJ* 1990; 301: 1348.
13 Medawar P. *Advice to a young scientist.* Cambridge: Harper and Row, 1979.
14 Friedman PJ. Correcting the literature following fraudulent publication. *JAMA* 1990; 263: 1416–9.
15 Holden C. NIH moves to debar cholesterol researcher. *Science* 1987; 237: 718–9.
16 Culliton BJ. Harvard researchers retract data in immunology paper. *Science* 1986; 239: 1069.
17 A statement on the draft report by OSI by Baltimore appeared in *Nature* (9 May 1991), with comments by Margot O'Toole the following week and replies by Baltimore and Eisen and a formal response by Imanishi-Kari two weeks after this (30 May).
18 Culliton BJ. Harvard psychiatrist resigns. *Science* 1988; 242: 1239–40.
19 Norman C. Stanford inquiry casts doubt on 11 papers. *Science* 1988; 242: 659–61.
20 Barinaga M. NIMH assigns blame for tainted studies. *Science* 1989; 245: 812.
21 Palca J. Scientific misconduct cases revealed. *Science* 1990; 48: 297.
22 Anderson C. NIH laboratory admits to fabricated embryo research, retracts paper. *Nature* 1992; 357: 427.
23 Aldhous P. Tragedy revealed in Zurich. *Nature* 1992; 355: 577.
24 Rennie D. Cited by Roark, cited by Kohn.[2]

25 Vaughn RG. Whistleblowing in academic research. Paper presented at the second AAAS-ABA National Conference of Lawyers and Scientists Workshop on Fraud and Misconduct in Science, 1988.
26 Green HP. Scientific responsibility and the law. *Journal of Law Reform* 1987; **204**: 1009.
27 Edsall J. *Scientific freedom and responsibility* (1975). Cited by Green.[26]
28 Association of American Medical Colleges. *The maintenance of high ethical standards in the conduct of research*. Washington, DC: AAMC, 1982.
29 Association of American Universities. *Framework for institutional policies and procedures to deal with fraud in research*. Washington, DC: AAU, 1988.
30 Royal College of Physicians of London. *Fraud and misconduct in medical research*. London: RCP, 1991.
31 Harvard Medical School. *Guidlines for investigators in scientific research*. Cambridge, Mass: Office of the Dean for Academic Affairs, 1988.
32 Greenberg DS. Science and the Dingell factor. *Lancet* 1992; **339**: 234–5.
33 Institute of Medicine. *The responsible conduct of research*. Washington, DC: IOM, 1989.
34 Hallum J, Hadley S. Scientific misconduct: the evolution of method. Professional ethics report *Newsletter of AAS* 1990; **3**: 4–5.
35 Greenberg DS. The "fraud squad" is ruled out of bounds. *Lancet* 1991; **337**: 289–30.
36 Anonymous. Court rule for NIH. *Science* 1992; **256**: 1137.
37 Hamilton DP. NSF's no-fuss investigation. *Science* 1992; **255**: 1346.
38 Hamilton DP. OSI: better the devil you know. *Science* 1992; **255**: 1344–7.

In describing many of the details of recent cases of research misconduct in the United States I have been considerably helped by the table of misconduct cases resolved by the Public Health Service in the last two years published in *The Chronicle Of Higher Education* (3 July, 1991, A7)

A pharmaceutical company's approach to the threat of research fraud

PETER BROCK

The increased concern since 1990 about fraud in pharmaceutical industry-sponsored research has been criticised by many people as being a gross over reaction to a minor problem. But the emphasis on fraud occurring in *clinical* research is a greater concern.

Clinical research is almost at the end of the research and development chain for a pharmaceutical product. Very many important decisions are made much earlier on the basis of one or two critical experiments. Often dosage recommendations for initial clinical work are based on pharmacokinetic data derived from a small number of animals, and often the results are not duplicated. The carcinogenic risk or toxic risk to humans is often extrapolated from one or two pivotal toxicology studies. On the other hand it is very unlikely that key decisions concerning the assessment of risk or dosage would be based on a single clinical comparative trial.

Thus, unreliable data, particularly in relation to toxicology or pharmacology, could have much more serious implications than fraud occurring in a single phase III or phase IV clinical study. Companies should therefore be equally vigilant with regard to preclinical experiments as to clinical experiments in man. Unfortunately, from the general public's perspective, this does not seem to have been the case.

Many of the cases of fraud which have been drawn to the public's attention have been relatively trivial examples occurring in postmarketing surveillance or large scale general practice studies. Few cases of fraud in earlier phase research come to public notice. This may reflect the higher standards of this research, and the inbuilt checks and balances within a company or contract research house, but this is not proved.

The relative importance of early phase research does, however, commit a company to having the most stringent checks and balances to ensure that all data coming out of early phase research are genuine and validated.

Despite the concern that undue emphasis has been placed on clinical research, as distinct from early phase research, most of the steps that companies are introducing to protect themselves against clinical research fraud are equally applicable to in-house or contract research.

In this chapter I will outline some of the approaches that can be adopted by companies in order to protect themselves against clinical fraud, because that is where most experience has been obtained.

Why commit fraud?

A thorough knowledge of the motivation to commit fraud could provide companies with a permanent cure to the problem. Unfortunately such a panacea does not exist but some of the factors that motivate investigators to commit fraud are obvious and well documented.

PEER PRESSURE

There have been numerous examples, mainly in academic research, of peer pressure leading to the need to publish a continuous stream of articles or to achieve "a breakthrough" in a particular topic. This is well documented but there seems little that can be done to ameliorate this academic peer group pressure.

UNREASONABLE EXPECTATIONS

The industry, in its constant drive to shorten the development time for new pharmaceuticals, exerts considerable pressure on its research and discovery group. Simple calculations can show that each month's delay in product licence approval, in a major country, can lead to loss of sales revenue of many millions of pounds. In the light of this pressure it is not surprising that there have been cases where short cuts have been taken in the development process. Sometimes these short cuts have led to the fraudulent generation of data.

An investigator, with a proved track record in a fairly simple and straightforward study, is asked by the company to do a second or third study. The new study, however, is a much more complex design, much more stretching scientifically, and requires much more commitment both of time and effort from the investigator. The investigator feels embarrassed to admit that he does not properly understand the study, the company assumes because he has done the earlier study well that he is "a good investigator" and does not take the time adequately to explain what is required of him. This is a recipe for disaster.

GREED

It is, however, a sad reflection on the standards of some investigators that the only motivation that can be identified for their committing forgery or fraud is straightforward greed. Many acts of fraud in clinical research have been linked to trivial studies involving small sums of money. It is therefore difficult to understand how greed could be a motivating factor. Further analysis does, however, show that quite often the company has conveyed the idea that these studies are trivial (occasionally postmarketing surveillance is the culprit here) and this has communicated itself to the investigator. The unscrupulous investigator feels, therefore, that as the study is trivial he will treat it trivially and has a licence to defraud.

It is obvious that company culture, approach, and attitude, or academia's approach and attitude, are common factors. In tackling the problem of fraud it therefore seems that a change in attitude on behalf of the company or academia should be the key to success.

Who commits fraud?

The distressing answer to this question is that all layers of company organisations from external investigators through trial monitors, people engaged in data resolution, data processing, and project management, to medical directors have all at one time or another been involved in allegations of clinical fraud.

This observation is very important for companies aiming to eradicate fraud from their research process. It means that companies must have systems that allow suspicion and checking of all levels of the organisation up to and including senior management. This is hard to achieve in practice.

The prime aim of every company must be to build in checks and balances which allow appeal to "a higher authority" if a complainant feels that his or her immediate line manager is not responding appropriately to the complaint.

The company's dilemma: between a rock and a hard place

Having concluded that a change in attitude on behalf of the company or academic department could be a key to success in combating fraud the obvious question to ask is "Why hasn't this happened before?"

To understand why the pharmaceutical industry has been loth, until recently, to tackle the problem of fraud one has to understand the unique relationship that exists between the pharmaceutical industry and its customers.

In the normal relationship of a company carrying out a process, a supplier of goods, and an end user or customer the supplier supplies the raw material, which is then processed by the manufacturer and sold to a customer. The transactions are one way. In this scheme the customer can impose standards on the manufacturer and the manufacturer can impose standards on his supplier.

The situation that the pharmaceutical industry finds itself in with regards to clinical research is that our suppliers—in this case clinicians—are normally our customers, prescribing doctors. This has been one of the prime reasons why the pharmaceutical industry has been loth to take an aggressive attitude to clinical fraud.

A case study might make the problem clear.

THE CASE OF DR X

The clinical research department of a large pharmaceutical company carried out a large postmarketing surveillance study on its new cardiovascular agent. In the routine screening of the data, suspicion was raised that a certain doctor, Doctor X, had fraudulently generated the data. A site visit was initiated and the site monitor confirmed that it was highly likely that Doctor X had committed fraud.

After documentation of the case it was drawn to the attention of the medical director, who decided to pursue the doctor for fraud. As was the company's custom, the medical director's intention to prosecute the case was drawn to the attention of the marketing and sales directors and the chief executive officer.

Three days after the joint staff meeting to discuss the case, a note was received from the national sales manager concerning Doctor X. The note read:

Doctor X is one of the best doctors that we have in the country for prescribing our whole range of products. Our local representative confirms that Doctor X is a "company friend" and any prosecution brought against Doctor X would have a major impact on our sales in that area. Not only is Doctor X a keen user of the company products but he has been used extensively to speak at local and regional meetings in support of our products particularly in light of his first hand knowledge of their use.

I therefore recommend to the CEO that no further action be taken against Doctor X despite the fact that the case seems proven against him.

The commercial decision not to prosecute Doctor X was upheld by the chief executive officer and no further action was taken. This, however, is not the end of the saga.

Unbeknown to the sales and marketing directors, the medical director had asked the research group to check their computer database to see if Doctor X had participated in other studies. Two or three days later it was confirmed that Doctor X had participated in at least two other studies and one large postmarketing surveillance exercise. The data were retrieved from these studies and checked, and a high index of suspicion that fraud had been committed in these studies was confirmed.

In addition the national sales manager, presumably out of interest, had been checking the representative call statistics to see how often Doctor X had been called on by the local representative. He was amazed to find that for the past two years Doctor X had been seen between 10 and 16 times a year despite the fact that the maximum call frequency allowed within the company was four to six calls a year even on high users of company products.

At this stage several people were getting extremely concerned and it was decided to check, through independent audit, whether Doctor X was in fact a high user of company products as he had claimed. *As far as could be told from an in-depth audit using third party sources, Doctor X was in fact not a user of company products at all.*

The myth therefore of the "company friend," the good doctor whom we do not want to upset, was in this case exploded. It was, however, serendipity that the investigation of Doctor X was carried further because of the interest of the medical director and the national sales manager. It is a salutory note that, despite the additional information, no further action was taken against Doctor X.

Not only was Doctor X defrauding the clinical research department, he was in fact defrauding the representatives and the company—particularly when it is borne in mind that the company was using him, and paying an honorarium, to speak about his first hand knowledge of company products to other doctors.

The dilemma posed by the unique relationship with the customer as the supplier, and the need to protect company friends, as illustrated by this case, is still a major hurdle to the industry's commitment to stamping out fraud in clinical research.

The position in the United Kingdom between 1989 and 1992 has improved considerably. The positive approach taken by the Association of the British Pharmaceutical Industry and the very firm line taken by the General Medical Council (GMC) have reinforced the British pharmaceutical industry's decision to eradicate fraud from clinical research. The GMC in its 1992 annual report makes the following comment:

The Council is bound to take a serious view of behaviour such as that outlined above [proved clinical fraud], in relation to clinical trials. Lack of care or dishonesty by doctors when participating in such trials is not only discreditable in itself, but is also a potential source of danger to patients, whose safety depends on the integrity and diligence of all those who participate in the testing of approved drugs.

This unambiguous statement has proved very helpful in convincing companies and organisations to adopt an aggressive approach to suspected fraud.

Prevention or cure

The old adage that prevention is better than cure applies to fraud in clinical research. The cost, inconvenience, and delays incurred by having to redo clinical studies because of lack of confidence in data obtained from a pivotal research project are enormous. Although this chapter will review some of the methods which have been used to detect fraud once it has been committed, the aim of a company should be to prevent fraud being perpetrated against it, not to detect when fraud has been committed. In fact the detection of a fraud perpetrated against a company should be seen as a failure of the company systems, and just as much a criticism of the company as of the person committing the crime.

In attempting to prevent fraud the attitude of the company and its employees is of prime importance. A full and frank discussion covering the company's approach to fraud and its methods used to detect it can act as a major deterrent to an investigator tempted to take short cuts with the study. To achieve this, trial monitors, clinical research associates, medical advisers, and all other people having contact with investigators must have adequate training to make sure that the right message is communicated. A company that gives the impression that a research project is "trivial" cannot expect it to be taken seriously by an investigator.

The application of the guidelines on good clinical practice and good clinical research practice[1-3] with the checks and balances they introduce, and the structured approach to the writing of protocol, design of case record forms, and archiving of documentation, have done much to convince investigators that clinical research is a serious issue for the pharmaceutical industry. This change in attitude, and the benefits that come with it, should be one of the main reasons for applying good clinical research practice to all phases of clinical research, not just studies being done for regulatory purposes

A way to further emphasise the company's insistence on reliable and accurate data is to have a formal contract between the investigator and the company. This is often called "The investigator agreement." This contract, as well as covering finance, timings, etc, should include the following items:
- A statement that the research is to be carried out according to the good clinical practice guidelines (GCP). (If necessary a brief guide to these could be attached to make sure that there was no uncertainty about what this meant)

- A statement that the company reserves the right to audit or do source data verification in order to check the accuracy of the data
- A statement that it is company policy to pursue all cases of suspected clinical fraud according to a standard operating procedure. If the standard operating procedure is attached the potential investigator is left in no doubt as to the consequences of fraud.

The role of the standard operating procedure

With the introduction of good clinical research practice, standard operating procedures now govern all aspects of clinical research. Every company should have a standard operating procedure outlining what is required of its employees in cases of suspected fraud.

Such a standard operating procedure achieves two objectives. Firstly, it can be used to show would-be investigators the company's approach to fraud and thus convince them of the seriousness with which this is viewed by the company. Secondly, it offers some protection, at least in English law, for people who act according to the standard operating procedure who may be threatened with litigation by persons suspected of committing fraud. This is particularly important in those cases where, on further investigation according to the processes laid out in the standard operating procedure, the suspicion is found to be unfounded.

In order for the limited protection offered by such a standard operating procedure to be maximised it should clearly and unequivocally state the exact process that should be adopted by someone who has a suspicion that clinical fraud has taken place. It should be unequivocal and allow no deviation from the steps outlined. Further protection can be obtained if the job descriptions of those engaged in clinical research state that compliance with the standard operating procedures currently in force (including the one on fraud) is a requirement for employment.

As well as offering the benefits outlined above a company standard operating procedure, if properly written, can offer the right advice and guidance to junior staff who have reason to use this procedure, which, we hope, is only rarely called on. The junior clinical research associate who is suspicious of the world famous professor at a time when all her senior colleagues are on holiday would find a clearly written standard operating procedure of tremendous use.

An example of a standard operating procedure is given in appendix A.

Detecting clinical fraud

The detection of clinical fraud is not easy. Some formal scheme is necessary particularly if approaches to the problem are going to be carried

forward into a training programme. A scheme that has been found to work well in practice is to consider the detection of fraud in four distinct steps:
- The visit, normally by clinical research associate, medical research associate, or medical adviser
- The return trial materials
- The case record forms, patient diary cards, etc
- The final report.

THE VISIT

For companies which have fully implemented GCP into everyday working, initiation visits are required before the setting up of a clinical trial. These visits provide the ideal opportunity to assess the reliability, effectiveness, and, sometimes, honesty of the centres being considered to participate in a research programme.

To fully exploit the opportunity presented by these early visits and the planning of clinical research a certain approach is necessary from the company representative. Many company representatives (clinical research associates or medical research associates) involved in the initiation visits for clinical research are new graduates in their first professional post. They need to be trained that if they have the slightest concern that something is not right with the centre or the investigator this should be communicated to the responsible person in the company. Many new graduates find this very difficult to put into practice, particularly if dealing with well known or prestigious investigators or centres. Strong reassurance from their management on the importance of this issue is needed.

In helping clinical research staff to identify the "giveaway signs" conveyed during a study initiation visit, training and the sharing of experience are the keys to success. With encouragement, trial monitors will rapidly build up a bibliography of relevant quotes or situations or attitudes which may indicate a possible future problem.

SOME NOTEWORTHY QUOTES

"I won't actually be doing the work, my ... will be, but you can't meet them today because they are off somewhere else."

(At a study or site initiation visit): "I'll be getting the patients from several other clinics/outpatients, but I am not quite sure which ones I will use yet, I will let you know."

(At a monitoring visit): "I don't have the patient's records here, but if you know what the questions are, I will follow them up and send the answers on to you."

It is common practice, in fact some people would say the norm, for the principal investigator not to be the person who will actually do the work.

Under these conditions it is essential that the company be given access to the staff who will be ultimately responsible for carrying out the studies. It is all too easy for a prestigious or busy unit to take on more and more work in the hope, without checking, that the junior staff can cope with it. Under these conditions unreasonable pressures are brought to bear on junior staff, fearful for their future, to complete the studies.

To illustrate some of the problems a further case study is useful.

THE CASE OF STUDY A

A British based pharmaceutical company was preparing to do a pivotal pharmacokinetic study on a new clinical lead. The study was aimed at establishing the pharmacokinetics of the new product in an elderly population.

The company had not carried out pharmacokinetic studies in elderly patients in the United Kingdom before and so had problems in selecting a suitable centre. A literature search was carried out and a centre was chosen on the basis of published work. The centre was visited by the clinical projects manager concerned to check that it was capable of doing the study according to the company's standard operating procedures.

At this visit the project manager spoke with the head of department, who reassured him by reference to previous work, both published and unpublished, and a review of the documentation from previous studies that the unit was equipped and able to do the work required. The principal investigator emphasised that the work would be carried out in a six-bedded unit which was an offshoot, separate from the main ward of another hospital. A protocol was developed, based on a protocol provided by the parent company and all the appropriate signatures were obtained.

At this time the medical director of the company was asked to sign the protocol but remembered the investigator's name from previous conversations with colleagues at a pharmaceutical function a few weeks before. On checking up with his colleagues he found that the centre had an unreliable track record over the past six months or so, but had been a reliable unit before that. The medical director refused to sign the protocol and instructed the project manager to return to the unit to confirm that it was suitable and able to do the work required.

On this occasion the project manager made an appointment to visit the unit concerned, although this was difficult. On arrival he was greeted by a rather harassed registrar, who explained that the "unit" was in fact a curtained off area in one of the main geriatric wards and was currently full of routine admissions because of a flu epidemic. The junior staff member also confirmed that there was a backlog of studies waiting in the unit but staff cuts over the past six months, owing to hospital cutbacks, had made it more and more difficult to carry out the work.

Needless to say the study never actually went ahead but it is problematical whether it would ever have been completed or, more importantly, whether, if it had apparently been completed, it would have been done fraudulently.

Sometimes visits by clinical research associates can produce unexpected results:

THE CASE OF TRIAL P: THE UNUSUAL CONSEQUENCES OF MONITORING VISITS BY CLINICAL RESEARCH ASSOCIATES

A large multicentre study of an injectable anti-infective agent for the management of intra-abdominal sepsis was being carried out by a European based company. Monitoring visits by the clinical research associate were, after the initiation and set-up visits, to be held at monthly intervals.

One particular centre caught the attention of the data administrator, who plotted out the recruitment rate for the suspicious centre and all other centres.

This showed that at the end of month two after the clinical research associates had been on a motivational campaign recruitment picked up from five per month to just about six per month for most centres and then returned down to the baseline recruitment rate of five per month until the visit at the end of month five. At this point the clinical research associates told the investigators that recruitment was closing in one month with the inevitable upswing in recruitment rate.

With the suspect centre the upswing in recruitment after the visit at the end of month two was a little above average but not suspicious. What was suspicious was the very dramatic (in fact in this case doubling) increase of recruitment of patients when the investigator was informed that the study would close for recruitment in one or two months' time and no further patients would qualify for payment. Further investigation revealed that at least four of the patients recruited after the visit at the end of month four were not included in the study.

Monitoring for patterns or trends in documentation which may raise suspicion

Historically, clinical research was often analysed by using accounting paper, pencil, and rubber. The volumes of data collected were limited and it was possible to look at complete data sets and get a very good "feel for the data." Many experienced statisticians still insist on obtaining this "feel for the data" before subjecting it to statistical analysis.

The introduction of modern computer methods has to a large measure removed manual manipulation of the data. The need to process case record forms as if they are items on a production line, to avoid peaks and troughs of workload in the data group, has exacerbated the problem. Monitoring visits by field staff are often spaced out over many weeks or months and case record forms will have moved on to the next level within the data processing organisation.

The first suspicion of fraud is often based on a "gut feeling" of primary or secondary monitors. In order to encourage this intuitive approach it is often useful to reacquire all the case record forms relating to a particular doctor or centre and to review them all together. This is particularly the case if there are other grounds for suspicion. This longitudinal review of the data, all in one place and at one time, may draw attention to suspicious similarities which have been missed when individual case record forms have been handled on a one by one basis as they move through the system.

There are many giveaway signs, too many to list here, which may point to forgery or fraud. In one example the use of a distinctive green colour ink to complete the case record forms on approximately 60 patients from three different centres over a six month period was suspicious. Patient diary cards, particularly those requiring the patients to enter data and symptoms or complete questionnaires or visual analogue scales, can be particularly revealing. Similarities in handwriting between "patients" or the way that the "patient" has marked the visual analogue line can often be the clue that initiates a fraud investigation.

Of particular interest is the wide variety of ways that patients choose to mark visual analogue lines if given a free choice, as they normally are; the use of a cross, tick, oblique or horizontal line, or even a bar commencing at one end of the visual analogue scale and finishing at the patient's preferred point will all be seen. Lack of this variability in patients' completed visual analogue scales allegedly coming from different patients should be viewed with great suspicion.

The dating game

Many cases of fraud are committed without much thought on the part of the person perpetrating the crime. Often the fraud is committed in a great hurry, particularly if the motivation is to complete the work by an agreed deadline. Under these circumstances quite obvious and silly mistakes are made. The person committing the crime is often more concerned to check that the follow ups actually occur 10, 14, 28, or 60 days—whatever the protocol dictates—after the previous visit than to ensure that these dates actually fall on days of the week that make sense. It is not unusual to find that some investigators seem to be doing a lot of clinics on a Sunday and even routine follow up outpatient endoscopies on Christmas Day have occasionally been noted. In one dramatic example a whole cohort of patients were claimed to have been followed up at a time when it was known that the unit was shut for refurbishment.

The trial materials

Good clinical practice requires that all unused trial materials be accounted for on completion of a clinical study.

Of all the aspects that clinical trial monitors and clinical research associates find most fascinating, the one that captures the imagination is the review or audit of returned clinical trial materials. Quite often the first hint of trouble occurs after the review of returned trial materials.

It pays to be suspicious—bearing in mind that trial materials normally have been in a patient's home, handbag, pocket, or kitchen cabinet—if they seem to be too clean, too exact, or too similar. From my experience, trial materials which are actually taken as prescribed are very suspicious indeed. Although it is generally accepted that compliance in clinical trials is higher than compliance in routine medical practice, materials taken exactly as dispensed should be viewed with a great deal of scepticism.

The widespread introduction of calendar packing and blister packing has also provided a fruitful area for investigation. Calendar packs which start on the same day are obviously worthy of investigation. It is sometimes particularly illuminating to check the day of the week that it seems the medication was started on against the start date as entered on the case record form.

One of the mainstays of the detection of fraud is the recognition that a person's habitual behaviour will be reflected in the case record forms or other activities associated with the study. The use of blister packaging has led to some interesting examples. In one particular study of an antidepressant, it seems that the medication was being taken properly but examination of returned blister packages from several different "patients" showed that they had all started their medication from the same physical location on the blister strip. Obviously this is very unlikely to occur in real practice.

Two more case studies will further illustrate possible approaches in reviewing returned trial materials.

THE CASE OF TRIAL Z

Trial Z was a study with a topical (gel formulation) of a non-steroidal anti-inflammatory drug carried out in the United Kingdom. It was a parallel group, multicentre, double blind placebo controlled study using 20 centres, with 12 patients per centre.

At the first follow up visit to one particular centre, when the first two to three patients entered a review, the trial monitor voiced some concerns suggesting possible fraud. The monitor had noted that the returned trial materials all seemed to have been handled the same way. The tubes had been squeezed in an identical fashion. The monitor commented, "There are four people living in our house, we all squeeze our toothpaste differently—how is it that the three patients enrolled into the study at this centre seem to have squeezed their tubes identically—not only that but the tubes seem to have been gripped in the middle and squeezed, very unlikely for a medication that was meant to have been given three to four times a day for five to seven days." At a subsequent visit the remaining tubes for the last nine patients from that centre all looked identical.

The returned samples for this centre were also unique in that their weights were a mean of 24 g $\pm$ 6 g, whereas the tubes returned from the other centres showed a mean weight of 8 g $\pm$ 12 g. Examination of all the tubes returned from the suspect centre showed that they had all been gripped and squeezed in an identical manner—making it very unlikely that the materials had been used in the clinical trial by 12 different patients.

THE CASE OF TRIAL Y

Trial Y was a study of an oral non-steroidal anti-inflammatory drug. It was a prospective, double-blind, placebo controlled, crossover study carried out as part of a phase III programme. Escape analgesia (paracetamol) was provided. The consumption rates for the escape analgesia were calculated on a daily basis and were one of the parameters of efficacy.

The centre carrying out the study had a proved track record in similar work and seemed to have carried out previous studies quickly and efficiently.

The company statistician was the first to point out an anomaly. It was obvious from reviewing the data that in those treatment periods when the patients should have been receiving the active drug their analgesic consumption seemed to remain the same as when they were receiving placebo. As previous studies had shown efficacy this was very suspicious.

There were three explanations: there had been problems in clinical trial materials—not unknown—and the active drug was in fact missing from the treatment schedules (that is, the patients received placebo all the time), or, secondly, the drug was not active, or, thirdly, the patients were not taking the medication.

Analysis of retention samples, of surplus materials unallocated from the trial programme, and of returned samples from the study confirmed that the active drug was present in the appropriate tablets. A review of the blister packaging of the trial materials suggested that the patients were in fact taking them as directed. A review of other clinical trial data suggested that the dose being given in this study was adequate to achieve an analgesic effect, which should have led to a reduction in the consumption of escape analgesia.

Audit confirmed that the patients actually existed but there was no evidence that they had participated in the clinical study (this study was carried out before GCP was widely introduced in the United Kingdom). Subsequently the investigator admitted that he had made up all the data and had disposed of the escape analgesia leaving "just a few" tablets in the bottle.

Routine examination of the data: a time consuming exercise

Once data have been loaded into a database, particularly with on line computer systems which are now widely available, it becomes simplicity itself to carry out comprehensive analysis of data sets. This can be a useful exercise and the chapter by Evans gives details of the principles behind such analysis and the various methods available. Many companies have introduced the routine review of data by such methods as part of their quality assurance procedures.

Interpretation of data derived from such comparisons should, however, be undertaken with extreme care. I have known several cases where suspicion was raised by the "atypical" nature of the data from a centre. Further investigation revealed, however, that the data were quite genuine and the difference was due to either an unusual age/sex distribution within that centre or particular referral patterns happening within a hospital or community. It is therefore, I think, unwise to base any case of suspected fraud simply on this sort of analysis.

THE RETURNED CASE RECORD FORMS

Case record forms are used and completed in a working environment. A data monitor from a major international company once said at a meeting that "The case record form returned without at least four coffee stains and four different pens used in its completion has invariably been fraudulently filled in". This is probably an extreme view but case record forms which are returned too quickly, too clean, too complete (with no data resolutions), and too uniform in terms of both the style of handwriting and pens used should be viewed with considerable suspicion.

Having given some indication of the methods that can be used for detecting fraudulent centres I must emphasise that by far the bigger problem is the detection of a single fraudulent entry, or series of entries, relating to a particular patient within a centre or to a particular visit. A missing value may be fraudulently completed when all other data are complete and when company employees are placed under excessive pressure to complete a study. Under other conditions fraud occasionally occurs if a particular patient, whose record is complete in all other respects, misses a follow up appointment for any reason; the data for the missed visits are then invented. The detection of this type of fraud is incredibly difficult. If the investigator, or company employee, has inserted clinically sensible values, taking into account an individual patient's previous and subsequent results, a fraud may be impossible to detect without source data verification.

THE STUDY REPORT

There has been much speculation over the past year or two as to whether fraud is ever detected by the time the final report is written. This has actually occurred but such cases seem to be few and far between. Quite often the observations that lead to the detection of fraud in a clinical report are serendipitous.

THE CASES OF COMPANY D AND F

Two medical directors of major international companies were discussing, over a gin and tonic, the cost of clinical pharmacology in contract research establishments in the United Kingdom. As is often the case both were talking from recent examples and the conversation progressed to discussion of the design of the studies.

It became obvious to the two directors that they were talking about almost identical studies, being carried out at the same contract house, with similar agents. Both of these were cardiovascular agents potentially useful in treating hypertension.

As the evening wore on it not only became obvious that they were talking about a similar study design with similar agents but that the results which they had obtained in their studies were similar if not identical. The two directors agreed, far into the night, to exchange final reports; they were not suspicious that any of the data had been fraudulently generated at this time.

At a subsequent meeting they compared notes because, on reading the reports, it was impossible to detect the difference between them other than that the name of the molecule had been changed. Even the shapes of the kinetic curves were identical and the calculated clearances and half lives were very similar.

To this date neither of the medical directors knows whether the data had been fraudulently generated. Needless to say both reports were abandoned, at substantial cost, both in terms of money paid to the centre and of delay in getting product licence approval.

The value of source data verification audit as a method for detecting research fraud

In theory 100% audit with source data verification should lead to a 100% detection of research fraud. In practice 100% audit is impossible within the bounds of reasonable costs. Most companies therefore have decided to introduce sampling methods, which by definition guarantee less than 100% verification.

At the present state of development in the United Kingdom of source data verification it cannot be relied on to detect all cases of clinical fraud. As the methods develop and GCP and source data verification become the accepted norm, it will undoubtedly be harder for clinical fraud to be committed in British research.

It is also particularly difficult, in the United Kingdom, to use all the information derived from source data verification audit in the prosecution of a case of suspected fraud. Quite often an audit report might contain a phrase as follows:

Careful inspection of the case notes showed that many (16/24) visited the surgery during the trial period for either flu vaccination, blood pressure checks, or for routine examination or follow up for prescriptions. Dr Y commented that the record keeping is not as complete as it should be but that this was a general practice surgery not a research organisation.

Many sets of case notes had a separate new "support card" filled in with the same pen and handwriting. Dr W commented that those who did not have a separate card were seen at home.

There are some doubtful details recorded in the notes, where for example some statements have been deleted and then written over with a different pen.

The role of ethics committees

A good case can be made for ethics committees to have a pivotal role in the detection and management of suspected fraud. Up till now this challenge does not seem to have been picked up by ethics committees.

One can envisage a situation where a protocol is submitted to an ethics committee for its consideration along with the name of the proposed investigator and centre. If an ethics committee had doubts that the doctor could recruit the number of patients required by the protocol, or perhaps had some concerns about the quality of work previously carried out by the centre or doctor, then it would seem to be ethically reasonable for it to draw this to the attention of the company before the initiation of the clinical study.

What should the pharmaceutical industry do about it?

The way forward for the pharmaceutical industry seems clear. To avoid clinical fraud being perpetrated the following process should be introduced and built into the control of the clinical research:

- The full implementation of GCP for all clinical studies
- The setting up of an investigator contract, signed by both investigator and company, which outlines the responsibilities of the investigator and company and specifies what action the company will take if it suspects fraud has been perpetrated against it
- A declaration that the company is willing to prosecute all cases of fraud
- The training of clinical research associates, trial monitors, data managers, and medical advisers to be alert to the telltale signs of fraud
- The building in of routine check statistics to the analysis of data
- The introduction of a standard operating procedure, signed by all levels of management, both commercial and clinical, which outlines unambiguously the steps to be followed in cases of suspected clinical fraud.

The next major step forward would be the generation and sharing of details of cases of suspected fraud among companies, the trade associations and the boards of health and ethics committees. This, because of the legal problems entailed, is something for the future rather than the here and now.

1 Harvard Medical School. *Guidelines for investigators in scientific research.* Cambridge, Mass: Office of the Dean for Academic Affairs, 1988.
2 Association of the British Pharmaceutical Industry. *Good clinical research practice guidelines.* London: ABPI, 1988.
3 Committee on Proprietary Medicinal Products Working Party on Efficacy of Medicinal Products. *Good clinical practice for trials on medicinal products in the European Community.* [111 3976/88-EN Final.] Brussels: European Commission, 1991.

Fraud in general practice research: intention to cheat

JAMES HOSIE

The possibility of fraud in clinical research seemed unlikely until recently. There had been several stories quoted; stories about unethical and criminal doctors in the USA taking names from tombstones and using them as "patients" for drug trials. Such things were not thought likely to happen in Britain. In the past few years, however, there have been several cases of general practitioners being removed from the medical register by the General Medical Council for acts of criminal fraud in clinical research studies.

This chapter provides an overview of fraud from the viewpoint of a general practitioner. It will examine the possible reasons for fraud, the current practices for detecting and preventing fraud, and also some of the complications arising from new guidelines for clinical research. Finally, it will consider some of the ethical questions raised by source document verification and examination of patients' medical records.

The opinions given in this chapter will be coloured by my own experience as an inner city general practitioner with an extensive interest in clinical research, working in a small practice. Over the years I have witnessed the development of good clinical practice (GCP) guidelines and have been amazed by the diversity of ways in which the pharmaceutical companies and contract houses have interpreted and implemented the changes. Finally, I have been concerned in a study, as principal investigator, in which an act of fraud was committed, discovered, and exposed.

General practice research

For the many conditions that require drug treatment, general practice is the obvious setting for clinical research. Firstly, the general practitioner has access to a large number of patients suffering from a particular condition with neither complications nor other illnesses, both of which would make it inappropriate to test new products.

Secondly, the general practitioner has a special relationship with his or her patients, and they are often very willing to help with research. Patients do this for altruistic reasons—a genuine desire to help others suffering from similar conditions—but also they do it to please the doctor. This desire to please the doctor might make them too willing to take part in research, and the general practitioner may need to protect them from this.

A new development in clinical research is source document verification. This is an alleged requirement to allow industry personnel, some of whom do not have a medical qualification, access to the patients' full medical records. The general practitioner must protect his or her patients' confidentiality.

Error versus fraud

It is important to distinguish between error and fraud. Error is an inevitable consequence of clinical practice. An almost infinite variety of mistakes can be made by all those engaged in research. The search for this error is a vital component of good clinical practice. It is only when mistakes are recognised that learning can occur. All our previous medical training has taught us to fear error, as error is associated with blame. This fear may lead to concealment and this in turn can lead to fraud.

Mistakes can occur at every stage in a clinical trial. Patients may over comply with treatment, they may lose diary cards and tablets, they may forget to attend for visits, and they may even move away during the trial. Doctors may forget to record basic information, make mistakes while entering data, include patients incorrectly (for example, those too old for the study), miscount tablets, mix up medication labels, etc. The monitors may confuse researchers by identifying mistakes and requesting changes in data and so compound further errors. Finally, the pharmaceutical companies may make mistakes in packaging and labelling study material and in the method in which they require data to be entered.

While GCP will reduce or eliminate error, it is much less helpful in detecting fraud.

TYPES OF FRAUD

There are two broad categories of fraud: acts of omission and acts of commission. Some examples of acts of omission are failure to note that the patient has a disease which is listed as an exclusion criterion, that the patient is on a drug which is listed as a contraindication or is outside the age range for the study population. Side effects, adverse events, and patient withdrawals may not be reported in order to avoid extra paper work and possibly to avoid loss of income. These last two are the most serious sins of omission.

Acts of commission are much less common. Blood pressure values may be rounded up—for example, diastolic blood pressure entry criteria of 100 may be rounded up from diastolic blood pressure of 99 or lower. Laboratory results and electrocardiograms may be used from other patients, compliance can be altered by throwing away extra tablets, and the dates of visits may be altered to suit the protocol.

REASONS FOR FRAUD

The relationship between the pharmaceutical companies and the general practitioner in contract with them is at times ambivalent. Ostensibly the company purchases the services of a general practitioner to research its product. Sometimes companies seem to be looking for a favourable result in order to justify the expenditure, but such an attitude should not be condoned. In order to encourage full information being sent to the Committee on Safety of Medicines, guidelines have been agreed; some companies, however, would still wish the investigators to report such adverse events only to them and not directly to the Committee on Safety of Medicines.

Within the companies there are various vested interests. Career advancement for clinical research associates may depend on good research and the pressure for favourable results can encourage pressure on the investigator. It can be demoralising as well as detrimental to individual prospects to spend years developing a drug which is later not marketed.

Recently, there has been a growing number of "contract houses" which organise and monitor research. These contract research organisations work on a commission basis and as a result tend to look for investigators to provide large numbers of patients for research rapidly. They have to balance speedy collection of data with adequate monitoring—which may be expensive. This factor alone can encourage error.

The recent increase in the number of general practitioners and other investigators committing fraud in clinical research is not surprising. The most obvious reason is financial gain. Other benefits might be scientific publications and, for those who recruit large numbers of patients, exotic travel to international meetings to present results. Others may commit fraud because of mental instability. An example of this was an investigator found to have "completed a study" before clinical supplies had even been delivered.

Surprisingly, it can take some time before an act of fraud is discovered and may take even longer before it can be proved. The reasons for this are numerous. Pharmaceutical companies do not wish to risk damaging their own reputations; if this one act by an investigator is discovered to be fraudulent, how many episodes before have gone unnoticed? This would cast doubts on the validity of previous research on products that may have already been marketed.

Fraud can be difficult to prove and unsubstantiated allegations are risky. They may expose the company to possible libel claims and bad publicity.

Finally, doctors themselves are reluctant to censure colleagues, believing that highlighting this problem will bring the profession into disrepute.

One example will suffice.

The case

In 1991 I was engaged in a study of an antihypertensive drug as principal investigator. This required that I assist with the design of the study and the analysis of the results but not the choice of clinical researchers. The study was a comparison of two calcium antagonists, one being currently available and the other the drug under investigation.

Towards the end of the study we were examining recruitment rates and withdrawals and it was noted that one investigator had had no withdrawals due to side effects despite having 22 patients in the study. This was surprising as calcium antagonists have a well documented incidence of side effects, especially early on in the treatment. These range from flushing, headaches, and peripheral oedema to constipation.

When the study monitor attempted to visit the surgery to check the data he discovered that the consent forms were missing. His inquiry was met with the explanation that they were at the doctor's home. No electrocardiograms were available for the same reason.

This study had used a local laboratory, and the initial test results were available for all patients except one. Subsequent results, however, were either missing or the laboratory form had had both patient's name and the date of the test removed. When asked to obtain copies of these laboratory tests the doctor refused, saying that he had not informed the laboratory that the patients were taking part in a clinical trial. The company was concerned about this failure and offered to pay for the tests and also to acquire copies of the results. The doctor then went on to explain that for the purpose of anonymity he had used fictitious names on the laboratory forms and he could not now remember them.

Further suspicion was raised by an examination of drug boxes. All were in pristine condition despite having been used by patients for some weeks. All had exactly the correct number of tablets returned, and all patients had had 100% compliance. All patients had attended on exactly the correct time interval and date and all quality of life questionnaires were completed with no mistakes or changes of mind. There were no adverse events and no withdrawals for any other reason.

By this time our concern was so great that the company organised an audit by senior personnel. The doctor was informed in advance of the date and purpose of this audit. On this occasion all the case sheets, electrocardiograms, and consent forms were available.

The consent forms seemed to have three types of very similar handwriting. The electrocardiograms showed that 25% of the patients in the study had left bundle branch block and a further 20% had lateral ischaemia. Comparison of the biochemistry reports for an individual patient showed that values differed greatly over the study period despite there being no adverse events or concurrent illness.

Lastly, it was noted that some of the haematology forms with the dates removed had been signed by a haematologist who had left the hospital some 18 months before the study began. The hospital normally destroys the signature stamp of any haematologist three months after he or she leaves.

This last finding proved to be the only piece of definite evidence, and consequently the company informed the Association of the British Pharmaceutical Industry (ABPI). The APBI received further details from a second company regarding a second trial, conducted suspiciously. The General Medical Council (GMC) was informed, and after an inquiry the doctor's name was removed from the medical register. (A further view of this case is given in the chapter by Wells.)

Detection

It is surprising that, given the above catalogue of "unusual behaviours," the doctor concerned was allowed to continue in the study for so long before suspicion arose. Detection of fraud is a relatively new concern both to the industry and the profession. It is still not considered likely that professionals will commit criminal acts of this nature.

In this case the experience of the clinical research associate who was monitoring the study proved helpful. He was well versed in the protocol, and had a broad based knowledge of the natural history of the disease under investigation and the pharmacology of the drugs being examined. The principal investigator's experience was also helpful. He had considerable skill in research and an awareness of the behaviour of patients in such studies, an understanding of the effects of the drugs over time, and a grasp of the likely and possible side effects of the treatments. Working together they were alerted to the probability of fraud. Almost every possible excuse was considered and then rejected. Despite this, it took considerably longer to prove to the satisfaction of senior personnel within the company and the disciplinary authorities that the doctor had committed fraud.

Prevention

Much work can be done to prevent error. The company should liaise with a principal investigator who has personal experience in running studies. He should be concerned in the writing of the protocol, will be able to predict likely practical problems in the running of a study, and the protocol should therefore be much more relevant. Unnecessary investigations, both in range of tests and in the numbers of times each test is performed, would be avoided. It is excessive, for example, to request three electrocardiograms during a 12 week study of non-steroidal drugs. Superfluous data recording is time consuming and can cause great confusion. One company requests information about all previous treatments for hypertension including the drug names in generic formulation. Such excesses do nothing to improve the study and serve only to demotivate investigators.

Investigators should be chosen with care. In the previous example the investigator's work was considered "dubious" by one company, yet another company commissioned work from him even after the medical director had been made aware of this fact.

Planning meetings with investigators and clinical research associates should be organised well in advance in order to allow the investigators to become conversant with the protocol. The meeting could then discuss pertinent problems. Investigators with previous experience should not be expected to perform the same tests—for example, Hamilton rating scales—time after time for different companies. The current insistence that each individual study be preceded by such a meeting is counterproductive. The current practice of research meetings simply to rehearse the protocol page by page benefits no one.

Clinical research associates need better training and should work with experienced company personnel before being given the responsibility of monitoring studies. Lack of experience can cause research associates to follow their interpretation of GCP guidelines too rigorously. This time consuming exercise is often at the expense of the researcher and his staff. Requests for the researcher to assist the associate in the exact coding of past medical history and concurrent disease such as back pain are an improper use of investigators' time. Again, this is detrimental to the scientific outcome of the study.

There is an urgent need for the industry, perhaps using the ABPI, to produce working guidelines on GCP. They should be clinically orientated, indicative, and explicit. The current confusion is compounded by the fact that the European Commission and the Food and Drug Administration have different requirements and interpretations of each other's regulations.

Reasonable expectations of the amount of time required to set up, recruit, and run a trial would greatly reduce errors. It would allow for proper training and monitoring and reduce the pressure on contract research organisations. This would in turn reduce the pressure on the researcher.

So much for error. It is much more difficult to prevent fraud. Investigators should be made aware of the possible risks incurred and the increasing probability of being caught. This can be done by better publicity of the GMC proceedings against doctors for fraud. Consideration could be given to developing computer software to give the probability of significant changes in laboratory values or electrocardiograms.

At present one company is working with a clinical investigator in order to draw up guidelines for detecting possible fraud in clinical studies at an early stage; additionally, the ABPI has published its own recent report, referred to in the chapter by Wells, which also tackles this issue.

Regrettably, many of the requirements of the new guidelines will not prevent criminal acts of fraud. These requirements include the use of source documentation verification. It has been suggested that if a monitor examines the patients' medical files he or she will be able to verify the data. This is not necessarily true. In the case of fraud described in this chapter the associate had access to the patients' case sheets and the data recorded in the case sheets corresponded to those in the study report forms. An improper investigator can make entries into patients' records which are false. No monitor would be able to detect the difference.

An alternative method of source data verification is the "back to back" method. This is carried out by both clinician and clinical research associates checking the information recorded in the research form against that in the patient's case notes. In this way the associate is prevented from seeing confidential patient records.

This method is very often preferred by the research associates, who are then saved from the task of having to decipher a doctor's handwriting. It may not, however, be preferred by the doctor as it is extremely costly of his or her time.

Patient confidentiality is greatly threatened by this new requirement. The medical record is a very valuable tool for good patient care. In it the doctor records many facts. He or she also records impressions about the patient's condition, and these are often no more than that. Later they may be confirmed or ignored by the doctor. Other facts may be recorded which are not strictly related to that patient's disease but will be important in the handling of that patient's problems now or in the future. Family factors may be recorded, and consent would be required from these people before the record is used by any third party.

Consent to enter a study may specify that the patient's file could be seen by a third party and that third party may not hold a medical qualification. I suspect that if this fact is made clear to patients recruitment will be seriously reduced, and rightly so.

Overall, the benefits to be gained from open access by the industry to patients' clinical notes are far outweighed by the considerable potential loss of this invaluable tool.

In conclusion, there is much work to be done on refining good clinical practice. This work will best be carried out by the ABPI, the GMC, the British Medical Association, and practising clinical researchers working together to produce realistic standard procedures. We must strive to prevent error and fraud by using clinical procedures. These procedures would be much more effective than excessive bureaucratic machinery and would reinforce the value of clinical research in general practice. If this were to happen research would become intellectually stimulating again and, more importantly, much more fun.

The pharmaceutical industry and contract research organisations

MALCOLM VANDENBURG, MARK DAVIS, HAROLD NEAL

The pharmaceutical industry now has many commercial reasons for wanting to be seen at the forefront of the fight against fraudulent data. The development of a new drug is very costly. To have data rejected when these are later discovered to be fraudulent wastes time and research investment and delays sales and profit potential. To have suspect data exposed after marketing causes more havoc. Additionally, data from fraudulent doctors usually overplay efficacy and underplay toxicity, creating false expectations of the drug which can have serious consequences. Most drugs withdrawn from the market are withdrawn because of the realisation of new adverse reactions. Thus any company wants to have every opportunity of discovering these at the research stages.

This would not have been the case in the 1970s, for many reasons. The first is that the pharmaceutical industry did not have systematic methods in place for discovering fraud. It was always felt that doctors were professional, above reproach; that doctors had signed the Hippocratic Oath, that they cared for life, and were sensitive, ethical individuals who had no interest in, or reason for, fabricating data. This belief is unlikely to have been true, but the pharmaceutical industry had always felt itself to be inferior to physicians, looked up to them, and needed them as supporters, influencers, and friends as well as ultimate customers. The researcher, often being from an academic department, was an especially courted individual. When suspected fraud was stumbled on (there being no system in place to discover it), usually nothing was done about it.

There were many reasons for this. Firstly, it was very hard, if not impossible, to prove that fraud had taken place. In pharmaceutical research, the investigator filled in case report forms with the patient's demographic data, as well as efficacy and safety variables, and handed these data to the sponsoring company, which trustingly accepted them. Should the company wish to check on the data in these forms, it was hampered by the investigator using the issue of patient confidentiality to prevent the company checking that the patient existed by reference to the doctor's files on patients, or confirming the data on the case report forms with those in the files. Should access be granted, the data contained on the case report forms were unlikely to be in patients' clinical files.

Secondly, because proving a falsehood is fraught with problems, companies who had suspicions felt constrained by the laws of libel and slander not to make the allegations in any way public, for fear of legal action. They were also scared of bad publicity within the profession—of being seen as the "Big Brother" pharmaceutical industry picking on the poor helpless investigator who was doing his best to help—with subsequent loss of prestige and, probably, prescriptions and, thus, profits.

Thirdly, the pharmaceutical industry usually wanted to believe the data produced by the suspect investigator because such data usually showed the drug under investigation to be good and free of adverse events. It also wanted to include the data in publications and regulatory submissions because each patient studied, or case report form submitted, represented a considerable investment in terms of time and money. More so, in that fraudulent doctors are seen usually to be the the fastest recruiters of patients or completers of case report forms. Discarding their data could leave a regulatory submission or publication considerably short of an adequate number of patients.

So what changed to encourage the pharmaceutical industry to go against this history and become one of the best promoters for the exposure of fraudulent data in the United Kingdom? There were many reasons; some commercial, some regulatory, some practical, and some personal. In addition, there was the growing globalisation of clinical research, implementation of guidelines on good clinical practice (GCP) and the growth of the contract research industry, all of which had an effect for the better. Let us now explore each of these parts.

The contract research organisation and fraud

The growth of the contract research industry has been one of the reasons why pharmaceutical companies now feel able to admit and prosecute fraud. It also explains why more fraud is being detected. Additionally, the problem of fraud is one that the pharmaceutical industry and contract research organisations have to come to terms with and agree how they will interact when fraud is suspected and/or proved.

Companies found it hard to face up to possible fraud in the early days not only because of the regulatory consequences of losing patient numbers, but also because:

- The research departments would have to admit that they had chosen wrong investigators for the study under suspicion
- They had probably been using the same investigators for years in many studies without them being suspected
- Raising awareness of the fraud after analysis and preparation of the report would possibly turn the spotlight on the deficiencies of the research department in not having picked up discrepancies earlier.

Some descriptions of examples of these early stumbles on to research fraud may be useful.

ONE PATIENT—TWO STUDIES

An investigator was simultaneously doing hypertension studies for a pharmaceutical company and an independent clinical research organisation. It just so happened that the data were analysed at the same time by the same person, who noticed that some of the patient initials, dates of birth, and results of blood tests were identical in the two studies with start and end dates which overlapped.

ONE PATIENT—TWO CASE REPORT FORMS

An investigator sent in to the drug company 10 case report forms having been given supplies for 10 patients. These case report forms arrived while the clinical research associate was on holiday and were placed in a file by his secretary. On his return from holiday the clinical research associate rang the physician to ask for the case report forms. The physician promptly sent in 10 new case report forms with the same patient numbers, but completely different data.

IMPROBABLE CLUSTERING OF BLOOD TEST RESULTS

A physician sent in data on 18 patients each of whose serum potassium was always, at each visit, between 4.0 and 4.4 mmol/l.

IDENTICAL ELECTROCARDIOGRAMS

A physician sent in identical electrocardiograms for each of six patients. This was easy to spot as the doctor had connected the arm leads round the wrong way on these six tracings, but *not* for other electrocardiograms.

With the growth of the contract research industry, there is now often distance between the fraudulent doctor and the sponsor company. One person chose him or her, another person monitored and, therefore, someone else should have discovered the fraud earlier. This triumvirate of people gives the pharmaceutical industry a scapegoat. It now feels able to expose the fraud without feeling blame attached to itself. Pharmaceutical companies can avoid having to contact doctors who are potential customers. The third party, the contract research organisation, distances the industry medical advisers from the potential rebuke of their professional colleagues.

There is also often no financial penalty to the pharmaceutical company when the data are discarded. Their answer is often not to pay the contract research organisation for those patients concerning whom fraud is discovered. It is the contract research organisation which suffers the financial loss. In one case in our early days of contract research when we found a doctor to be fraudulent, we observed that both blood samples and electrocardiograms had been split between patients, as well as many errors on source document verification. The pharmaceutical company was confident enough of the fraud to exclude the data from analysis and regulatory submission, paid the doctor to prevent professional hard feeling, but refused to pay us, the contract research house.

More data are probably found to be fraudulent by contract research organisations for many reasons:

- Most contract research organisations want to have a reputation for quality. Quality now entails a tight system of GCP, monitoring, quality controls, and independent quality assurance. Additionally, the data are usually remonitored and reaudited by pharmaceutical companies. Thus, there are more stages at which to pick up hints of potential fraud that need investigation
- Pharmaceutical companies, for all the reasons outlined, expect and demand higher standards of monitoring from the contract research organisation than from themselves. They are also more able to be critical of the data
- The frequency of detection of fraud at the moment is probably at its highest. Many investigators have been used to going undiscovered for many years and they are performing studies to their "old" methods while being inspected much more intensely than ever before. Most contract organisations have highly experienced personnel with knowledge of many physicians, particularly "fast recruiters." It is a sad fact that a "fast recruiter" is now one of the people in whom fraud is most often discovered. Contract research organisations also have, on average, more experienced staff monitoring to GCP than European pharmaceutical companies have, although this is changing rapidly.

It is essential that the contract research organisation and the pharmaceutical company have a clear understanding of how they will deal with the many issues between them when fraud is uncovered.

Europe has, for many years, assumed that physicians would not falsify data. It is part of the European culture to be trusting of professionals, to respect them and, in the case of physicians, raise them to near deity. This situation has never been the case in the United States, which, by nature, is a very suspicious country and believes in openness as well as a system of checks and counterbalances to try to gain assurance that data quality is believable. This system with regard to clinical research has been called good clinical practice. There are two main tenets of GCP: protecting the rights of an individual and ensuring validity of data. The second is achieved through a system of monitoring by the pharmaceutical industry personnel concerned with the study and inbuilt systems of quality control and assurance as well as a final audit of the data by the regulatory authority, the Food and Drug Administration (FDA). Such systems include source document verification, in which the data on the case report form are checked against the investigator's patient files for completeness and accuracy. Such a system discovered several episodes of fraudulent data in the United States in a systematic manner and has resulted in both criminal proceedings and suspension of the ability of physicians to undertake research that will be used for submission to the FDA. The FDA publishes a blacklist of such physicians (p 129). As research became globalised, American companies exported the system of GCP into Europe, where fraud began to be discovered much more often.

As this happened, the European Commission, through the committee on proprietary medicinal products, has produced guidelines of its own for GCP, and data for European submission should now be to this standard. In addition to this activity several industry professionals, led by Frank Wells at the Association of the British Pharmaceutical Industry (ABPI) have mounted a crusade to stamp out this problem, prosecuting British doctors at the General Medical Council with considerable success when fraud has been suspected and documentable (p 77).

Detecting fraud in clinical research

In dealing with the detection of fraud it is important to identify the scope of the problem. Fraud can appear in many forms but no distinction should be made between these different forms. The purpose of all fraud is to gain some advantage by deception or providing false information. In the context of all clinical trials the end result of this is to place patients at possible risk. Thus no difference should be considered between the clinical investigator who manipulates data to satisfy certain requirements or the one who simply invents data.

In the first case could be considered examples where data have been altered to allow inclusion of patients in a trial when criteria have not been met or, alternatively, where data which would mean withdrawal of a patient already entered have not been reported. In the second there would be situations where measurements have not been carried out and the data have been made up, ranging to where the total information has been invented, including the existence of patients.

The advent of GCP has, it is hoped, made the perpetration of fraud more difficult and its discovery more likely. Greater emphasis is placed on checking documentation, although the main purpose of this attention to detail is not to detect fraud but merely to ensure the accuracy and completeness of the data. Care should be taken not to confuse genuine, if erroneous, data with fraudulent data. Mistakes can be made, and a lack of understanding or incompetence does not constitute fraud. What is required in this case is better training of investigators and more careful monitoring.

With effective monitoring of clinical trials and independent audit at investigators' workplaces any suggestion of fraud should be more easily identified. However, in many cases firm evidence of fraud is difficult to obtain. Often the evidence found is circumstantial, but where several such items are found they can be used together to raise suspicion.

The main weapon in the hands of the monitor is the requirement to carry out source document verification. This investigation is much more likely to reveal the first category of fraud mentioned above, where entry criteria have been misreported. If the monitor is carrying out true source document verification with full access to the source data much greater confidence can be placed in the genuine nature of the data. However, in many cases full access is not allowed for various reasons, which means that the monitor must use other methods of obtaining the information. Interview methods are employed which depend on the monitor trusting the investigator to provide accurate answers, but if the investigator cannot trust the monitor with the source data why should the trust operate in the opposite direction? A further practice that is developing is the generation of a trial-specific source document which contains all information relevant to the trial but which cannot be considered as a true source document in the same way as the general practitioner's or hospital notes. In essence this document is worthless and can only encourage the fraudulent investigator. The only purpose it serves is to prove that the investigator is capable of copying information from one document to another and it does nothing to convince the monitor regarding the accuracy and veracity of the data. However, it should be remembered and emphasised that source document verification is not intended to be used in the detection of fraud; its prime purpose is to ensure the accuracy of the data.

Several items can be used as pointers to the monitor that all is not as it should be in a trial. Patient recruitment can often be an early indicator. Excessive numbers of patients recruited by an investigator or rapid recruitment, especially when approaching a closing date for a trial all warrant further investigation. A common mistake made when inventing data is to make the data too good or consistent. All patients are not the same in their responses, and in practice wide variations may be expected rather than values neatly arranged around a mean. In this respect the measurement of blood pressure is perhaps a good example. Significant variability in this parameter may be expected and, when repeating measurements in the same patient, it is unlikely that blood pressures will all fall within a few mm Hg of each other.

Similarly it would not be expected that the patient population recruited by an investigator would be well balanced. The distribution of patients regarding age and sex should not be equal. Likewise the investigator who enrols patients with little, if any, medical history and whose patients do not suffer any adverse events or take concomitant medication should be regarded with suspicion.

Good clinical practice has brought about changes in obtaining patient consent for a trial, with written consent now almost universally the case. This provides the means of comparing the patients' handwriting. If signatures are being forged it is likely that some similarities can be seen among them. Some studies also require the completion of diary cards by patients and these again offer the possibility for comparison. It is unlikely that all patients will use the same colour pen. Occasionally a mistake in the completion of the diary cards is reflected across all patients, which again is unlikely to occur with genuine data. The condition of the diary cards can also be taken into account. Cards which have been issued to patients are invariably creased and crumpled, so cards in perfect condition should be viewed with suspicion.

A similar situation may exist with medication. It is unlikely that patients will keep the drug containers in pristine condition. Containers may be expected to show some signs of wear and tear, labels on bottles may be grubby, boxes damaged around the edges, and foil strips bent with pushing out tablets. Clean, unused-looking bottles and boxes and strips where the tablets have merely been cut off should act as warnings to the vigilant monitor that perhaps all is not in order.

The attitude of the investigator to the monitor can also be revealing. Thus the investigator who is often not available and is difficult to arrange monitoring visits with should be avoided. If he is genuinely busy it could be questioned whether he has the time to conduct the trial, which may lead to the temptation to invent data to complete his obligations. Alternatively he may be being uncooperative because he has something to hide.

In many cases it will prove difficult, if not impossible, to obtain incontrovertible evidence of fraud. Unless suspicions are followed up with higher authorities the only outcome will be that the sponsor may not use that particular investigator again. Good clinical practice offers the opportunity to ensure high quality clinical trials, and effective monitoring and auditing as required by the guidelines provides the means to minimise the risk of fraud. However, adequate follow up must take place in those, one hopes relatively few, cases where fraud does seem to have occurred.

WHAT TO DO IF FRAUD IS SUSPECTED

The person most likely to discover fraud in a clinical trial or to become suspicious is the monitor since he or she will have most direct contact with the investigator. However, other members of the clinical research team may become suspicious, for example at the data entry stage. Whoever does suspect that fraud has taken place should make these suspicions known to his or her superiors within the organisation. Ideally, the steps to be taken should be documented as a company standard operating procedure. The next logical step to take is to get a second opinion, and it would be most appropriate to ask the quality assurance department to carry out a for-cause audit. This would involve an in-depth review of all documentation relating to the particular investigator and of the procedures followed. If the audit supports the initial suspicions further action is indicated.

In the case of a contract research organisation there is a responsibility to keep the client company informed and this should be done immediately after the audit. The clients may wish the contract research organisation to continue with any action or alternatively may wish to visit the investigator themselves with their own monitor or quality assurance department. This may, however, serve only to antagonise the investigator. The future course of action should be agreed between the contract research organisation and the client and in the majority of cases the client will be happy for the contract research organisation to act on its behalf. However, close contact should be maintained and the client kept aware of any developments.

Further options may be available for obtaining more information. If the data are being entered on to a database regularly it should be possible to run comparisons of the data from the suspect investigator with the database as a whole or with similar investigators who are above suspicion. This could be particularly useful in cases where the patient population seems too well balanced or where there seem to be significant differences in occurrence of adverse events and levels of concomitant medication.

It was at this point in the past that companies then took the easy option of not taking any further action except for possibly not using the data and certainly not using the investigator again. It was felt that it was a stigma on the company to have used a fraudulent investigator. The pressure on contract research organisations was even more, with client companies taking the attitude that it was a failing of the contract research organisation to use a fraudulent investigator. Thus for a contract research organisation to admit to this was likely to lose it business. Fortunately this situation has now changed and with the encouragement of the ABPI there is much more openness. It became obvious that many companies were aware of fraud and, perhaps because of the greater emphasis on documentation brought about by GCP, fraud was becoming easier to discover. It was also apparent that to simply keep quiet about the problem was in no one's best interest. Investigators do not tend to carry out clinical trials for a single company and, therefore, if one company discovers fraud it is morally unacceptable not to make this information general knowledge. Any company would be disturbed to discover that an investigator they were using was fraudulent and then find out that another company had been aware of this for some time but had covered it up. Only with a more open acceptance that certain investigators, albeit only a few, are not producing genuine data can the full benefits of GCP be found. In this way a pool of trustworthy investigators will become available for clinical trials and the quality of the trials will be assured.

It was the recognition of this that caused the ABPI to encourage its member companies to notify it of any suspicions. Although one company may not have enough evidence to take further action against an investigator it may be that another company has also expressed its suspicions, or may do so in the future.

In the United States the FDA has powers to act against fraudulent investigators by barring them from clinical trials or by action through the courts. At present in Europe there is no such possibility. However, in the United Kingdom it is possible to report investigators to their own professional body, the General Medical Council (see the chapter by Wells). If a case goes to the professional conduct committee it is possible to obtain much stronger evidence. The solicitors acting for the General Medical Council are able to gain access to patient registers through the family health service authority and also to interview patients regarding their involvement in the trial. These options are not available to pharmaceutical companies.

Key issues for the clinical research organisation and the pharmaceutical industry

We admit to our pharmaceutical industry colleagues that it is impossible to guarantee that we will not discover the possibility of fraud despite using only reliable investigators we know and performing a full initial site visit to determine the suitability of investigators. The best way to counteract fraud is to prevent it happening. This check list provides ideas to ensure as far as possible that reliable investigators are recruited into studies.
(1) Examine the latest available information on FDA "blacklist" doctors plus fraud cases before the General Medical Council in the United Kingdom and other professional institutions in other countries.
(2) Check the credentials of each doctor enrolled against the information provided in the current or appropriate professional membership lists.

(3) Obtain "grapevine" information from industry peers, colleagues, and pathology laboratories, when possible, on which doctors are reliable investigators. The tags "good investigators" and "fast recruiters" have become associated with fraudulent doctors. Caution has to be observed in any "open discussions" with peers, etc, so as not to contravene the laws of libel and slander in identifying suspected fraudsters. Keep discussion positive to identify and confirm the reliable investigators.
(4) Keep meticulously detailed records on investigators and their clinical trial performance records.
(5) During the initial site visits discuss and agree the steps that need to be taken to identify and deal with suspect patient information or data during a study.
(6) Get a commitment for direct access to patient notes by the monitor during all monitoring visits and, as necessary, at other times.
(7) Make it clear in the protocol and investigator agreements that source documentation verification will be performed.
(8) Emphasise to potential investigators that fraudulent, suspicious, or even careless data will NOT be paid for and could even result in litigation for breach of contract.

CONTRACT BETWEEN CONTRACT RESEARCH ORGANISATION AND SPONSOR COMPANY

Initial discussion between the contracting parties should dwell on "what if..." to explore all possible eventualities by:
(1) Sharing their experience of suspected and proved fraud.
(2) Sharing knowledge of reliable physicians, as well as the so called "good investigators" and "fast recruiters" to maximise the potential success of a study.
(3) Defining and mutually agreeing what circumstances and situations would be regarded as:
  (a) proved fraud
  (b) suspected fraud
  (c) careless data.
(4) Reaching agreement prospectively on the implications of what to do and how to proceed when fraud is either suspected or proved:
  (a) suspect patients/data to be discarded or entered into study results
  (b) additional patients to be entered into a study if feasible
  (c) financial arrangements for such contingencies
  (d) legal responsibilities and obligations of both parties.

While it is very difficult to account in contractual terms for every possible situation a full discussion on the above points should bring the key issues to the surface to provide a basis for a formal mutual agreement.

Any contract, whether it is an exchange of letters or a legal document, should ensure that the following points are included in any agreement to provide services to a sponsor company:

Standard operating procedures—A contract research organisation should have standard operating procedures for dealing with the cases of proved or suspected fraud, or careless data. Such standard operating procedures could be attached to any agreement as appendices to set out what principles and circumstances are accepted as either proved or suspected fraud or possibly careless data; and, how both parties will deal with the practical, regulatory, and financial consequences.

Delays—Any contract should require the sponsor company to supply documents, data, records, and cooperation to the contract research organisation. Furthermore, the contract research organisation should not be responsible for errors, delays, or other consequences arising from the failure of the sponsor company to provide appropriate information and cooperation. The sponsor company should also be required to acknowledge that a contract research organisation cannot be responsible for any default for any cause beyond its reasonable control.

Indemnification—While a contract research organisation must commit itself to use all reasonable care and skill in preparing accurate information supplied for a sponsor company, it must also ensure that it does not claim, represent, guarantee, or warrant that any such information will be accurate in every respect. An all embracing statement should go on to say that if any information programmed or results produced should contain errors or omissions then the contract research organisation, without prejudice to any other right or remedy of the sponsor company, will use reasonable care and skill to correct promptly any discrepancies. It should be emphasised that in no event will the contract research organisation be liable for special, indirect, incidental, or consequential damages for any liability to a third party. The sponsor company should also be asked to agree to defend, indemnify, and hold harmless a contract research organisation against and from any third party claims, proceedings, or investigations arising out of the contract. Provided adequate discussion has been given to preparing and agreeing the standard operating procedures before the start of the contract, this indemnification requirement will be a mere formality.

In costing contract research organisations will need to consider whether it is necessary to include in overhead calculations money for time spent:
- Monitoring fraudulent investigators
- Investigating the fraud
- Prosecuting the fraud, if necessary
- Adding more investigators to a study to achieve target numbers.

Statistical aspects of the detection of fraud

STEPHEN EVANS

Round numbers are always false—SAMUEL JOHNSON

Introduction

The very use of the word "data"—from the Latin "given," suggests that those who receive data for analysis do so in the spirit of a gift. To question the veracity of data is then to look the gift horse in the mouth. It may be wise, however, to have at least the level of suspicion that was advised to the Trojans when confronted with their gift horse.

The emphasis in statistical textbooks and training is on analysing the data assuming that they are genuine. Checking the data is sometimes mentioned[1,2] though this is directed mainly at the possibility of accidental errors rather than deliberate falsification. Altman notes that "it is the large errors that can influence statistical analyses."[2] Accidental errors which are large clearly affect the analysis, but alteration or invention of data will usually be done in a way that tries to hide any large effect so that the features of these data will not be the same as ordinary errors. In spite of this, careful use of the best procedures for data checking with some simple extensions will go a long way to detecting many instances of fraud. This chapter will outline routine methods for checking data that will help to correct accidental errors as well as the problems which are the target of this book. The accidental errors in data are (one hopes) more frequent than deliberate ones so that effort expended in checking data will result in better quality reports of medical science even in the absence of attempts to cheat.

The power of modern computer programs for statistical data analysis is a great help with this type of data checking, but also facilitates fabrication of data. More emphasis in the training of statisticians needs to be given to this aspect of data analysis, since a perfect analysis of the wrong data is much more dangerous than an imperfect analysis of correct data.

Types of fraud

Relatively little has been published about the particulars of fraudulent data, so that most statisticians have little or no experience of this. From what is known we can divide the problems into two major groups.

STATISTICAL ASPECTS

(1) Data *manipulation* to achieve a desired result or increase the statistical significance of the findings and affect the overall scientific conclusions.
(2) *Invention* of data for non-existent or incomplete cases in clinical studies.

The motives in the first case are to achieve publication, or to produce results confirming a particular theory, rather than financial considerations. The motives in the second instance are usually almost entirely financial. Most of the well known cases of fraud in the United Kingdom fall into this category.

Publication bias is a well known feature of the scientific literature, in which results that are highly statistically significant are more likely to be published than those which show non-statistically significant effects. Hence some fraud is directed at obtaining statistical significance of the results. Several publicised cases of this type have occurred in the United States though they are also known in Europe. This is the type of fraud which tends to occur in academically related research, where career advancement is the ultimate motive. More details of known instances of fraud are given in the first chapter by Lock.

Characteristics of genuine data and their analysis

In biological, and especially in medical, investigation there is almost always considerable variation in any phenomenon studied. A major contribution of statistical methods is in quantifying variability and in distinguishing random variation from genuine effects. Statistical significance tests (or confidence intervals) are one way of classifying genuine as opposed to spurious effects. The object of most fraud is to demonstrate a "statistically significant" effect which the genuine data would not show.

Most medical research looks for evidence of some effect such as a new treatment for a disease. The effect will be shown by differences between a treated and a control group. In a statistical significance test (or confidence interval) there are three components which are combined to show the strength of the evidence:

(1) The magnitude of the effect.
(2) The variability of individuals showing the effect.
(3) The number of individuals studied.

Evidence for the existence of an effect is when (1) and (3) are as large as possible and when (2) is as small as possible. Most fraud consists of reducing variability and increasing the number.

STATISTICAL ASPECTS

Birthweight Distribution

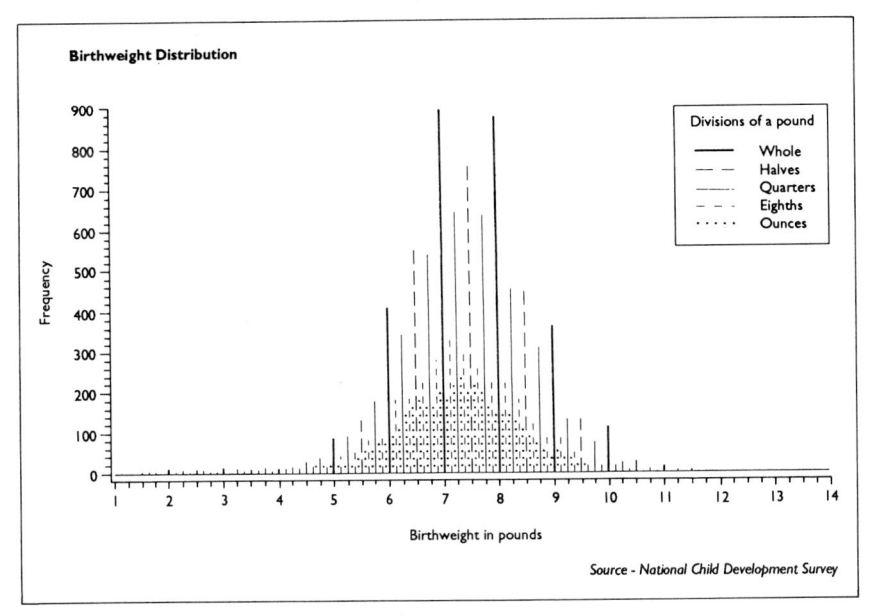

Divisions of a pound
— Whole
– – Halves
——— Quarters
– · – Eighths
· · · · Ounces

Source - National Child Development Survey

FIG 1—*Value preference in recording babies' birth weights*

The large amount of variability in genuine data not only makes the use of statistical methods important in medical research, but also tends to be hidden when summary statistics of data are presented. Whenever summaries of data are presented, they should be accompanied by some measure of the variability of the data.

Wherever measurement entails human judgment, even in reading data from an instrument, the data show special features. One of these features is "digit preference." This is well known in measuring blood pressure, which tends to be recorded to the nearest 5 mm Hg or 10 mm Hg. Where recording is to 5 mm Hg, it is still more usual to find values with a last digit of 0 than of 5. In research, measurements may be made to the nearest 2 mm Hg.

Another example is in recording babies' birthweights. Figure 1 shows an example of data from a large national study done in 1958, where, when the weights are shown to the nearest ounce, it is clear that certain values are much preferred to others. Whole pounds are the most frequent, with half and quarter pounds and two ounces being progressively less popular, while very few weights are recorded to the nearest ounce. In more recent data the preferences are for values recorded to the nearest 500, 250, or 100 g.

Errors of measurement and of recording occur in all genuine data, and some individuals show an idiosyncratic response. These factors result in "outliers" occurring in the data. When they are genuine values they should be included in the analysis, but when there is good external evidence that

63

STATISTICAL ASPECTS

they are errors (for example, age = 142 years) they should be corrected or eliminated. Most effort in data checking is directed towards these values as noted above.

Characteristics of fraudulent data

MANIPULATED DATA

Fraudulent manipulation is likely to attempt to show a desired effect by manipulating the data in any or all of the three ways which affect the statistical significance of the results noted above:

- Larger differences between groups appear
- Variability of results is reduced
- Extra data are invented.

The main way is by reducing variability, so that observations which do not fit the desired result are deleted or amended. Simple invention of data tends to result in a series of values which are too close to each other. It needs considerable familiarity with the subject of the study, or the examination of other people's results, to be able to recognise this reduced variability.

The number of changes made on original record forms may also be excessive when manipulation of the data is done by changing the record forms.[3]

SIMPLE INVENTED DATA

In some ways this type of fraud is harder to detect when reading simple summaries of the data because the values themselves will not be manipulated with any target result in mind. The fabricator in this instance will not usually be quite as sophisticated in his or her approach to data and so there will be special characteristics seen in the ersatz which are not seen in the authentic.

There are two main characteristics of this type of data. Firstly, there tends to be too little variation and an almost total absence of outliers. The second is that because human intervention is totally responsible there will often be digit preference and rounding of values in measurements which would not normally show these features, such as when results have been obtained by an entirely automatic process (for example, sodium concentration in urine, measured by an autoanalyser). The shape of the invented distribution tends to be relatively flat with values being generated in an even spread over a limited range.

The record forms where invented data have been created from the start do not have many alterations at all, and have too regular writing. That all the forms have been completed in the same pen may be spotted by those entering or checking the record forms from a clinical trial.

Methods for detecting problems

In some senses the methods for detecting problems are simply an extension of the usual methods for checking data, combined with an awareness of the characteristics shown by altered and fabricated data. There are some purely statistical methods, and some graphical methods which supplement the numerical ones. Familiarity with the research subject is also important, which will be true for a medical investigator and referee, but may not be true for the statistician analysing the data. This knowledge will include a sensitivity to look for relationships that should exist and for the absence of relationships that should not.

EXAMINING DATA: ONE VARIABLE AT A TIME

The features of fraudulent data such as excessive digit preference or alteration of record forms will not usually be visible to the reader, referee, or editor but may be detected if looked for by a colleague or statistician processing the invented data. Digit preference itself is neither a sensitive nor a specific test of fraud.

Statistical methods—The methods described in textbooks aimed at medical research such as those by Altman[2] and Gardner and Altman[4] are entirely appropriate and, though they have an implicit assumption that the data are genuine, the presentation methods they suggest will be a first step in preventing fraud.

The guidelines that were previously published in the *British Medical Journal* and that have been updated as chapters 9 and 10 of Gardner and Altman[4] are particularly pertinent. The use of standard deviations and percentile ranges (such as 25th–75th or 10th–90th) may be helpful. The range itself is subject to error, and increases with increasing sample size. It may be helpful in detecting outliers (or their absence) but should not be a substitute for measures such as the standard deviation which can be used for comparative purposes across different studies. The range is more popular in the medical literature than it should be, and is often the only measure of variability quoted in published reports.

Original data should be summarised wherever possible rather than only derived variables. A confidence interval or a standard error may allow for the derivation of the standard deviation provided the sample size is clear to the reader. Provided this is possible, then constraints on space may allow for standard deviations to be omitted, though they can often be included with very little space penalty.

Authors (and editors) should be encouraged to present raw data if possible rather than just summary values, and, where practicable, diagrams which show all the data should also be presented. Bad data tend to lie too close to the centre of the data for their own group.

Graphical methods—These are part of statistical science and require careful thought for scientific presentation. The advent of business presentation graphics on personal computers has led to a decline in the quality of published graphs. Inappropriate use of bar graphs for presenting means is a typical example. The use of good graphics is particularly useful in looking for patterns in data which are under suspicion.

Some techniques may be used for exploration of data but may not be the best for final communication of the results. An example is the use of the "Stem and leaf" plot. This is like a histogram on its side, with the "stem" being the most significant digits, and the "leaves" being the least significant digit. This can be constructed by hand very easily, and many of the statistical computer programs can produce it. Because it retains all the data—unlike the histogram, which groups the data—the last digit can be seen, and instances of digit preference can be seen clearly. It was such a technique which showed that doctors did not always use the Hawksley random zero sphygmomanometer correctly.[5] This example itself illustrates that, as with the title of that paper, it is always easier to blame a machine than human failing.

Figure 2 gives a stem and leaf plot of blood pressure recorded in another study where although the measurements were theoretically made to the nearest 2 mmHg some digit preference may be seen.

Stem and leaf plots might be used in publications more than they are, and for further details of their construction see Altman[2] or Bland.[6]

EXAMINING DATA: TWO MEASUREMENTS OF THE SAME VARIABLE

As an example, consider a trial comparing two treatments (A and B) for hypertension. A way of analysing the data is to look at the individual changes in blood pressure and compare these changes between the two groups.

The basic data consist of the values of blood pressure for each individual at randomisation (r) and at final assessment (f). A t test or confidence interval is calculated by using the changes (f-r), and comparing groups A and B.

Statistical methods—Ordinary data checking will look for outlying values (values a long way from the mean) of blood pressure at r or f, and in the changes (f-r). Fraudulent data will not usually have outlying values, rather the reverse. Outliers will increase the variability of the data more than they affect the mean, so statistical significance will be reduced. When data have

```
Depth    Stem  · Leaves         Plot of DBP
  2      5 •   | 68
 12      6 ★   | 0222224444
 16        •   | 6666
 33      7 ★   | 00000022222222444
 (8)       •   | 66668888
 37      8 ★   | 00000022244444
 23        •   | 666888
 17      9 ★   | 000024
 11        •   | 666
  5     10 ★   | 000
  3        •   | 88
        11 ★   | 4
        HIGH   | 118, 140
```

FIG 2—*Stem and leaf plot of diastolic blood pressure. The first two values are 56, 58. Note that there are 21 values ending in zero, while 11 values end in 8. This is only slight digit preference. (The values are not expected to be measured to better than 2 mm Hg)*

been manipulated by either removing or changing values which are inconvenient from the fraudster's viewpoint, or when data are completely invented, the range of data will not be extreme. The data will have the outliers removed or "shrunk" towards the mean, and the values will have small changes to increase the differences between the groups.

A sensitive test of fraud will be to find noticeably reduced variability in the changes in the blood pressures. For blood pressure, and for many other variables that are measured in research, there is good knowledge of this variability. It tends not to be examined as carefully as the mean or median values which are reported. Extreme values of the mean or median will be noticed easily, but the usual reader and even the referee and editor of a paper are less likely to examine the variability. For blood pressure, the between person variability in most studies has a standard deviation of close to 10 mm Hg. This variation increases with increasing mean value, so that in studies of hypertensive patients the variability will be rather larger.

The within person standard deviation varies with the length of time between the measurements concerned, tending to increase as the time between measurements increases. An alternative way of looking at this is to state that the correlation between the two measurements tends to decrease the further apart they are in time. This will happen without treatment, but will also happen in the presence of treatment. Two measurements repeated within a few minutes tend to have a correlation which may be as high as 0·8, while measurements a week or so apart tend to have a correlation of about 0·6 to 0·7. Values several years apart tend to have lower correlations, falling to about 0·3 at 10 years. The within person standard deviation then tends to be about 7 mm Hg for values from one week to a few months apart, which is the typical range of time encountered in much research. The reports of studies, whether genuine or not, often tend to neglect the reporting of the variability of differences. Sometimes it is only a summary p value which is given. If this is given exactly (rather than $p < 0.05$), then it is possible to work back to the original standard deviation of the differences and hence to be able to see if there is a hint of data which do not have the expected variability.

When changes are examined, which will always be the case when any paired statistical significance tests are done as well as when changes are compared between groups, then the variability of the changes should also be given. It is well known that comparisons in a table are made more easily by going down a column than across a row. This means that the same values in different groups should be given in columns so that comparisons may be made more easily.

The issue of variability of changes, where the change is the outcome of interest and where a statistical significance test is done by using the changes, is not examined carefully enough. All too often the baseline and final means and standard deviations are presented with just a p value for the comparison of the changes. This, firstly, makes detection of bad data more difficult; secondly, in order to plan further studies using those changes, especially when you want to calculate sample size, the key information is not available in the publication. This must be one of the most frequent problems encountered by the consulting statistician helping to plan new research.

Graphical methods—Graphical methods tend not to be used for pairs of observations, though when the pairs of points are shown joined by lines then it is possible to see when variability is too little by noting that all the lines are parallel. When the same variable is repeatedly measured this type of graph can be used, though it is rarely done, and the usual graphs do not indicate anything of the within person variability. There is considerable scope for improvement in the methods available for graphical presentation of data from repeated measurements; this requires research by creative statisticians.

EXAMINING DATA: TWO OR MORE VARIABLES AT A TIME

Statistical methods—When data are invented to manipulate or show an effect that is not present or not present so clearly in the genuine data, then a skilled manipulator will perhaps be able to produce data that are convincing when viewed in one dimension. It is very much more difficult to retain the nature of real data when viewed in two dimensions. The relationship between variables tends to disappear. In a well documented example,[7] a laboratory study on animal models of myocardial infarction included several variables. The simplest example of this problem was the data on weight of the dogs versus the weight of the left ventricle. In this case of very elaborate forgery the range and variability of left ventricle weight were high, in fact higher than in the genuine data, with a similar range for the weights of the dogs. The correlation between these two measurements was very much weaker. The situation with infarct size versus collateral blood flow was even worse, where the variability in collateral blood flow was very much less than expected and the relationship which should have existed was absent.

This type of problem is not as easy to detect by reading a paper, but ought to be detected by a statistician with access to the raw data and familiar with the science of the study. In some cases a correlation matrix may be presented, and careful examination of this may show unexpected findings which raise the index of suspicion.

In the example quoted,[7] the study was being carried out in several laboratories simultaneously so that the differences between the laboratories could be studied very easily. In fact the study itself was set up because of previous inconsistencies in the results from different laboratories.

In many cases this advantage of multicentre studies is not possible and considerable experience may be necessary to detect the problem.

The situation with regard to several variables is an extension of that seen with two. The variables on their own tend to show reduced variability, but even when this is not so, the relationships among many variables become much weaker than they should be.

Examination of the correlation matrix may also show where relationships are too weak (or, on occasions, too strong) for genuine data. This approach essentially examines the relationships between pairs of variables. There are true multivariate methods which are able to look at the effect of many variables simultaneously, which are of use in complex data checking.

The first method is fairly well known among statisticians and examines the "influence" of individual observations. It is of most help where data errors have been made and for ensuring that single observations are not distorting the results of an analysis too much.

The basic idea is to have a single outcome variable which is the measurement of greatest importance. This is used as the outcome (dependent) variable in a multiple regression analysis, with several possible predictor variables, including one for the treatment group if a comparative study is being analysed. The first step is to use standard methods of multiple regression. This entails obtaining as good a fit to the data as possible which makes biological sense. For these purposes it may be reasonable to obtain the best fitting equation (also called a "model") regardless of how sensible it is in biological terms. The inclusion of variables which are not thought to be medically relevant may indicate that

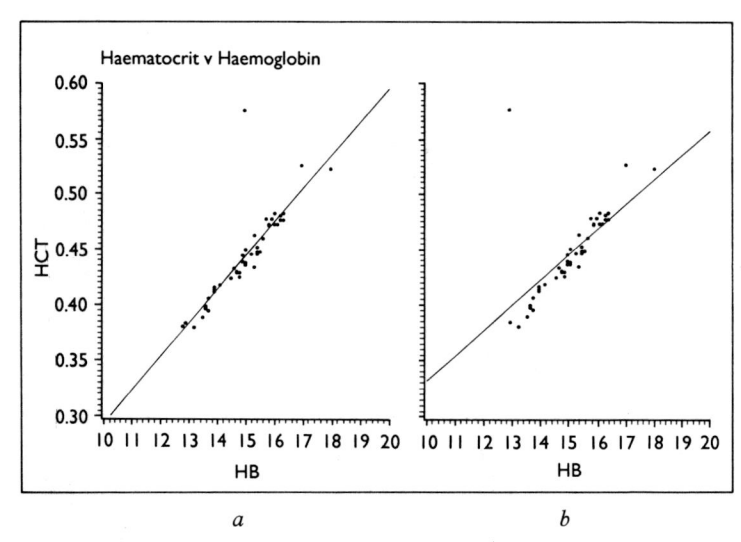

FIG 3—*Use of Cook's distance to measure the influence of an outlying point*

there are problems with the data. The relationships with such variables may merit further investigation.

There are several measures of "influence" available, of which probably the best is called "Cook's distance." This is like a residual in multiple regression: the distance between an observed point and the value predicted for that point by the regression equation. An ordinary residual may not be very informative, since outliers may have small residuals in that they "attract" the regression line towards them. An alternative is a "deleted" residual, which entails calculating the equation for the regression line excluding that point, and obtaining the residual from the predicted value with this regression equation. This will be very effective when a single outlying point is present in the data. An outlier can influence the regression equation in two ways. It can influence the "height" when it is in the centre of the data, but it influences the slope when it is also an outlier in the predictor variable(s). This effect is known as "leverage," and is illustrated in figures 3a and 3b, where, other than the outlier, identical data are shown. Cook's distance for the outlier in 3b is very large because it has leverage altering the slope as well as being an outlier, while it is an outlier in 3a without leverage.

The problem with invented data is that they are unlikely to be outliers in any dimension; in fact the exact opposite is true. Invented data are likely to have values which lie close to the mean for each variable that has been measured. In one instance of invented data of which I had experience, the perpetrator used the results of an interim analysis of means of all the measured variables to generate four extra cases for which either the original

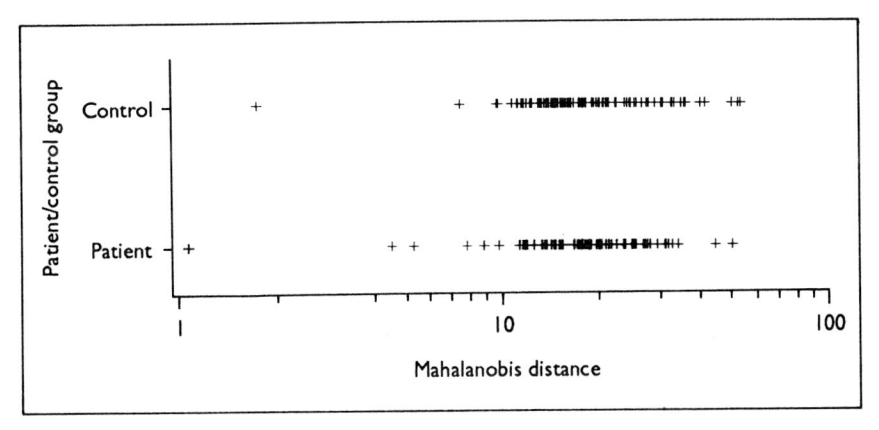

FIG 4—*Distribution of Mahalanobis distance for a set of data to which two "inliers" have been added*

data were lost, or the results did not fit the desired pattern. The means of the two "treatment" groups had been provided for all haemodynamic and biochemical measurements. The perpetrator used these means as a guide so that the invented data consisted of the nearest feasible numbers close to the relevant group mean with minor changes so that the data for the four individuals (two per "treatment" group) were not absolutely identical.

These data have the effect of increasing sample size and reducing the standard deviation of every measured variable. This can have a noticeable effect on the p values—it can change $p = 0.07$ to $p = 0.01$.

Such data cannot be detected by any of the usual checks. However, one method for looking for outliers can also be to detect "inliers." It is not unusual for a value of one variable for any case to be close to the mean. It is less likely that it will be close to the mean of an entirely unrelated variable. The probability of it being close to the mean of each of a large number of variables in any individual case is then very low. The distance of a value from the mean for one variable can be expressed in units of standard deviation—a Z score. This distance can be generalised to two dimensions when the distance from a bivariate mean (for example, diastolic blood pressure and sodium concentration each expressed as Z scores) can be calculated by using Pythagoras's theorem. A measure of the distance from a multivariate mean, equivalent to the square of a Z score is called the Mahalanobis distance. The distribution of this distance should follow a χ^2 distribution, approximately. Very large values—outliers—can be detected in this way.[8] Although not mentioned in textbooks, this can also be used to detect "inliers," looking for much smaller values of Mahalanobis distance. Figure 4 shows the Mahalanobis distances for a set of data to which two "inliers" (with low values) have been added. It is possible to use formal statistical tests which may be used to indicate the need for further investigation, but cannot in themselves prove the existence of fabrication.

A similar approach for categorical data was used by R A Fisher in his examination of the results of Mendel's genetic experiments on garden peas. Several experiments had observed frequencies that were too close to the expected ones. The usual statistical test for comparing observed and expected frequencies uses a χ^2 test and looks for small p values to indicate departure from a null hypothesis. This form of the test looks for p values very close indeed to 1—for example, 0·99996. The probability of observing a χ^2 as small or smaller then becomes $1 - 0·99996 = 0·00004$, which is strong evidence that the usual chance processes are not at work. Some geneticists have doubted Fisher's suggestion that a gardening assistant was responsible and that the data are reliable, but as Fisher concludes "There is no easy way out of the difficulty."[9]

Graphical methods—With data in two or more dimensions the publication of scatter plots should be encouraged whenever space permits. Modern statistical computer graphics programs can show a large number of data points in fine resolution, which are very useful for data screening. There are circumstances where such "clouds" of points can be helpful in a publication, rather than just showing a summary statistic. The mean and standard error can conceal more than they reveal.

In data checking, graphs tend to be very much more useful than numerical statistical methods, and the plotting of unusual variables against one another can show problems not found in any other ways. The time sequence of the data is a particularly important aspect. Altman and Royston[10] have noted the influence of time on several aspects of a study, though they did not mention the issue of fraud in that context. Bailey[7] shows some dramatic pictures where the data collected by an individual extended over a time period that included both genuine and invented data, and where the time when the fraud was suspected could be seen clearly on the graph (figure 5—the variability increases to the level seen in site A).

The graphs which use the "residuals"—that is, the variation remaining when all the systematic and known aspects have been removed—are especially helpful. It is in this aspect of invention that the reduced variability is seen most clearly.

Hints for referees and editors

It is a controversial point, but as a referee I have often wanted more data than are intended to appear in the final article. Sometimes the raw data themselves may be necessary for a proper review to take place even if, because of pressure of space, they cannot appear in the final journal article. In most cases this request for the data has been met with alacrity since

STATISTICAL ASPECTS

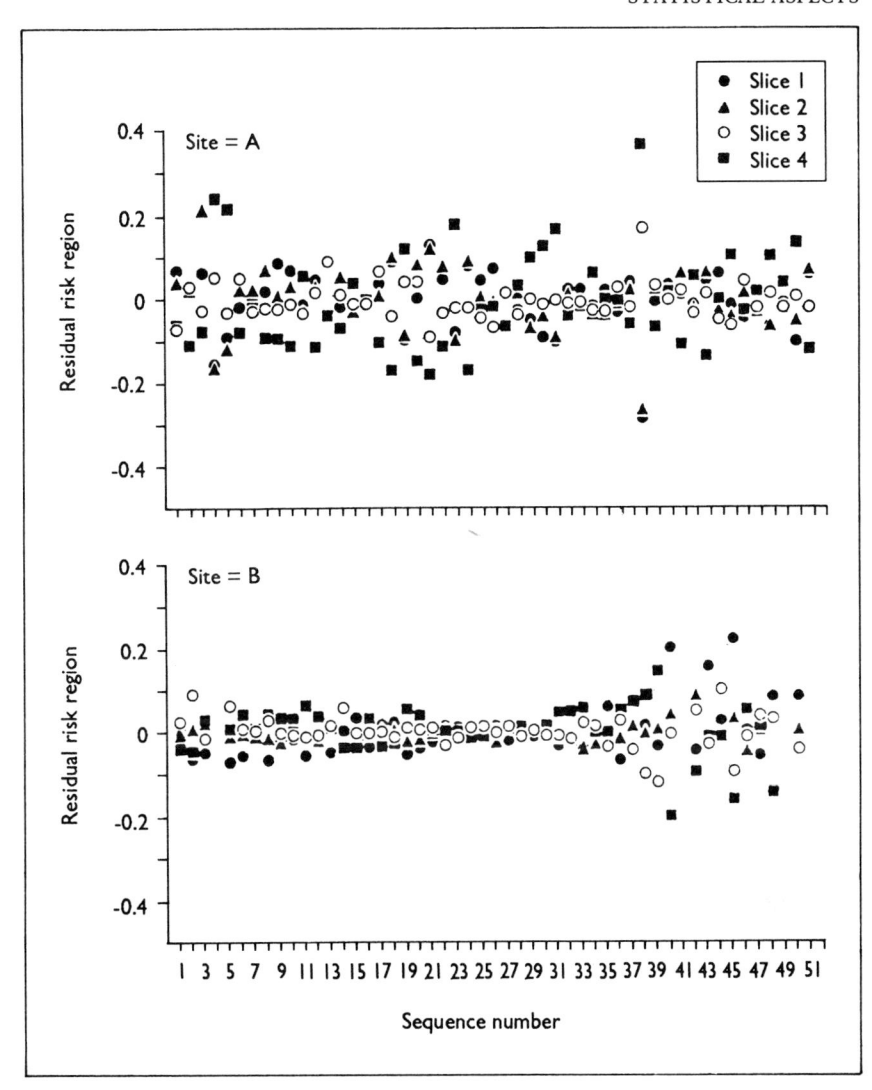

FIG 5—*Residual risk region by sequence. Reprinted by permission of the publisher from "Detecting fabrication of data in a multicenter collaborative animal study" by K R Bailey (*Controlled Clinical Trials **12**: 741–52*). Copyright 1991 Elsevier Science Publishing Co, Inc*

anything that helps publication is usually of interest to the author. In a very few instances nothing more has been heard from the author(s), which leads to definite conclusions about the quality of the work. I have had one instance where the data were supplied quickly, but where I could not reproduce the statistical significance of the findings. Again, after I raised a query, nothing more was heard by me from the authors.

73

Some points which are indicators of problems are:

- Numbers that do not add up across a table
- Graphs with different numbers of observations from those quoted in the text
- p values quoted without the data necessary to estimate them
- Statistically significant effects in small studies where most investigators need larger ones
- Absence of measures of variability or standard errors.

However, it is also important to realise that with any diagnostic procedure there are false positives and false negatives. If we regard a false negative as failing to recognise fraud or manipulation when it is present, then there is also the possibility of the false positive—accusing someone of fraud when it is absent. Obtaining extra evidence is the only way of reducing the rate of both these errors simultaneously.

1 Armitage P, Berry G. *Statistical methods in medical research.* (2nd ed.) Oxford: Blackwell Scientific, 1987; chap 11.
2 Altman DG. *Practical statistics for medical research.* London: Chapman & Hall, 1991; chap 7.
3 Neaton JD, Bartsch GE, Broste SK, Cohen JD, Simon NM. A case of data alteration in the Multiple Risk Factor Intervention Trial (MRFIT). *Controlled Clinical Trials* 1991; **12**: 731–40.
4 Gardner MJ, Altman DG. *Statistics with confidence.* London: *BMJ*, 1989.
5 Silman A. Failure of random zero sphygmomanometer in general practice. *BMJ* 1985; **290**: 1781–2.
6 Bland JM. *Medical statistics: an introduction.* Oxford: Oxford University Press, 1987.
7 Bailey KR. Detecting fabrication of data in a multicenter collaborative animal study. *Controlled Clinical Trials* 1991; **12**: 741–52.
8 Tabachnik BG, Fidell L. *Using multivariate statistics.* 2nd ed. New York: Harper Collins, 1989; chap 4.
9 Freedman D, Pisani R, Purves R, Adhikari A. *Statistics.* 2nd ed. New York: Norton, 1991.
10 Altman DG, Royston JP. The hidden effect of time. *Statistics in Medicine* 1988; 7: 629–37.

The British pharmaceutical industry's response

FRANK WELLS

Introduction

This book deals in depth with the subject of fraud and misconduct in the context of clinical research as a whole. This specific chapter deals with the response of the pharmaceutical industry in the United Kingdom to the detection of such fraud, and the role of the British trade association—the Association of the British Pharmaceutical Industry (ABPI)—in dealing with it.

Recently the ABPI has taken an important action. This was to produce a report, intended to alert its member companies and others to fraud and to provide guidelines for its detection, prosecution, and prevention. Such a report would not have been possible, or even acceptable, until recently, although some companies do have standard operating procedures which outline the steps to be adopted by any employees suspecting fraud, and which emphasise the philosophy and management commitment of the company. But even these companies have adopted these procedures only during the past two years, before which the industry was in a dilemma as to what best to do. The ABPI report was therefore intended to encourage and assist companies to establish clear policies.

Ideally, fraud ought never to occur; agreed high standards should exist for clinical research, to which everyone involved should stick. But if standards slip, and fraud is suspected, plans must exist to deal with it. Within the British pharmaceutical industry, policy guidelines which set such standards for clinical research have existed since 1988,[1] and have been accepted by virtually all British pharmaceutical companies. The position has if anything been strengthened by the adoption of similar guidelines by the European Commission, which have therefore assumed the status of "rules," as from July 1991.[2]

Historical aspects of fraud

Until recently there was only one published case of clinical research fraud in the United Kingdom.[3] However, for some time there has been an impression among British pharmaceutical physicians, clinical research associates, and quality assurance professionals that a small but significant amount of data supplied by British clinical investigators is fraudulent. This view was shared by the Royal College of Physicians, which in 1990 set up its own working party on fraud and misconduct in clinical research, following the publication of a leading article in the *British Medical Journal*.[4] This initiative of the Royal College of Physicians recognised that the problem is important, and raised the suspicion that several serious instances had occurred which had not been investigated or reported. Publication of the Royal College of Physicians working party report[5] led to the ABPI deciding to set up its own working party referred to above. Both the ABPI and the Royal College of Physicians acknowledge that it would be wrong to believe that fraud is rife, but it does occur, and its very existence is a cause for serious concern.

Following publication of the industry guidelines on good clinical research practice (GC(R)P) by the ABPI in 1988,[1] the working party recognised that much time and effort had been spent in explaining the principles of good clinical research practice to the leaders of the medical profession, as well as to individual investigators. These guidelines specifically underline the importance of monitoring, and of audit procedures. More recently the European Commission has approved the guidelines on good clinical practice produced by the committee on proprietary medicinal products, and these have been operative from 1 July 1991.[2] The need for this information to be promulgated, and for investigators to be trained in the principles of GC(R)P, is therefore as important as ever; and fraud is more likely to be prevented if investigators, and their colleagues, are fully aware of GC(R)P standards, of the requirement for the industry to operate to them, and of the commitment of companies to act vigorously against any irregularities.

That said, why is there so little mention of clinical research fraud in the literature coming from the pharmaceutical industry? The probable reason is that, until recently, pharmaceutical companies suspecting fraud were greatly concerned about all sorts of risks: recrimination, adverse publicity, and loss of favour, support, and indeed prescriptions, if they were seen to be critical of the medical profession. These concerns have some justification: in the very first documented case in the United Kingdom activated by a pharmaceutical company, as a result of which the doctor was struck off the medical register, the company which had been defrauded was immediately boycotted by the doctors in the district, albeit only temporarily.[3] The details of this, the Siddiqui case, are set out later in the chapter.

Such concerns have fortunately now largely been overcome, and the ABPI working party therefore began its deliberations against a background of increasing confidence on the part of pharmaceutical companies to take action against doctors who had been proved to have submitted fraudulent data, but also of uncertainty how best to investigate or to handle suspicions in the first place that data might be fraudulent. The working party recognised that a mechanism was needed to make it easier for member companies to pursue such suspicions without prejudice. Details of procedures to be adopted by companies or contract research organisations in those circumstances are set out in the chapters by Brock and VandenBurg.

Sharing information

One of the most frequently reported problems arising from the detection of suspected fraud is deciding what to do with the information which has been gathered; might there be other cases of suspected fraud which other companies have detected from the same investigator, but is it right and proper to contact other companies at random to raise such queries, and would company pharmaceutical physicians be laying themselves open to the laws of libel or defamation if they suggested to others that a doctor might be acting fraudulently?

The ABPI working party considered this at length because no mechanism existed for sharing such doubts outside the company in which the doubts were generated. It concluded that it is in the public interest for pharmaceutical physicians to report to an independent third party any serious concerns which they may have, in good faith, regarding a specific investigator. A way forward, on which legal advice has been given, has been to give to the ABPI, and specifically the ABPI medical director, this third party role, and a "possibly suspect doctor name-holding" responsibility. Companies may ask whether the name of a possibly suspect doctor had already been given to the ABPI by another company, and be given the answer "yes" or "no." No list of names is promulgated, and the information is not held on computer, thus exempting it from the provisions of the Data Protection Act. On a doctor to doctor basis, the name of the company medical director who had first provided the ABPI with evidence of suspicion about an investigator is given to the company medical director making a subsequent inquiry with similar evidence of suspicion. The ABPI medical director is also in a position to advise companies when, in his opinion, evidence reported from more than one company has, when accumulated, created a strong enough case to submit to the General Medical Council (GMC), even if the evidence from one company alone did not. A round table discussion may then be held, particularly when more than two companies are suspicious of the same investigator, as has happened on at least two occasions.

Prosecuting fraud

Once an investigator has been shown beyond all reasonable doubt to have submitted fraudulent data to a pharmaceutical company or contract house, it is essential in the interests of the public, the profession, and the industry that that doctor should be dealt with. In the United Kingdom this is usually by referral to the GMC for possible consideration by the professional conduct committee. Alternatively, the doctor may be prosecuted for the criminal offence of deception, and the chapter by Hodges which follows is devoted to legal issues. In the United Kingdom the GMC is preferred as it works more quickly than the courts of law.

THE GENERAL MEDICAL COUNCIL

Disciplinary powers were first conferred on the GMC by the Medical Act 1858, which established the council and the medical register. The council's jurisdiction in relation to professional misconduct and criminal offences is now regulated by sections 36 and 38 to 45 of, and schedule 4 to, the Medical Act 1983. This act provides that if any medical practitioner registered with the GMC

- Is found by the professional conduct committee to have been convicted in the British Isles of a criminal offence, or
- Is judged by the professional conduct committee to have been guilty of serious professional misconduct

the committee may if it thinks fit direct that his/her name shall be erased from the register, or that his/her registration be suspended for a period not exceeding 12 months, or that his/her registration shall be conditional on his/her compliance, during a period not exceeding three years, with such requirements as the committee sees fit to impose for the protection of members of the public or in his/her interests.

Cases submitted to the GMC must be presented as a statutory declaration, a model for which appears in appendix B. Most cases submitted to the GMC by pharmaceutical companies recently have been mediated through the ABPI. The simple statutory declaration must be accompanied by a report setting out the details of the case, including a description of the clinical study, the method of recruitment of the doctor to whom the report refers, the monitoring process, how suspicions were first raised, how they were investigated, and how the conclusion was reached that led to the case being presented to the GMC. Supporting documents are required, though these best follow the declaration and the report. These supporting documents include the clinical study protocol, the recruitment letter(s) to the doctor concerned, the formal agreement with the doctor, including details of the financial arrangement, and copies of all the clinical report forms, laboratory or other reports, and/or diary cards which may be suspect.

The GMC secretariat will acknowledge receipt of the statutory declaration, and will subsequently request any additional documents considered necessary to process the case before or after it has been considered by the preliminary screener. Every complaint is scrutinised meticulously, and if it seems that the evidence submitted is insufficient, the council's solicitors may be asked to make inquiries to establish additional facts. Cases recently submitted by the industry have nearly all provided sufficient evidence for this stage to be unnecessary. Nevertheless, before deciding to refer a matter to the GMC it may not be possible for a pharmaceutical company to obtain access to patients itself—for example, to verify whether the patients had completed diary cards submitted by the doctor concerned. If the GMC considered such verification necessary, it would advise the pharmaceutical company accordingly, and do what it could to assist.

A decision whether action shall be taken on an allegation of serious professional misconduct is then taken by the president or by another member of the council appointed for the purpose (the preliminary screener). If it seems to the president that the matter is trivial, or irrelevant to the question of serious professional misconduct, he will normally decide that it shall proceed no further. However, to date, none of the cases referred by or in conjunction with the ABPI has come into this category. If it is decided to make allegations of serious professional misconduct, the doctor is informed of the allegations against him/her and is invited to submit a written explanation. If the doctor responds to this invitation, the explanation offered, which may include evidence in answer to the allegations, is placed before the preliminary proceedings committee, which next considers the case.

After considering a case of alleged serious professional misconduct, the preliminary proceedings committee may decide:

- To refer the case to the professional conduct committee for inquiry; or
- To send the doctor a letter; or
- To take no further action.

The letter referred to above may be a warning letter or a letter of advice, when it seems that the conduct of the doctor has fallen below the proper standard but not to have been so serious as to necessitate a public inquiry. A few cases referred by the pharmaceutical industry have been dealt with in this way. The names of the doctors concerned remain confidential.

Additionally, if it seems to the preliminary proceedings committee that the doctor may be suffering from a physical or mental illness which seriously impairs his or her fitness to practise, the committee may refer the case to the health committee instead of to the professional conduct committee. This safeguard for the doctor concerned is important, and has been used in at least one case referred to the GMC by the industry.

The rules governing the operation of the professional conduct committee require that any allegation of serious professional misconduct, *unless admitted by the doctor*, must be strictly proved by evidence, and the doctor is free to dispute and rebut the evidence called. This means that it is essential that cases referred by companies to the GMC are supported by the strongest possible evidence. The doctor is entitled to submit evidence and witnesses to rebut the allegations, and to call attention to any mitigating circumstances and to produce testimonials or other evidence as to character. Pharmaceutical companies may be required to provide witnesses for cross examination, but the case may be so strong that such witnesses are not needed. This is what has happened in the eight cases referred by pharmaceutical companies in conjunction with the ABPI which, to date, have been considered by the professional conduct committee.[6-9] If the facts alleged are found by the committee to have been proved, then it is up to the committee to determine whether, in relation to those facts, the doctor has indeed been guilty of serious professional misconduct.

At the conclusion of an inquiry in which a doctor is found guilty of serious professional misconduct, the professional conduct committee must decide on one of the following courses:

- To conclude the case without affecting the doctor's registration (but it may admonish the doctor)
- To postpone its determination
- To direct that the doctor's registration be conditional on his/her compliance, for a period not exceeding three years, with such requirements as the committee may think to impose for the protection of members of the public, or in the doctor's own interests
- To direct that the doctor's registration shall be suspended for a period not exceeding 12 months; or
- To direct the erasure of the doctor's name from the register.

Doctors who are suspended or erased have 28 days in which to give notice of appeal against the direction to the judicial committee of the Privy Council.

In the eight cases referred to above, all eight doctors were found guilty of serious professional misconduct; three were admonished, one was suspended for six months, and four were erased from the medical register. None of them appealed.

OTHER LEGAL ROUTES

If a company decides for whatever reason that it does not wish to use the GMC procedure, or if, for example, in another European country, a company wishes to prosecute a doctor who is not registered with the GMC, it is always open to that company to use a legal process. The GMC made it clear that it would not seek to usurp the proper authority of the police or of the Crown Prosecution Service where a criminal offence may have been committed. Alternatively, a company which considered itself fraudulently exploited by a doctor could take out a civil prosecution. A prosecution, however, would take considerably longer to process through to conviction than the GMC procedure, and, if successful, would automatically (in the

United Kingdom) lead to the GMC disciplinary procedure being invoked. The ABPI therefore strongly recommends that companies should consider it most appropriate that offending doctors in the United Kingdom should be submitted to the professional disciplinary proceedings laid down by law for the GMC.

The following cases are typical of those recently submitted by pharmaceutical companies in conjunction with the ABPI to the GMC:

THE CASE OF THE DURHAM PSYCHIATRIST

During 1986, Reckitt and Colman undertook a clinical trial on a new antidepressant medicine, for which it required a number of consultant psychiatrist investigators. One such doctor, much respected in Durham, the city where he was employed as a hospital consultant, was Dr V A Siddiqui.

This doctor presented all the data needed for the 15 patients he had entered into a clinical trial after a long session one Saturday afternoon when he had sat down and invented much of it. The record forms were all too neat, and were all submitted at the same time; this raised doubts in the mind of the clinical research associate, and thence of the medical adviser in charge of the trial. Dr Siddiqui happened to be one of several consultants taking part in a pivotal study for a new tricyclic antidepressant—sadly, unbeknown to the clinical research associate, he was involved in seven other trials at the same time, many of them potentially sharing the same patient population. The local ethics research committee had expressed mild surprise that he had submitted so many trial protocols for approval, but had never queried whether he could manage them all at the same time. His reputation in his home city was one of great dedication to duty.

When the data arrived, unexpectedly complete in view of the recruitment difficulties that the doctor had reported, the clinical research associate went to great lengths to check the source data—and found considerable difficulty in doing so. For some reason, the doctor chose to refer his haematology and biochemistry specimens to two different laboratories—one in Durham and one in Bishop Auckland. Neither laboratory had any data at all for one patient, though both laboratories had some data for all the other patients—but not what the investigator had submitted to the company. When challenged by the medical adviser, he denied that he had fabricated any of the information, claiming that, under stress at the time, he had handed the management of this particular trial to his registrar. But he could not remember her name, and she had now left. At this stage the regional health authority was asked for its help—not to investigate a possible crime, because there was no evidence of harm to any patients—but to supply the name and new address of the registrar. She was written to by the company at this address, which was several hundred miles away, and in her reply she indignantly denied that she had anything whatsoever to do with her previous consultant's research projects. Because he had so many, she and her colleagues never had time to do anything other than look after all the NHS patients, who, she implied, rather suffered from her erstwhile chief's involvement in other things.

The case was a strong one, and the ABPI helped the member pharmaceutical company to bring the doctor's activities to the attention of the GMC in a simple statutory declaration. The case was considered by the professional conduct committee. The doctor concerned was found guilty of serious professional misconduct, and his name was erased from the medical register.

* * *

The immediate aftermath was most unfortunate, and undoubtedly temporarily set us back. Because there was no local mechanism for investigating this sort of misconduct, no one locally knew anything about it, and the doctor involved certainly did not talk about it. When the news broke that evening, the local paper carried banner headlines—and the local medical community was horrified and incredulous. How dare the ABPI and a pharmaceutical company do this to one of their highly respected colleagues? That was the last time they would have anything to do with that particular company—and they banned it from access to the postgraduate medical centre forthwith. Fortunately, the postgraduate dean and the clinical tutor agreed to a meeting with the ABPI, which was held on site in Durham, and we were able to relate the facts to representatives of the local doctors. The situation was restored as a result, but the immediate effect had been disastrous. No pharmaceutical company was going to go through this again if it were to be jeopardised as a result.

Much the same happened when an eminent American physician faced trial in the biggest case of fraudulent drug research in the history of the Food and Drug Administration, which had his licence to practise revoked. He had "a great following among his patients and people could not believe what had happened." The incredulity of his colleagues was also profound, and many of them made representations on his behalf to have those who had "betrayed" him brought to task.

THE CASE OF THE WIMBLEDON GENERAL PRACTITIONER

During the spring of 1990, the clinical research organisation Medical and Clinical Research Consultants (MCRC) was commissioned by Glaxo

Laboratories to undertake a clinical trial in general practice comparing controlled release salbutamol with controlled release aminophylline in the treatment of obstructive airways disease.

Doctors were invited by personal letter to take part in this study, and Dr Lakshmi Pandit of Wimbledon, whose name had been given previously to Medical and Clinical Research Consultants by another client pharmaceutical company as a potential investigator, was sent such a letter on 4 July. He responded to this invitation not only by immediately returning a proforma in a prepaid envelope but by writing a separate letter, dated one month later, both indicating his willingness to take part in this clinical trial. The form which Dr Pandit signed stated that he had read the study protocol, including the Declaration of Helsinki and the code of practice for the clinical assessment of licensed medicinal products in general practice, and agreed to conform with the relevant requirements.

He was visited by the clinical study monitor for the trial in the usual way and provided with supplies and documentation for him to treat and report on four patients. The clinical study monitor telephoned Dr Pandit two months later and was told that he had recruited all four patients, and a monitoring appointment was then made for two weeks later. At that visit, and as a result of monitoring all the report forms eventually submitted, some unexpected features and inconsistencies were noted:

(1) The information on the initial clinical report forms showed that the four patients were all enrolled on the same day and the patients' details were all very similar—non-smoking, non-drinking, manual workers, all aged between 45 and 60, but including a 60 year old woman. All four had arrived on the same day, all suffering from asthma, but none of them taking any medication for it.
(2) The patient information on subsequent clinical report forms showed that, throughout the trial period, for none of the patients was any concomitant medication given, and no adverse events were recorded; that the peak flow readings on the clinical report forms were often widely different from those recorded on the diary cards (supposed to be completed by the patients) for the corresponding day; that the distances patients travelled (to the surgery) varied considerably from visit to visit, and that some of the initial reports on distances and time taken were probably inconsistent with a diagnosis of asthma—including the 60 year old woman walking a mile (1·6 km) to the surgery in 15 minutes. Four miles (6·4 km) per hour is quite a fast rate, but the next two visits were apparently achieved at a speed of 7·2 (11·5 km) mph over a distance of 1·2 miles (1·9 km)—highly unlikely for a patient with asthma.

It was concluded that this picture showed a remarkably consistent profile of the patients, with unbelievable travel information. It is

exceedingly unlikely that the four patients, recruited on the same day, would have this consistency of profile.
(3) The diary cards raised further suspicions. Patients taking part in this trial were expected to complete diary cards on such matters as breathlessness, tablet count, and peak flow readings. However, the method of completion cast considerable doubt on the validity of the information, quite apart from all the entries seeming to be in the same handwriting, with the same idiosyncrasies of style; for instance, all the diary cards when required to show the number 0, showed the mark X. One card had been completed in different pens horizontally rather than vertically, suggesting that all the data were filled in at the same time, but with an (erroneous) attempt made to make it look as if they had been completed on different dates. The instructions on the diary card indicated that the first day of completing the card should be the day after visiting the general practitioner. All four patients made the same mistake of starting on the day of the visit, and none of these points was consistent with the cards being filled in by the patient on a daily basis.
(4) Next, on the visual analogue scales, patients were asked to measure, at each visit, how they felt compared with their previous visit, and to mark a horizontal line with a cross. There was a remarkable, highly unlikely, consistency in the writing of all four patients. One patient, however, wrote very spidery crosses for three of the visits, and managed a very firm one for the fourth visit. This does not happen in practice.
(5) Patients were given either two treatment packs (for salbutamol) or six treatment packs (for aminophylline). The two patients on salbutamol, had they taken the dose indicated, would have returned six tablets from one pack, and 14 tablets from the other pack. Both patients returned these amounts, but both had cut the unused tablets for pack 1 off the strip-and-blister pack, when predicted behaviour would have been to press out the doses as required, and then to return the whole strip.

This raised doubt as to whether the medication was distributed to patients.

Once all these suspected irregularities had been identified, the clinical study monitor and regulatory compliance quality assurance manager for Medical and Clinical Research Consultants attempted several times to contact Dr Pandit requesting an audit visit. Four phone calls between 17 January and 31 January 1991 requesting that he should call back and five letters between 15 January and 25 Feburary were all unanswered, except for two occasions when Dr Pandit insisted that he wanted copies of the case record forms so that he could "get his records ready."

The inconsistencies, unlikely patient profiles, handwriting anomalies, and the failure to permit verification of original data led to the conclusion that the data submitted were fraudulent, which justified referral of this doctor to the GMC. At a hearing before the professional conduct committee, Dr Pandit was found guilty of serious professional misconduct, and his name was erased from the medical register.

THE CASE OF THE COVENTRY DOCTOR

Towards the end of 1989 the clinical research organisation, Medical and Clinical Research Consultants, was commissioned by Glaxo Pharmaceuticals to undertake a clinical trial in general practice comparing cefuroxime axetil with amoxycillin in the treatment of lower respiratory tract infections.

Doctors were invited to take part in this study, and a Dr K Francis of Coventry responded to the invitation by returning a prepaid card indicating that he would like to participate in this antibiotic study. The card also stated that he had read the protocol, the Declaration of Helsinki, product information details and the code of practice for the clinical assessment of licensed medicinal products in general practice and agreed to conform to the relevant requirements. His acceptance of this invitation to take part was followed by the despatch of protocol and clinical materials in mid-January. At that time he was supplied with sufficient drugs and case report forms to treat four patients.

The case report forms for all four patients were returned on 7 February 1990, when they were the subject of internal review; three of the patients had been recruited on 19 January and the fourth on 23 January 1990.

For all four patients several discrepancies from the requirements of the protocol were identified and these were queried in a letter sent to Dr Francis two days later. Four letters were in fact sent, each dealing with a specific case, and with each letter a photocopy of the relevant pages of the case report forms was enclosed, with the discrepancies highlighted. All these discrepancies referred to dates of birth and the age of patients, the protocol specifying that one inclusion criterion was that the patient must be aged 50 years or over, or in one of four additional "at risk" categories. For none of the four patients did Dr Francis refer to the other four "at risk" categories, and therefore his sole inclusion criterion was "aged 50 years or over." Dr Francis responded to these four letters, but the returned case report forms contained further errors, which were drawn to his attention in writing without delay, again with photocopies of the relevant pages.

Review of all the data submitted by the doctor confirmed serious unexplained inconsistencies in the information supplied, and a pharmaceutical physician on the staff of Medical and Clinical Research Consultants conducted an on site audit at Dr Francis's surgery. At the site visit, Dr Francis would not allow this physician access to the original patient records, nor would he himself refer to the records in the physician's presence, and it was not therefore possible to confirm or corroborate the information given.

What the contract house was left to deal with, therefore, was a series of report forms, in which many of the data were inaccurate or inconsistent. The inconsistencies, the errors in interpreting the protocol, and the failure to permit verification of the original data, specifically patients' dates of birth, led to the conclusion that the data submitted were fraudulent, which justified referral to the GMC. At a hearing before the professional conduct committee, Dr Francis was found guilty of serious misconduct, and his registration was suspended for six months.

THE CASE OF THE PLAISTOW PRACTITIONER

In the autumn of 1990 Fisons contracted with Data Analysis and Research Limited, of Cambridge, to undertake a multicentre clinical trial entitled "An open crossover study to compare the acceptability and efficacy of Tilade Mint (4 mg qds) delivered by the Autohaler with Tilade Mint (4 mg qds) delivered by the standard metered dose inhaler."

Fisons suggested to Data Analysis and Research that, among others, Dr R B Gonsai, a single handed general practitioner in Plaistow, London, E13, might have an interest in this trial. On 8 November 1990 Data Analysis and Research wrote to him inquiring whether he would be interested in participating in the trial, enclosing a form on which he was to indicate his interest or lack of interest, and a summary of the protocol. He completed and returned the form confirming his interest. He was visited two months later by a clinical research associate from Data Analysis and Research to discuss the trial, after which he was confirmed as a suitable potential investigator.

An initiation meeting was held on 5 June 1991, at which the study design was again discussed with a detailed review of the case record forms. At that meeting Dr Gonsai signed a formal agreement to participate in the trial, the protocol, an indemnity letter, and a receipt for the investigator brochure. These documents clearly stated that the trial was to be monitored by authorised people with respect to current guidelines on GC(R)P. Clinical supplies and documentation were provided for five patients.

A routine monitoring telephone call to Dr Gonsai was made on 4 July 1991, when he confirmed that he had recruited four patients, although he had not returned their enrolment cards. During this telephone call, an appointment was made for a monitoring visit 9 July 1991. On 8 July, when a call was made to confirm this appointment, the doctor cancelled the appointment, and it was not possible to hold the first monitoring appointment until 19 August 1991. At that meeting the data for four patients were reviewed. For one patient the documentation seemed satisfactory. The data for the other three patients showed an anomaly regarding the dates of assessments: the third assessments for each of these three patients were dated 20 August 1991, 24 August 1991, and 28 August 1991, respectively— dates in advance of the monitoring visit.

THE BRITISH INDUSTRY'S RESPONSE

Dr Gonsai explained that his wife, who helped with completion of the clinical report forms, had dated these assessment forms in advance, but that the appointments book confirmed that the patients had visited the surgery on 16 or, in two cases, 17 August 1991. However, verification with the NHS notes of these patients showed no record of these visits having taken place.

Regarding the diary cards, required to be completed by each patient, further anomalies arose. The entries for two of the four patients were completed up to 20 August 1991 and 24 August 1991—when reviewed on 19 August 1991. Dr Gonsai could offer no explanation for this.

A further monitoring appointment was made so that the company might seek a written explanation from Dr Gonsai on the completion of diary cards by patients beyond the dates of their last visits, and to check the appointments book. This appointment was duly fulfilled early in September 1991, when it was noted that Dr Gonsai had recruited one further patient into the study.

Several further issues were raised which required clarification at a subsequent meeting:

(1) For the fifth recruited patient no diary cards were available at all. Dr Gonsai stated that the patient had not returned them, and additionally that he had issued old cards to the patient, from a previous study.
(2) The forced expiratory volume and forced vital capacity values were identical for all three visits for three patients, and for two visits for the fourth and fifth patients. These results are beyond reasonable bounds of statistical coincidence.
(3) The evening peak flow readings recorded by one patient were outside the range of the peak flow meter.
(4) The morning and evening peak flow readings were identical for all patients on all the diary cards; there is usually a variation between morning and evening readings in real life, and the chances of finding this constant uniformity of data in practice are beyond belief.
(5) The contract house queried further the state of the diary cards. They were in pristine condition, without any of the usual evidence of handling found on their return from patients. It was also queried why two sets of the diary cards seemed to be in the same handwriting, and, again, why some of the data had been completed on diary cards beyond the date of the final visit of the patient to the doctor.

On the strong grounds of probability it was concluded that the data submitted by Dr Gonsai to Data Analysis and Research included entries which were not compatible with the facts concerning the patients to whom they were supposed to refer, and that this constituted serious professional misconduct, justifying referral to the GMC. At a hearing before the professional conduct committee Dr Gonsai was indeed found guilty of serious professional misconduct, and his name was erased from the medical register.

THE CASE OF THE GENERAL PRACTITIONER FROM GLASGOW

In February 1991 the Astra Clinical Research Unit set up a four-centre general practitioner clinical trial in Glasgow, designed to compare felodipine ER once daily and nifedipine SR twice daily given as monotherapy for patients with mild to moderate hypertension. One of these four practitioners was Dr David Latta. The data submitted to the company by Dr Latta during the course of this trial were so at variance with what would be expected, and with what were in fact submitted by the other centres, that a source verification audit was conducted.

The following results were obtained:

(1) All 22 patients had exactly 100% compliance.
(2) All 22 patients had returned all the empty blister packs in which the trial medication was supplied.
(3) All 22 patients had kept drug boxes in pristine condition.
(4) 21 of the 22 patients had exactly 28 days on treatment.
(5) All 22 patients completed qualify of life questionnaires, which were all in pristine condition. There were no changes of mind or mistakes in the questionnaires.
(6) No patients in the study reported any adverse experiences.
(7) No patients withdrew from the study, and all 22 patients completed the study according to the protocol.
(8) The range of blood pressure readings was very small, and an exceptionally large proportion of patients maintained a heart rate of 74.

All the above points were not in accord with usual trial experience, in which considerable variation in patient behaviour is seen, and this in itself raised suspicion. However, subsequent points were of greater concern:

(9) Most of the blood test results were on forms which had had the patient's name or sample date cut off the source documents. Some of the documents had been stamped by the laboratory with a date preceding the date on which the sample was supposed to have been taken; some of these dates had been altered in pen to the correct date.
(10) The doctor claimed to have used pseudonyms for the samples he submitted, but had forgotten them, and so copies of the damaged laboratory report forms could not be obtained.
(11) Some of the damaged laboratory report forms seemed to have been signed by a doctor who had left the laboratory in December 1990, three months before the first patient was recruited.
(12) The consent forms were all produced retrospectively and several of these forms seemed to have been signed by the same hand.

(13) No record of any of the patient data generated during the course of the trial was entered into the patients' NHS records; separate NHS record cards were generated, retrospectively, from data recorded in the clinical trial record forms, some in the presence of the trial monitor. These were therefore meaningless as source data.
(14) The electrocardiograms for eight patients seemed identical; for a further four patients they seemed differently identical; and for a further seven patients again seemed identical. This implies that for 19 patients just three tracings were used.
(15) The study file had not been used, and no record of drug accountability was taken.

The sum total of these points was so at variance with what would be expected that it was highly likely on the grounds of probability that some of the data generated by Dr Latta in this trial were fraudulent, and the evidence was therefore submitted to the GMC. At a hearing before the professional conduct committee, Dr Latta was found guilty of serious professional misconduct, and his name was erased from the medical register.

THE POLICY OF THE ASSOCIATION OF THE BRITISH PHARMACEUTICAL INDUSTRY

The working party made several recommendations, all of which have been adopted by the ABPI as policy. These are:
(1) Every member company should be reminded of its obligations under the principles of GC(R)P, and asked to state its commitment to reporting all cases of fraud and to taking appropriate action.
(2) Every member company should introduce standard operating procedures for the handling of suspected fraud, which should include at least the following items:
   (a) A clear statement of the company's policy towards the handling of suspected fraud.
   (b) A stated policy that any cause for concern regarding suspected fraud must be referred to the medical director or other independent person at the earliest possible stage.
   (c) Clear guidelines as to the path to be followed if fraud is suspected.
   (d) Clear guidelines as to the right of appeal if a complainant feels that his/her concern is being inappropriately dealt with within the company.
   (e) The existence, within the company, of appropriate statistical screening methods which can be used effectively on a routine basis.
   (f) A policy that all cases which give rise to serious concern regarding a specific investigator should be notified at an early stage to the ABPI's director of medical affairs.

The association is committed to giving all possible assistance to its member companies in advising on action against fraud, with appropriate publicity given to the outcome of such action, to act as a deterrent, in its determination to stamp out fraud in clinical research which is sponsored by pharmaceutical companies, if it possibly can.

Only the utmost vigour in applying this policy will be successful; we hope others will adopt similar policies throughout the world.

1 Association of the British Pharmaceutical Industry. *Good clinical research practice guidelines*. London: ABPI, 1988.
2 Committee on Proprietary Medicinal Products Working Party on Efficacy of Medicinal Products. *Good clincal practice for trials on medicinal products in the European Community*. [111/3976/88-EN Final.] Brussels: European Commission, 1991.
3 Anonymous. GMC professional conduct committee. *BMJ* 1988; **296**: 306.
4 Lock SP. Misconduct in medical research: does it happen in Britain? *BMJ* 1988; **297**: 1531–5.
5 Royal College of Physicians of London. *Fraud and misconduct in medical research*. London: RCP, 1991.
6 Lock SP. Research fraud: discouraging the others. *BMJ* 1990; **301**: 1348.
7 Anonymous. Doctors struck off register for drug test misconduct. *Scotsman*, 11 December 1991.
8 Dillner L. GMC gets tough with fraudulent doctors. *BMJ* 1991; **303**: 1493.
9 Anonymous. Sex, scandal, and fraud. *BMJ* 1992; **305**: 272.

Investigating, reporting, and pursuing fraud in clinical research: legal aspects and options in England and Wales

CHRISTOPHER HODGES

By comparison with the history of money and avarice, in which fraud has often played a part, the history of modern clinical research is of recent origin as, therefore, are known cases of fraud in clinical research. So not surprisingly, virtually no legal provisions have been developed to deal explicitly with fraud in clinical research. To state the relevant law one must therefore analyse the relevant provisions of a wide range of pre-existing general law, in particular criminal law, civil law, and regulatory law (which is itself in this context a recent development, effectively dating within the European Community only from 1965).

In considering the subject of fraud in clinical research, it is all too easy to proceed on the assumption that fraud has been investigated, established, and proved in the appropriate tribunal. This is not, of course, the situation that presents itself in practice. The usual chain of events is that information will come to the attention of someone (usually a colleague of an investigator engaged in research, or a clinical research associate, or other employee of a pharmaceutical company sponsoring the research project) which will raise questions, uncertainties, or perhaps suspicions in that person's mind. That person may often not have access to information or sufficient authority to investigate the matter further so as to verify whether the initial concern was or was not well founded. Proper investigation requires communication with others and access to further information or data before valid conclusions can be drawn. What is required of the law is therefore not only rules under which verified fraudulent conduct may be officially declared to be such and appropriate sanctions applied, but also appropriate protection and powers for those who need to communicate and investigate suspicions.

LEGAL ASPECTS AND OPTIONS

The various aspects of relevant law will now be examined in turn, starting with the investigation of fraud within a company or institution and analysing the available options for proceeding further with criminal, civil, and professional sanctions and punishments. As will be seen, the existing English legal system can provide options which offer satisfactory solutions to many of the problems of dealing with fraud in clinical research, if the procedures are properly applied. The following detailed discussion will be easier to follow if it is borne in mind that the options which are available to a person who has suspicions are:

- To do nothing
- To set investigations in progress, either personally or by informing appropriate authorities;

and the main options which are open to a senior manager who has confirmatory evidence of fraud are:

- To do nothing
- To institute criminal proceedings
- To institute civil proceedings
- To institute professional disciplinary proceedings
- To institute internal disciplinary proceedings.

Investigation of fraud

DEFAMATION

Consideration first needs to be given to the civil law of defamation. This is for two reasons. Firstly, the investigative procedure must leave adequate scope for communication of relevant information and suspicions among those who need to communicate and must protect them from an unwarranted civil action for defamation which would hamper proper inquiries. Conversely, as a matter of public policy, communication of unjustified statements should be restricted and discouraged. A person who realises that he or she is under investigation or against whom disparaging remarks are directed may threaten to bring a civil claim for damages for defamation. Such a claim may be entirely justified. Anyone who is investigating fraud must exercise caution and good sense in making allegations about a person against whom nothing has been established. At this stage, one is solely concerned with verification of facts. Conclusions based on those facts as to whether or not fraudulent conduct or serious professional misconduct may have taken place are to be made by the appropriate tribunal. There is no need for a person investigating suspected fraud to accuse anyone of being fraudulent or to state that conclusion or opinion to anyone else; since the objective is basically to verify facts and validate data, the inquiries may be entirely factual. It may, after all, be the case that uncertainty and suspicions are unfounded, in which case any accusations or voicing of suspicions may have been entirely unnecessary and unwarranted. It is often difficult for someone who suspects or believes that another person has done wrong to carry out a factual investigation dispassionately and fully objectively, but this is what is required. Equally, personal experience has generally led to the conclusion that a person who threatens to sue for alleged defamation often, but not invariably, issues a threat as a defence mechanism and has something to hide (or has an over inflated ego). The law of defamation clearly has its place in order to protect genuine reputations. Nevertheless, it is striking that the general perception of defamation is distorted by extensive media reporting of a few celebrated cases involving public personalities (such as entertainers and politicians) whose commercial reputation is often enhanced as a result of the increased media exposure which trial of a defamation action often attracts.

The tort of defamation is committed when a person publishes to a third party words containing an untrue imputation against the reputation of another. There are three distinct causes of action. These are:

- Libel, where the words are written or broadcast
- Slander, where the words are spoken
- Slander of goods or malicious falsehood, where the words may be spoken or in writing but disparage another's goods as opposed to another's reputation.

Libel—Broadly, libel is the publication in writing or by broadcasting of matter which is likely adversely to affect the reputation of a person or company in the estimation of reasonable people.[1] The words complained of must lower the estimation of the complainant and not, for example, merely disparage his goods.[2] If words disparage goods, they amount to libel of the company only if they impute carelessness, misconduct, or want of skill in the conduct of the management of the company, including the research of a product, or injure the reputation of its business.[3] If the words impute serious misconduct they will give a cause of action in libel.

Where the words are written the plaintiff does not have to prove special damages—that is, loss of money: the loss of reputation consequent upon the libel is sufficient. If the plaintiff is a company, although it need not prove special damage, its injury must be related to money but its loss is not necessarily confined to loss of income (for example, its goodwill may be injured).[4] It cannot seek recompense for injured feelings, as can an individual.

The plaintiff need show only that the words are libellous. There is a presumption that the words are untrue and the burden of proving that the words are true therefore falls on the defendant. However, there are several particular defences to a libel action including:

(1) Justification. It is a complete defence to show that the statements are true in substance and fact.[5] This is sometimes a matter of opinion based on the interpretation of scientific data.[6]
(2) Fair comment. This is a defence in the nature of qualified privilege: the comment must be of public interest, must be an expression of opinion (not an assertion of fact), and must be fair (for example, based on true fact).[7] However, it can be an honest but wrong, exaggerated, or even prejudiced opinion. Comments are usually considered fair if they are the expression of honestly held opinion, however obtuse or unreasonable that opinion may be.[8] The defence is destroyed if the defamed person can prove malice (see below).[9]
(3) Qualified privilege. This defence applies where the publisher is under a duty to communicate on a subject in which he has a legitimate interest, to a person having a corresponding interest.[10] The defence is intended to protect the public interest but persons should be free—even encouraged—to speak openly on occasions when they have a duty to speak. Malice also defeats this defence.

Malice—If a statement which is otherwise privileged (for example, fair comment or qualified privilege) is published "maliciously," the privilege is destroyed. Malice does not necessarily mean spite or ill will but can include publishing something recklessly or knowing it to be false or for some other improper motive.[11] It can include attempts to promote a company's goods over a competitor's by unfairly criticising a competitor. The motive most commonly relied on is an intent to injure the plaintiff; that intent must be the dominant purpose of the publication; knowledge that it will have that effect is not enough if the author is acting bona fide in protection of his own interests.[12]

A plaintiff will not be able to establish malice unless he proves that the author did not believe what he published was true or was indifferent as to its truth or falsity unless:

- He instead establishes evidence of malice in conduct extraneous to the publication complained of (for example, other actions by the defendant, such as telling a third party that he would "destroy the plaintiff's career")[13]
- What is published contains defamatory matter not really necessary to protect the interest for which privilege is founded (for example, including gratuitous comments irrelevant to the topic discussed in the document purely to damage the plaintiff).[14]

Slander—Slander is the publication by the spoken word of matter which is likely to affect a person's reputation adversely in the estimation of reasonable people. When preparing a statement of claim in an action for slander it is necessary to quote the precise words spoken by the defendant.[15] However, it is not necessary to prove that they were the precise words used.

It is sufficient to prove a material part of them or words which are substantially to the same effect.[16] The person who spoke the words and the company in whose employ and/or on whose behalf he made the statement may both be defendants to the action.

The principal distinction between libel and slander is that an action for slander can be brought only if the plaintiff can prove resulting damage arising from the publication.[17] There are certain exceptions to this rule, one of which is that it is not necessary to prove special damage where the words are calculated to disparage the plaintiff in any office, profession, trade, or business.[18] Therefore a slander of a limited company in the way of its business, such as statements by sales representatives that a product is unsafe, is actionable without proof of special damage.[19]

The defences to an action in slander are identical to those in libel.

MODE OF TRIAL

Actions for libel, slander, and/or slander of goods are usually heard by a judge and jury, as either party has a right to trial by jury. However, the court may order trial by judge alone if concerned that the trial requires any prolonged examination of documents or accounts.[20] As it is most unusual for a defamation trial (unlike all other civil actions) to be by judge alone, a material consideration when deciding whether to sue is the question whether the issue will involve detailed technical, scientific, and/or medical expert evidence which a jury would find difficult to follow.

Principles of natural justice

Before drawing practical conclusions on the relevance of the law of defamation to investigative procedures, it is important to be aware of two principles of natural justice that need to be observed in judicial or quasi-judicial proceedings. A procedure in which either principle is not observed may be declared invalid on review by the High Court.[21] The principles are:

- No person should be a judge on his own cause (*nemo judex in re sua*).
  Thus, a person who acts as prosecutor or accuser in formal proceedings (even internal disciplinary proceedings as well as judicial or professional proceedings) may not also fulfil the functions of adjudication on guilt or innocence, or of imposing a sanction. For example, the General Medical Council (GMC) cannot fulfil functions of both investigation and judgment
- Hear the other side (*audi alteram partem*).
  Under this principle, both accuser and accused must be allowed equal opportunity to put their case to the tribunal hearing the matter. In a criminal case, this principle is developed into complex and detailed procedural rules for exchange of evidence, rights of audience, etc. In a

less formal setting, where the potential consequences may be less serious, this may not be necessary.

Conclusions for investigation procedures

What procedures should an organisation employ in the investigation of suspicions? The following conclusions may be drawn from consideration of the legal rules discussed above.

GENERAL MATTERS

The need to establish a duty to report suspicions in order to qualify for qualified privilege points to the need to establish this as a contractual or professional obligation. It is questionable whether a general custom and practice is sufficient to attract qualified privilege. Thus, it is advisable to specify this duty in contracts of employment, standard operating procedures and contracts between sponsoring company, clinical research organisation, and investigator. (An example of a standard operating procedure is given in appendix A.) It is also advisable to establish and follow an accepted written procedure for investigating irregularities which conforms to the principles of natural justice. This would name the various different people who are to fulfil the necessary investigative and judicial functions.

In the absence of an explicit contractual obligation, communications to those up the chain of authority within a study, company, or institution, or by a member of a royal college to that college or perhaps by a member company to the Association of the British Pharmaceutical Industry (ABPI) stand a fair (but not definite) chance of being subject to qualified privilege, if made without malice, on the basis that they are made pursuant to an implied contractual duty or professional duty. The actual result in any given case would depend on the facts and in particular on the strength of the obligation to report. The result might be uncertain.

Qualified privilege may well not cover communications "outside a chain"—for example, by an industry employee to the ABPI or to the Royal College of General Practitioners over the conduct of a GP. If such a complaint is to be made, it should be strictly factual so as not to be defamatory in the first place ("I have seen the following evidence" is preferable to "and the implication is . . ."). There remains the question of whether such a communication will provide enough information to merit further investigation and, if so, investigation by whom. Perhaps the British Medical Association and royal colleges should have some role in providing an active investigatory and complainant function in taking a complaint to the GMC. Without such a mechanism, there is perhaps a danger that fraud will not be properly policed.

MATTERS AFFECTING INDIVIDUALS

An individual should communicate only with another to whom he or she has a duty to communicate (under a contractual or professional obligation) and who has a legitimate interest in receiving the information. One should be careful to choose one's words carefully: it is preferable to restrict communication to stating facts (which one knows to be true) and not venture conclusions or opinions (which might be wrong). Thus a statement such as "The date of the entries on this case record form precede the date of supply of the product" are preferable to "Prof X is a fraudster!" It may also be advisable to seek legal advice, since communications with a lawyer for this purpose are privileged from production in subsequent civil litigation on the ground of legal professional privilege.[22] This ground of privilege, however, is available only if the communication (including any document in which it is contained) is for the sole or predominant purpose of seeking legal advice.[23] It must not be for any other predominant purpose, such as mere information in dealing with other topics.

The advantages of reporting and investigating suspicions

There may, after all, be an entirely innocent explanation for what seems suspicious. If that is so, it could be argued that the general European climate is moving towards encouraging both investigator and monitor to welcome the audit and verification of the true position, rather than to see this as unwarranted interference. The closer the monitoring is to raw data and their development, and the more a monitoring function is required and accepted, the greater should be the pressure for uniform adherence to acceptable quality standards and the smaller the temptation for fraudulent or questionable conduct.

Regulatory considerations

The holder of a product licence or a clinical trial licence has certain obligations under regulatory law, including obligations to report certain information to the licensing authority. There are no references in these statutory provisions to reporting fraud as such, but certain provisions may be relevant. As will be seen, the reporting requirements are quite widely drawn.

UNITED KINGDOM LAW

The legal obligations for the holder of a clinical trial certificate (CTC) to report safety information to the licensing authority under The Medicines (Standard Provisions for Licences and Certificates) Regulations 1971 Schedule 1 Part II are as follows:

(2) The certificate holder shall forthwith inform the licensing authority of any information received by him that casts doubt on the continued validity of the data which was submitted with, or in connection with, the application for the clinical trial certificate for the purpose of being taken into account in assessing the safety, quality or efficacy of any medicinal products to which the certificate relates for the purpose for which the certificate holder proposed that it may be used.
(3) The certificate holder shall forthwith inform the licensing authority of any decision to discontinue the trial of any medicinal product to which the certificate relates and shall state the reason for the decision.
(4) The clinical trial in respect of which the clinical trial certificate has been issued shall be carried out in accordance with the outline of the clinical trial contained in the application for that certificate subject to any changes thereto the licensing authority may from time to time approve.

Similar provisions are contained in the regulations relating to exemptions from licences (CTX):[24]

4(1)(c) ... the supplier has given an undertaking to the licensing authority that he will inform them forthwith of—
(i) any adverse reactions or effects associated with the administration of the medicinal product,
(ii) any other matter coming to his attention which might reasonably cause the licensing authority to think that the medicinal product could no longer be regarded as a product which could safely be administered for the purposes of the clinical trial or as a product which was of satisfactory quality for those purposes,
(iii) any change in respect of any of the matters specified in Schedule 2 to this order, and
(iv) any refusal to approve the clinical trial by an [Ethics] Committee ....

The authorisation of a medical or dental practitioner to carry out clinical trials on unlicensed products (a DDX authorisation),[25] imposes no obligations relevant to the current situation on the manufacturer of the products.

After a medicinal product has been granted a product licence, the relevant reporting provision is that

The licence holder shall forthwith inform the licensing authority of any information received by him that casts doubt on the continued validity of the data which was submitted with, or in connection with, the application for the product licence for the purpose of being taken into account in assessing the safety, quality or efficacy of any medicinal product to which the licence relates.[26]

The Medicines Control Agency has stated that it does wish to be informed of suspicions or evidence of fraud. It does, of course, have the option in appropriate subsequent cases, to refuse to issue a CTC or CTX or DDX where a particular investigator is concerned.

LEGAL ASPECTS AND OPTIONS

EUROPEAN PROVISIONS

There are currently no European legal provisions equivalent to or governing the United Kingdom's CTX, CTC, or DDX rules. Neither is there an equivalent in European law of the reporting requirement for a licensed product. However, there are some, albeit indirect, provisions in the European Commission's guidelines on good clinical practice (GCP).[27] The prevention of fraud is implicitly a particular function of the monitor. The specific responsibilities of the monitor include, among others:

2.4
- (a) to work according to a predetermined SOP, visit the investigator before, during and after the trial to control adherence to the protocol and assure that all data are correctly and completely recorded and reported, and that informed consent is being obtained and recorded from all subjects prior to their participation in the trial.
- (c) to ensure that all staff assisting the investigator in the trial have been adequately informed about and comply with the details of the trial.
- (d) to enable/ensure communication between the investigator and sponsor promptly at all times.
- (e) to check the CRF entries with the source documents and to inform the investigator of any errors/omissions.
- (i) to submit a written report to the sponsor and the steering committee (if any) after each visit (monitor report) and after all relevant telephone calls, letters and other contacts with the investigator (audit paper trail concept).

The specific responsibilities of the investigator include the following:

- (j) to establish a system ... to ensure that deliveries from the sponsor ... are correctly received ... recorded ... handled and stored safely and properly; that investigational products are only dispensed to trial subjects in accordance with the protocol; that any unused products are returned to the sponsor ....
- (k) to manage code procedures and documentation with meticulous care and ensure that the treatment code is only broken in accordance with the protocol and that the monitor is consulted/informed when this is done.
- (l) to collect, record and report data properly.
- (m) to notify (with documentation) the sponsor and when applicable the Ethics Committee (and relevant authorities where required) immediately in the case of serious AEs and to take appropriate measures to safeguard subjects.
- (n) to make all data available to the sponsor/monitor and/or relevant authority (where required) for verification/audit/inspection purposes.[28]

Chapter 3 of GCP deals with data handling. The investigator is required to:

Ensure that the observations and findings are recorded correctly and completely in the CRFs and signed.

Although these are only guidelines, Directive 91/507/EEC, which amended the annex to Directive 75/318/EEC, does make reference to the need to carry out clinical trials in accordance with good clinical practice and it is likely that considerable reliance will be placed on the EC guidelines.

Concern has been expressed about the lack of control of clinical trials within the European Community. This led the commission to issue a discussion paper[29] in January 1991 on whether it is necessary to have a specific directive dealing with the conduct of clinical trials. Among the points for consideration were concerns about fraud and whether it would be better to adopt the American system, under which inspections are mandatory. Contributions were invited from interested parties on this and other issues. A compilation of comments was issued in July 1991, which showed a very mixed view among member states. No further progress has been made since then on this subject.

Lastly, it should be remembered that it may be a condition of the grant of ethical approval to inform the ethics committee of relevant subsequent events. The GCP guidelines contain an obligation to inform the ethics committee of "serious or unexpected AEs occurring during the trial likely to affect the safety of the subjects or the conduct of the trial."[30] The United Kingdom's health service guidelines on local research ethics committees[31] state that "Reports to the Committee should also be required once the research is underway if there are any unusual or unexpected results which raise questions about the safety of the research."

Offences, consequences, and sanctions

Once investigations have produced sufficient prima facie evidence that reprehensible behaviour has occurred, the question for senior management is what to do. As suggested earlier, there are several options, the first of which is to do nothing. No doubt much could be said on this option and, without discussing it in detail, it is stimulating to consider whether one would prefer a system in which the highest standards of GCP are not only achieved but seen to be achieved, and high standards are consistently encouraged by openness and thorough audit, or a situation in which public, professional, and industry confidence is open to undermining by the possibility of fraud, innuendo, and uncertainty.

The legal options under criminal and civil law will now be considered.

Criminal law

Fraud has never been given precise legal definition. Fraud usually takes the form of a dishonest statement of what is false or a dishonest suppression of what is true, or dishonestly depriving someone of something which is his or to which he would or might be entitled. There is possibly not a crime of fraud itself[32] but there are specific criminal offences which may generally be described as fraudulent, such as:

- Dishonestly obtaining property belonging to another by deception, with the intention of permanently depriving the other of it[33]
- Dishonestly obtaining a pecuniary advantage by deception.[34]

The sentence which a court might pass in any given case depends on an infinite range of variables. The maximum sentence for the former offence is 10 years' imprisonment, although for cases in which the amount involved is less than £1000 a compensation order has on occasion been thought appropriate. The maximum for the second offence is five years' imprisonment.

Although an individual citizen may commence a criminal prosecution against any other citizen (by "laying an information" before magistrates), unless the Attorney General objects, it is usual for the investigation and collection of evidence to be commenced by the police if they receive a complaint from an individual. If the Crown Prosecution Service considers that the police have assembled sufficient evidence, the service will prosecute the case through the criminal courts. A minor case may be heard before magistrates but for certain offences (those triable "either way," that is, in a magistrates' court or a crown court) a defendant has a right to elect for trial in the crown court before a judge and jury.

The criminal process may take months and sometimes years to complete. Its progress is entirely in the hands of the official authorities and the complainant is not involved other than in making the initial complaint and in providing evidence to the authorities and the court. The process is based on explaining to magistrates or a judge and jury the context of clinical research and in persuading them that an offence has been committed "beyond reasonable doubt." It is entirely right that appropriate cases of antisocial conduct should be dealt with through the criminal courts, which constitute society's official mechanism for dealing with antisocial conduct. However, use of the criminal process is generally effective only in cases in which the evidence is clear and unequivocal. One should not underestimate the difficulties of explaining to judges and lay juries the context and intracacies of clinical research and, for example, complex techniques of data analysis.

Concern is sometimes expressed as to whether the police need to be informed of actual or suspected fraud. There is no specific obligation on an individual to notify the police of possible criminal behaviour of others.[35] However, where a crime has been committed, a person who discovers it must take care not to become personally involved. Participation in a crime essentially committed by others may constitute the separate crime of aiding and abetting the first crime.[36] Aiding and abetting has even been extended to inactivity in circumstances where a person has a right to control the actions of another but deliberately refrains from exercising it. Inactivity has been taken for positive encouragement in decided cases. Examples in decided cases have included a husband who stands by while his wife drowns their children[37] and a public house licensee who stands by watching his customers drink after hours.[38] In addition, there are the following relevant statutory offences:

- "A person who, where an arrestable offence has been committed, knowing or believing that offence or some other arrestable offence has been committed, and that he has information which might be of material assistance in securing the prosecution or conviction of an offender for it, accepts or agrees to accept for not disclosing that information any consideration other than the making good of loss or injury caused by the offence, or the making of reasonable compensation for that loss or injury"[39]
- Committing an act which tends to pervert or obstruct the course of justice (such as making a false statement to a constable[40] or stealing and destroying evidence[41]) in relation to actual proceedings or once an investigation has started which might lead to proceedings
- Acting with the intention of impeding the apprehension or prosecution of a person knowing or believing him to be guilty of an arrestable offence.[42]

Civil law

Under civil law, it is open to a person who has suffered claimable damage to sue for financial compensation in the form of an award of damages. Potential civil claims in this context could be based on causes of action in fraud and breach of contract.

FRAUD

In contrast to the position under criminal law, there is a long established civil wrong (known as a tort) of fraud. A person who is proved to have committed fraud is liable to pay the foreseeable damages of the plaintiff which flow from that fraud, which may be substantial, as referred to below. Although the tort of fraud or deceit is analysed in terms of making false representations, this would seem to include the recording of fictitious information by an investigator. The requirement that the representation must be intended to be acted on would not seem to present great difficulty in clinical research.

The origin of this tort dates back to the eighteenth century case of Palsey v Freeman,[43] where the plaintiff was held to have an action in deceit following a false representation made to him about the creditworthiness of a third party.

To succeed in such an action, several points must be established:

- That the defendant made a representation by words or conduct
- That the defendant made the representation, either knowing it to be untrue or being reckless as to its truth
- That the representation was made with the intention that the plaintiff should act on it
- That the plaintiff did in fact act upon the representation and suffered damage by so doing.

The plaintiff will then be entitled to be put back in the position he would have been if the tortious act had not been committed.

The misrepresentation, which may be either express or implied from conduct, must be a representation as to a past or existing fact.[44] A deliberate concealment of a defect will be sufficient for a false representation, being equivalent to a positive statement that that fact does not exist,[45] as is the leaving uncorrected of a false statement[46] and the making of fragmentary statements which may be true as far as they go but suggest that which is false.[47] Whether a statement of opinion involves a further implied representation of fact—for example, that the person stating the opinion has reasonable grounds for his belief—will involve a consideration of various factors such as the reasonable meaning conveyed to the representee, knowledge of the parties, and so on.

The defendant must have knowledge that the statement is false. This was established in the leading case of Derry v Peek.[48] The false representation must be made:

- Knowingly
- Without belief in its truth, or
- Recklessly.

The test is a subjective one. The existence of a genuine belief in the truth of the statement may raise difficult issues of proof for the plaintiff. A merely negligent, even grossly negligent, misrepresentation will not suffice for fraud.

The representation must be intended to be acted on by the plaintiff; others accept it at their own risk.[49] However, given that the false statement need not be made directly to the plaintiff,[50] those subsequently injured as a result of fraudulent research may have a claim. It is sufficient if the defendant's apparent intention was that the plaintiff should act on his statement. If it is relied on, it is no defence that the plaintiff was negligent or foolish in doing so, or that he had a full opportunity to discover the truth for himself.

A mere attempt to deceive is not actionable; there must be damage to the plaintiff. The test of remoteness of damage is directness and not reasonable foresight. In claiming damages for deceit, as with all civil as opposed to criminal actions, the lower standard of proof of the balance of probabilities is required. Since it concerns proof of fraud, however, a higher degree of probability will be required to satisfy this civil standard.

The Misrepresentation Act 1967[51] extends the tort of deceit. It enables a person to recover damages for loss under a contract entered into on the strength of the misrepresentation if the party making the misrepresentation would have been liable in damages if that misrepresentation had been made fraudulently. The plaintiff can recover damages without proving fraud provided all the other requirements of the tort of deceit are present. The burden of proof is on the defendant to prove that he reasonably believed the representations to be true.

BREACH OF CONTRACT

A claim for damages may be brought for breach of a term in a contract. The term may be express or implied. Express terms will obviously vary from contract to contract and it will be unusual to have a contract which provided expressly that an investigator or an employee would be liable for fraud. Express contractual terms which could, however, usefully be included in a research contract with an investigator or clinical research organisation might be obligations that the investigator, investigator's staff (and, equally, the monitor and sponsor) would:

- Observe all relevant legal and professional guidelines and codes of conduct, such as the European Community's guidelines on good clinical practice, the various reports of the Royal College of Physicians of London in relation to clinical research, and the guidelines of the ABPI
- Carry out their functions in accordance with the best currently prevailing standards of practice
- Observe good professional conduct
- Engage in no illegal acts in relation to the research project.

If the contract with the investigator contains no express terms which are relevant to this subject, terms will be implied under the Supply of Goods and Services Act 1982 for any contract for the supply of a service. The most important relevant term is that the supplier (if he is acting in the course of a business) will carry out the service with reasonable care and skill.[52] This statutory and implied term may be negatived or varied by express agreement, or by a course of dealing between the parties, or by such usage as binds both parties, but an express term does not negative this statutorily implied term unless inconsistent with it.[53]

Initiation of civil litigation is entirely at the discretion of an individual plaintiff, provided he has or can obtain appropriate funding, since the costs of funding litigation are borne by the parties (unless they are eligible for and obtain legal aid). The losing party is generally ordered to pay a percentage (generally around 70%) of the costs of the winning party. Civil litigation may be slow and costly. It is generally advisable to initiate litigation only where large amounts of money have been lost or are at stake and the defendant has sufficient assets against which a judgment might be enforced. This option is therefore not a first choice in pursuing fraud in clinical research unless the investigator and/or his employer has significant assets. However, civil litigation may well be a useful option where the defendants do have significant assets and it can be shown that the plaintiff company has suffered significant loss. While failure to recruit the agreed number of patients to a protocol might constitute a technical breach of contract (although an investigator might argue a defence of force majeure) and failure to complete all case record forms in the appropriate fashion might also be a technical breach of contract, it would often be difficult to establish that a company had suffered significant loss as a result of these breaches of contract. On the other hand, a company might well be able to show that reliance on fraudulent data had caused it very significant financial loss. The issue of which losses may or may not be claimed as damages is complex and beyond the scope of this chapter. Potentially claimable financial loss might include not only the cost of repeating the study but also lost profits on delayed marketing for the product or on its subsequent withdrawal, which in certain instances might be very substantial sums.

If an investigator's attention is drawn to the significance of provisions in contracts or standard operating procedures which indicate that evidence of fraud will be investigated, wrongdoers pursued, contracts terminated, and losses reclaimed, this can have a salutary effect on the investigator's attitude to observing high quality standards in performing a study. It can therefore be advantageous to use contracts and standard operating procedures which state this policy unequivocally. A further useful provision to include in a contract with an investigator is a right of inspection of appropriate records at any time on reasonable notice. The aim of this provision is to ensure that there is proper access to data so that verification and investigation can take place and any uncertainties be confirmed or refuted without delay.

Professional disciplinary procedures: referral to the General Medical Council

In view of its importance, this option is discussed as a separate topic in the chapter by Wells.

There are considerable advantages in the GMC's disciplinary procedure over the available criminal and civil remedies. These include time (from start of investigation to GMC decision usually takes only about six months); cost (minimal in terms of legal expenses and, after the initial investigation of the matter by the company concerned, minimal further disruption by an investigating authority such as the police); less formal procedural rules than a law court, and the fact that the tribunal concerned already has extensive familiarity with the subject matter with which it will be dealing (a great deal of time and effort would have to be expended in explaining the nature, purpose, and intricacies of clinical research as well as the specific problem to a court of law). The third and fourth of these factors might certainly be expected to result in the GMC having less hesitation in reaching a conclusion that fraud had been perpetrated on appropriate facts being presented to it than would a law court.

Conclusions

Suitable procedures are available to cover the proper and fair investigation of suspicions in research sponsored by industry. Use of appropriate obligations in contracts and standard operating procedures is important. Greater difficulties might exist in pursuing suspicions in non-industry sponsored research.

Legal considerations suggest that explicit contractual and professional obligations should be developed in relation not only to observing GCP but also to reporting irregularities to defined personnel in accordance with a specified procedure and certain personnel (for example, the monitor) and that professional bodies should accept an obligation to investigate such information and take such disciplinary action as may be necessary. Obligations under regulatory law to report to the licensing authorities should not be overlooked.

Options for taking positive action against people against whom there is clear evidence of fraud include criminal prosecution, a civil claim for damages, and, if a doctor is involved, a disciplinary complaint to the GMC. A damages claim is appropriate where significant claimable sums have been lost and making a claim is commercially sensible. The GMC's professional disciplinary procedure has advantages over a criminal procedures in terms of speed, and in practice the resulting sanctions are effective.

1 Sim v Stretch (1936) 52 TLR 669.
2 Evans v Harlow (1844) 5 QB 624.
3 South Helton Coal Co. v North-Eastern News Association Ltd. [1894] 1 QB 133.
4 Thorleys Cattle Food Co v Massam (1880) 14 Ch D 763.
5 M'Pherson v Daniels (1829) 10 B&C 263. "The law will not permit a man to recover damages in respect of an injury to a character which he does not possess."
6 Wakley v Cooke (1849) 4 Exch 511. It is necessary to show that what is shown to be true is the same as that which the defendant's statement is interpreted to mean.
7 Grech v Odhams Press Ltd [1958] 2 QB 275. Kemsley v Foot [1952] AC 345. It is necessary only to establish sufficient facts in support of the comment.

LEGAL ASPECTS AND OPTIONS

8. Merivale v Carson (1887) 20 QBD 275.
9. McQuire v Western Morning News Co. [1908] 2 KB 100 (also Merivale v Carson above).
10. Webb v Times Publishing Co Ltd [1960] 2 QB 535 (at 563).
11. Clark v Molyneux (1877) 3 QBD 237.
12. Winstanley v Bampton [1943] KB 319.
13. Turner v MGM Pictures Ltd [1950] 1 All ER 449 (at 455).
14. Cooke v Wildes (1855) 5E & B 328.
15. Collins v Jones [1955] 1 QB 564.
16. Tournier v National Provincial Bank [1924] 1 KB 461.
17. Michael v Spiers and Pond Ltd (1909) 101 LT 352. Threat of material loss is insufficient.
18. Defamation Act 1952, section 2.
19. D & L Caterers v D'Ajou [1945] KB 364. A corporation may bring an action without proof of special damages.
20. Supreme Court Act 1981, section 69.
21. Anisminic v Foreign Compensation Commission [1967] 2 AC 147.
22. See Rules of the Supreme Court, Order 24, rule 5.
23. Waugh v British Railways Board [1980] A.C. 521.
24. The Medicines (Exemption from Licences) (Clinical Trials) Order 1981, SI 1981, No. 164.
25. The Medicines (Exemption from Licences) (Special Cases and Miscellaneous Provisions) Order 1972, SI 1972, No. 1200.
26. The Medicines (Standard Provisions for Licenses and Certificates) Regulations 1972, SI 1971 No. 972 as amended.
27. Committee on Proprietary Medicinal Products Working Party on Efficacy of Medicinal Products. *Good clinical practice for trials in medicinal products in the European Community.* [111/3976/88-EN Final.] Brussels: European Commission, 1991.
28. Ibid, section 2.5.
29. EC discussion paper on the need for a Directive on clinical trials, III/3044/91.
30. Ibid, paragraph 1.4.
31. HSG (91) 5, paragraph 2.14.
32. The common law misdemeanour of cheating was abolished by Section 32(1) of the Theft Act 1968, save as regards offences relating to the public revenue. This might conceivably be relevant to publicly funded (that is, NHS) research although the offence has been invoked only in relation to fraud against Inland Revenue.
33. Theft Act 1968, Section 15.
34. Theft Act 1968, Section 16.
35. Scott v Metropolitan Police Commissioner [1975] AC 819.
36. Accessories and Abetters Act 1811 section 8 as amended by Criminal Law Act 1977 section 1(1).
37. Russell (1933) VLR 59.
38. Tuck v Robson [1970] 1 All ER 1171.
39. Criminal Law Act 1967, section 5(1).
40. Field [1965] 1 QB 402.
41. Welsh [1974] RTR 478, CA.
42. Criminal Law Act 1967, section 4(1).
43. Palsey v Freeman [1789] 3 TR 51.
44. Yorkshire Insurance Co v Craine [1992] 2 AC 541.
45. Gordon v Selico *The Times*, Feb 26 1986, CA.
46. N Bank Finance Ltd v Charlton [1979] I R 149.
47. Peek v Gurney [1873] LR 6 HL 377.
48. Derry v Peek [1889] 14 App Case 337.
49. Peek v Gurney [1873] LR 6 HL 377.
50. Commercial Banking Co of Sidney v Brown & Co [1972] 46 ALJR 297.
51. Section 2(1).
52. Supply of Goods and Services Act 1982, section 13.
53. Supply of Goods and Services Act 1982, section 16.

Fraud in clinical research from sample preparation to publication: the French scene

D LAGARDE, H MAISONNEUVE

Until recently, French scientists did not seem to be concerned about misconduct in medical research. Specific guidelines for preventing fraud, disclosure, or publication of proved cases, and review papers, are still rare in France. Meanwhile, misconduct or fraud in southern Europe have been suspected by British authors, as stated by Stephen Lock quoting one anonymous informant: "The amount of fraud was lower in Britain than in the rest of Europe".[1] But times are changing, and French scientists and French authorities have already taken action to prevent misconduct.

This chapter will focus mainly on drug research conducted by academic institutions or pharmaceutical companies. Because of the huge economic pressure in this specific field of medical research, from sample preparation to final publication, negligence and misconduct may be easily encountered. The possibility of fraud in sample preparation had already been closely explored in France before the generic scandal happened in the United States. So, in a way France could be considered to be in much the same state as the USA in the early 1980s (S Lock, personal communication).

The implementation of government guidelines on good manufacturing practices and good clinical practices has been fast. These guidelines changed the status of medical research and had an impact on all kinds of research, not only clinical trials. Besides these guidelines, the Ministry of Health extended the mission of its inspectors to overseeing the application of the law regulating biomedical research in 1989[2] and the scientific community started to hold meetings on fraud, publishing the proceedings of such meetings.[3]

Identification of fraud in France

Private discussions between investigators, and between personnel of pharmaceutical industries, easily bring up suspicious cases. These suspected cases were never really investigated and remained unclear. Some international pharmaceutical industries started, five to 10 years ago, to apply standard American guidelines for good clinical practice, upsetting many investigators. As usual, the borders between negligence, misconduct, and fraud are difficult to assess.

SAMPLE PREPARATION

In the past the preparation of trial samples and delivery of drugs were too often neglected. They were neglected by both sponsors (study monitors, product managers) and investigators. Surprisingly, hospital pharmacists were not concerned. Access to trial codes was not protected, and blinded studies were sometimes understood as being blinded for the patient only.

Inspections in pharmaceutical industries clearly indicated that it was difficult to trace all steps of trial sample preparation afterwards. A lot of clinical trials have been conducted without carefully checking the prescribed drug from sample preparation to the final step of prescription by investigators. That does not mean that misconduct was happening, but the gap is sometimes narrow between negligence and misconduct.

In France, batches used for clinical trials do not need to be as sold. So, in many trials, drugs come from pilot batches. Meanwhile, excipients could slightly differ between the drug used in trials submitted for an application and the batches later put on the market. Few scientists are really aware of this. Only some pharmacists try to attract attention to these facts, which could cast doubt on the results of trials.

CONDUCT OF THE TRIAL

Our discussions with clinical research associates easily uncovered strange but efficient "cleanings." Modification of clinical data, absence of missing data exist everywhere. What is negligence? What is intentional? What is fraud? In France, it is still easy to find borderline decisions with a satisfactory explanation. There are always good reasons for eliminating outliers. As in other countries, pharmaceutical companies are never in a position to officially disclose cases of fraud by well known investigators. Disclosing fraud could damage the image of the pharmaceutical sponsor in the scientific community. Meanwhile, in some medical specialties it is acceptable to talk about fraud and to know which team was involved but official disclosure is not common.

We have encountered classic cases of misconduct during trials. We have been shown an audit of a suspicious trial. In this trial, patients had to fill in daily forms to evaluate symptoms. 120 daily reports were obtained from 120 patients. Samples from the handwriting of all 120 patients were submitted to a graphologist. He answered that all 120 patients were

THE FRENCH SCENE

probably left handed. The principal investigator was left handed. This observation is convincing proof that fraud occurred. The case has never been officially disclosed. The clinical reports showing such efficacy were not reported to an authority, and never confirmed by later trials with the same drug.

What leads to misconduct in clinical trials is usually the chance to make money. In another case, we faced an "ethical reason" for getting money. This investigator, in the south of France, was enrolled in a large multicentre trial for two years of follow up with complete clinical and biological check up every month for six months and every three months for 18 months. He completed three times the required number of observations with complete follow up for all patients. None of the other investigators enrolled the required number of patients, and about 30% to 40% of the patients did not complete the two-year follow up. Monitoring was difficult, as this investigator never allowed access to original laboratory data, or electrocardiograms. He was well protected by senior university personnel. As he was expecting a big amount of money in respect of the work done, he was impatient to be paid. We refused to pay him, telling him that he would receive 50% of the fees if the firm was given a clear explanation of the situation. Six weeks later, he "confidentially" made a private call out of working hours and explained that the patients did exist, but that data had been partially invented or misreported in order to comply with the protocol. He urgently needed money because he and his partner had a sterility problem, and had to afford several long trips abroad in order to adopt a baby. He had never realised the impact of faked data, thinking that, with large numbers of cases, some invented ones would never change the final results. His cases were excluded from the final analysis of the study by the firm.

Sometimes misconduct is difficult to differentiate from absence of knowhow. There have been cases, as in other countries, of firms developing drugs for many years without checking the first hypothesis on the first data. All the development may be conducted without reporting each finished study. Investigators are under pressure to publish and they submit papers without complete data and proper statistical analysis. When finally the time comes to write and edit final reports for a submission, in some centres it is difficult to retrieve all the data previously published. Years of clinical research may be carried out on a false basis, and be ultimately useless. Good clinical practice should avoid such situations but it is expensive, and French companies still find it difficult to apply.

PUBLICATION

There are cases of misconduct and fraud in France at publication level. Owing to the Latin mentality, and to the way French scientific journals are run, these cases are never disclosed. We have attended board meetings where it was decided to hide such fraudulent situations. Instead of publishing letters from scientists contesting other colleagues' findings, editorial boards prefer to recommend against such a dialogue. Only "positive" letters, with congratulations or acknowledgments, are accepted for publication. We have attended meetings where an investigator was giving an oral communication based on faked data submitted as an abstract six months before the congress. Instead of retracting the communication, this person preferred to give an unsubstantiated lecture. Duplicate publications are really poor quality generics, consisting of multiplying publications of the same data. Duplicate publication, especially of review papers, is sometimes not considered as fraud. It is rather considered as a way for a doctor to attract patients by being known by GPs, or to increase his or her number of publications. There is duplicate publication in French journals and we have seen many examples of such misconduct. French journals are clearly linked to pharmaceutical companies, which are needed to fund them. Only one journal, La Revue Prescrire, is free from this business, but it had been supported by government funds for many years and is now entirely supported by subscribers. Only French journals supported by scientific organisations, publishing papers in English in order to increase their readership, can afford editorial boards, using the peer review process. This probably adds to the poor quality of the journals published in French.

Mechanisms for dealing with fraud

As identification of fraud is not organised in France, and known cases remain confidential, no mechanism for dealing with it exists. There are no scientific committees dealing with fraud; no "a posteriori" investigations are conducted. If a large fraud was suspected at an academic organisation, reaction would be rather similar to that in the USA in the early 'eighties. What was seen in well known American cases, such as the Darsee affair, during the first investigational years could be repeated in France. Sophisticated dishonesty could escape detection by peers. Once suspicion arises, by accident or by deduction, scientists will delay investigation, and probably some of them will try to hide everything. Answers like, "We have lost the files since we moved," "Trainees were not closely supervised," "Our team is too busy to closely take care of such investigations" could be faced by inspectors.

If fraud is detected, no official academic committee is organised to deal with the case, which will probably be considered as an epiphenomenon rather than give rise to an in-depth investigation of the career of the perpetrator, or of all work done in the institution. We know of no examples of demands for return of funds allocated for research in France, as has sometimes occurred in the United States.

THE FRENCH SCENE

Starting an internal audit in an academic institution is still not easy. Suspected investigators do not answer questions, claiming medical confidentiality, lack of time, absence of files, etc. Verbal aggression is not unknown. "I will never prescribe your firm's drugs," "I will destroy your image in the city," etc. These menaces are unlikely to have much impact. Inspectors are officially authorised and ready to take decisions about legal action, official disclosures to professional institutions, or refusals of registration. We think that the French authorities would have the power to investigate such cases. For example, in French law, penalties do exist; but we have no knowledge of the application of this law in specific cases.

Mechanisms for dealing with fraud at the publication stage do not exist. Papers disclosing misconduct or fraud, such as those published by British or American journals,[4] seem unlikely to be published in France in the next decade.

Prevention

When fraud is not officially recognised, prevention seems rather problematic. Meanwhile, a lot of progress has been made. The quality of work has been improved since the publication, by the French Ministry of Health, of *Bonnes Pratiques de Fabrication* and *Bonnes Pratiques Cliniques*.[5,6]

Some other initiatives have also been taken by the Ministry of Health. The next step would be the publication of specific guidelines against fraud as was done in the United Kingdom, or by some national agencies in the United States. No guidelines have been published either by pharmacology departments (JP Boissel, personal communication), or by the Ministry of Health, or by national research agencies or even by the French medical association, the Conseil de l'Ordre (M Detilleux, personal communication). The French agency for medical evaluation, Agence Nationale pour le Développement de l'Evaluation Médicale, has not published guidelines for preventing fraud (Y Matillon, personal communication).

The French Ministry of Health has taken some steps to prevent malpractice, appointing medical and pharmacist inspectors to ensure compliance with the law, to check preparation of sample drugs carefully, and to monitor biological laboratories. Creating a special agency, such as the Office of Scientific Integrity in the United States[7], is not at all a priority in the scientific community. Such an agency may be created in France in the coming years (or decades?).

SAMPLE PREPARATION AND PRESCRIPTION

France has always been a leading country for the control of drug preparation, so that many trials have been performed with the highest clinical and statistical standards, without controlling the drugs given. Inspection of clinical trials conducted in France showed that it was difficult to track down afterwards which drug (the study drug or placebo) was in fact administered to patients. Focusing on this specific and major part of a research is important. The *Bonnes Pratiques de Fabrication*[5] lists specific recommendations for controlling the quality of drugs. These recommendations are not included in the EC guidelines.

There are safeguards against fraud at this first step of trials. Legislation has been passed in France to protect people submitted to biomedical research.[2] In January 1992 the programme and the main goals of pharmacist inspectors were published.[8] In this document concerning the inspection of pharmaceutical companies, the delivery of drugs in hospitals, and the standard format for inspection reports, chapter 3 concerns the application of the French law on biomedical researches.[2] This chapter has three subheadings:

(1) Manufacturing and labelling of drugs for clinical trials: inspectors should focus on this aspect and consider the European guidelines submitted for approval to the working party on "control of medicines and inspections." This draft[9] was appended to the French directives.[8] These supplementary guidelines specifically concern investigational products. All steps in the preparation of drugs for trials are precisely described. French pharmacist inspectors are clearly required to inspect the manufacturing of drugs.
(2) Requests for inspections on the *Bonnes Pratiques Cliniques*[6] coming from central administration should be considered as urgent, and be conducted by a medical inspector.
(3) Dispensing of drugs for clinical trials should be closely investigated. A decree ("arrêté") was issued on 9 August 1992 on the dispensing of toxic drugs.[10] The text thoroughly describes all steps from medical prescription to dispensing pharmacist and patient administration. All files should be kept, in good condition, with clear identification of drugs, prescribers, and so on.

Pharmacist inspectors were given priorities in 1992.[8] They should inspect first of all companies manufacturing drugs for human use; secondly, hospital pharmacists; thirdly all people and/or places involved in biomedical research. These priorities permit the tracking down not only of drugs for clinical trials, but all drugs dispensed for treatment.

In France, normally, pharmaceutical industries should have autoinspection. Each company should issue an internal inspection report on the whole manufacturing process. These reports should be done at regular intervals, and could be shown, on request, to representatives of the Ministry of Health, such as pharmacist inspectors.

CONDUCT OF THE TRIAL

The first way to prevent fraud is to make investigators aware of good clinical practice. They should understand the guidelines and agree to work to them. Good methods need to be taught. Many investigators do not think that it is necessary to learn methods, and they fear losing time doing so. In the past five years, specific training has started to be organised and soon we expect that each university will have courses on methods in clinical practice and scientific experiments.

Medical inspectors have been appointed by the French administration. They have a four-day training course at the Ecole Nationale de la Santé Publique (Rennes). The *Bonnes Pratiques Cliniques* and the French law on biomedical research have been published but a detailed protocol for medical inspections still needs to be set out.

Quality control is organised all over France for laboratory data from private and public biological laboratories. This control is under the supervision of the Laboratoire National de la Santé. This central organisation dispatches biological controls for diagnosis. Each laboratory has to test blinded and send back its result. This quality control applies to all laboratory tests and is supposed to be a guarantee for all patients. Medical research could be conducted, for example, in private practices with GPs using data issued by private biological laboratories. This, however, is probably not enough to ensure that no fraud could happen.

PUBLICATION

Prevention of fraud at the publication level does not really exist in France. Papers on publication bias are rare, papers on fraud are not published. Congresses such as the Second International Congress on Peer Review in Biomedical Publication get no publicity in France and only a few French scientists seem to be concerned. Fraud could be prevented by a good peer review system, but only a few journals have one.

1 Lock S. Misconduct in medical research: does it exist in Britain? *BMJ* 1988; **297**: 1531–5.
2 Loi n° 88-1138 du 20 décembre 1988 relative à la protection des personnes qui se prêtent à des recherches biomédicales. *Journal Officiel de la République française* 1988 December 22.
3 *La fraude dans les essais cliniques*. Proceedings of "Medicament et Santé. Drug and Health." 10 October 1991. Dijon: STS, 1991.
4 Engler RL, Covell JW, Friedman PJ, Kitcher PS, Peters RM. Misrepresentation and responsibility in medical research. *N Engl J Med* 1987; **317**: 1383–9.
5 Arrêté du 20 janvier 1992 relatif aux "Bonnes Pratiques de Fabrication." Paris: Ministère des Affaires Sociales et de l'Intégration.
6 Bonnes Pratiques Cliniques. Avis aux promoteurs et aux investigateurs pour les essais cliniques des médicaments. Paris: Ministère des Affaires Sociales et de l'Emploi, Ministère chargé de la Santé et de la Famille. (Bulletin Officiel n°87-32 bis) 1987.
7 Hallum JV, Hadley SW. OSI: why, what and how. *ASM News* 1990; **56**: 647–51.
8 Circulaire DPhM/13/cc n° 92-24 du 29 janvier 1992 relative au programme et aux modalités de travail des pharmaciens inspecteurs de la santé pour l'année 1992. Paris: Ministère des Affaires Sociales et de l'Intégration. (Bulletin Officiel 1992 April 24 no 548.)

9 Working Party on Control of Medicines and Inspections. *Draft supplementary guidelines for the manufacture of medicinal products for clinical trials.* [111 3004/91 EN.] Brussels: European Commission, 1991.
10 Arrêté du 9 août 1991 portant application de l'article R 5203 du Code de la Santé Publique dans les établissements mentionnés à l'article L 577 du même ordre. *Journal Officiel de la République française* 1991 October 10.

Fraud in medical research: the Danish scene

POVL RIIS

Scientific misconduct has accompanied scientific progress as long as we have had public reports on the results, and have had access to control public experiments or control observations. Such misconduct, often in its extreme form, scientific fraud, has been seen in polar explorers who claimed to have been the first to get to certain points, when later evidence established that they could not have been there, in geneticists claiming that the genome could adapt to certain physical life circumstances, and in travellers who described—and drew—fancy sea-monsters, unicorns, and mermaids.

Nowadays scientific misconduct is still known in all scientific disciplines. It has, however, attracted most attention in the health sciences, owing to this research sector's magnitude, clearcut homocentricity, and relation to such fundamental human conditions as life and death. This is a fact that all working in health sciences research must face, even if it is strange that only the biomedical sciences are in the focus of public interest—for diagnosing and preventing scientific misconduct must be important too in sociology, psychology, criminology, education, chemistry, physics, etc. Here the consequences, at least for society, can be as serious as in the health sciences. I predict a similar development in preventing and diagnosing scientific misconduct outside the biomedical sciences within the next decade or two.

When the North American reports on scientific fraud began to appear, many countries, including Denmark, considered the phenomenon to be an isolated American problem of no other relevance to them than a feeling of "how satisfying that it not has happened here," and even referred to the geographical distance as a measure of prevention, as if we were talking about foot-and-mouth disease. These attitudes reflected national self deception or habitual disinclination to face realities, also known as national escapism. After this phase of "what you do not see, does not exist" several countries have discovered that scientific misconduct is a universal phenomenon, and consequently also happens in their own scientific circles. That examples from the United States still dominate the scene shows rather that the American media and agencies are more disposed to self flagellation than many other nations.

In Denmark rare but well known cases of scientific misconduct in the health sciences have appeared over the past three to four decades. Some of them have been reported in public, others have been known only in the scientific community, sometimes because they were dealt with as were pregnancies in unmarried young women a few generations ago. With few exceptions none of these cases was investigated and reported according to the standards that are now considered appropriate. Their preventive effect was limited to that of horror stories, and their messages to new generations of scientists were never systemised and transferred to formal research education or to guidelines for good scientific practice in laboratory or clinical research.

A small group of Danish university teachers involved in courses for young scientists-to-be on ethics and honesty felt with increasing strength, a few years ago, that the many group discussions with the young participants pointed to a need for more systematic measures. One of these teachers happened to be chairman of the Danish Medical Research Council (DMRC), and one a former chairman. Consequently the idea that the DMRC ought to take an initiative was soon fostered. If scientific dishonesty had happened in Denmark and certainly could reappear, why not start working in a scandal-free period—that is, while there are no prominent national cases—as international experience has shown that systems created as a reaction to current cases have often been influenced by panic, conflicts of interests, or just a lack of necessary time for analysing this complicated topic.

The Danish Medical Research Council's initiative

Early in 1991 the DMRC decided to set up a national commission with the purpose of:
- Defining the term "scientific misconduct"
- Proposing procedures for establishing ad hoc investigatory committees in cases of suspected scientific misconduct
- Proposing rules for such committees' work
- Proposing requirements for research institutions regarding research protocols and storage of data
- Proposing further management of investigatory reports at the research institutions
- Proposing measures for preventing scientific misconduct—for instance, in the form of guidance and publication practices.

The commission consisted of representatives of the DMRC (with its chairman, Professor Daniel Andersen, as commission chairman), the medical faculties, the Danish Medical Society, the Royal Dental Colleges, the Royal Danish School of Pharmacy, the *Journal of the Danish Medical Association*, the central scientific-ethical committee, and a few special experts. The commission ended its work early in 1992 by publishing a comprehensive report in both Danish and English.[1] The steps taken to implement the commission's recommendations will be discussed later.

CONCEPTS AND SCOPE

The commission started to evaluate the terms most commonly applied to cases of scientific activity that diverge from written or unwritten ethical norms. *Fraud* and *misconduct* were considered, and so was the North American euphemism *scientific integrity*. While the first term comprises only the most serious cases, *misconduct* is broader, but alludes to medical etiquette. The preferred term was *scientific dishonesty* (in Danish "videnskabelig uredelighed"), covering a wide spectrum of ethical transgressions within the health sciences, referring to all fraudulent actions from idea, through experiment or trial, to publication. The commission included instances of negligence that were so grave as to represent a similar strain on scientific credibility. In such cases it is often difficult to disprove intent, just as in legal terminology, where the concepts of intent and gross negligence are juxtaposed. The Anglo-Saxon term *whistleblower* was translated to the Danish word for *informant* to avoid an unnecessary import of anglicisms.

The scope of the phenomenon was extended to all types of "forgery or distortion of the scientific message or a false claim of the researchers' contribution." The spectrum covers all deliberate:

- Fabrication of data
- Selective and undisclosed rejection of undesired results
- Substitution with fictitious data
- Erroneous use of statistical methods in order to draw conclusions diverging from those warranted by the study data
- Distorted interpretation of results or distortion of conclusions
- Plagiarism of results or entire articles of other researchers
- Distorted representation of other researchers' results
- Wrongful or inappropriate attribution of authorship
- Misleading scientific grant or job applications.

The commission decided to underline supplementary types of dishonesty, even if they would probably not be dealt with by a future investigatory system. These other types do not concern the scientific messages to any major degree. Instead they often distort the scientific community's perception of the scientist concerned through omissions or serious exaggerations:

- Covert duplicate publication and other ways of boosting the personal list of publications

- Presentation of impressive results directly to the public, thus bypassing the professional control system of scientific societies, editorial reviewers, etc
- Deliberate omission of original observations by other scientists
- Exclusion of people from a group of authors, despite their scientific contribution.

Examples of minor transgressions, which merely jam the international information network of the health sciences, include the *salami technique*, where one larger study is cut up into thin slices, each with its multiple, identical authors combined in new ways. The commission also considered the *imalas technique*. This anagrammatic term describes the opposite of the salami technique: deliberate polluting of the scientific literature by multiple publication of the same phenomenon "in two more cases." Another example is *data massage*—that is, authors' secret, repetitive application of a larger number of statistical tests in order to obtain the much desired low p value.

The last examples represent borderline cases, merging into the concept of collegiate etiquette, whereas the main categories of the worst kind (fraud, forgery) correspond to (and may well be) transgressions of criminal law, and plagiarism to breaches of civil law.

The etiquette types of offence usually result in a tarnished reputation, but most countries, including Denmark, have until now had no system for dealing with the more serious transgressions.

REPRESENTATIVE EXAMPLES

Examples from the United States, Europe, and Australia were analysed in detail in order to ensure that the conceptual system outlined was both exclusive and exhaustive.*

The McBride affair, concerning McBride's claim that imipramine and, later, Bendectin would cause fetal damage, illustrated the effect of deviations from the usual sequence of research phases: idea generation, hypothesis testing, projection of study results to the global network of knowledge, and publication after a phase of critical reading by colleagues, editors, and editorial referees, with a subsequent free discussion in the journal's correspondence column. It further emphasises the influence of a strong media charisma, not in itself fraudulent, but a temptation to short circuit the scientific process. The critical attitude to McBride's results was partly paralysed because of the lack of an easily accessible, independent investigation system (see also the chapter by Swan).

The Alsabti affair,[3,4] concerning Alsabti's claim to have constructed a unique diagnostic test for cancer, shows how political relations can twist the scientific process and silence critics in an authoritarian society. It

---

* Many of these cases are also discussed by Lock in the first chapter.

THE DANISH SCENE

further shows that the production of 60 articles in two years is incompatible with a normal honest scientific process.

The Gullis affair,[5,6] concerning Gullis's fraudulent findings that morphine and encephalins influence the concentration of cGMP and cAMP in nerve cells, illustrates the necessity of reproduction before publication when results are sensational. The affair was tackled fiercely and fast by the Max Planck Institute.

The Buck and Goulsmit affair,[7–9] concerning the two authors' claim that modified DNA could prevent HIV entering cells and the resulting wild fantasies that AIDS could be treated in a few years, underlines how critics and informants within an institution have a hard time trying to disclose scientific dishonesty. This Dutch case was well handled in the long run. It shows the well known negative effects of an autocratic management style. It further illustrates the negative influence of strong scientific competition in sensitive subjects in which the public has a strong interest, and the importance of including for investigation the grey zone between dishonesty and gross slovenliness.

The Soman affair,[3,10] disclosing V R Soman's plagiarism of Helena Wachslicht-Rodbard's manuscript, shows how important it is that referees stick to the rules for their work,[11] because this work gives them access to original observations when the true author's priority has not yet been established.

The often analysed American cases of Imanishi-Kari and Baltimore[12] and Gallo[13] show several aspects of scientific dishonesty. Most important is the light they shed on the university systems reacting in panic and self defence, the time and resources spent on multiple—obviously non-conclusive—investigations, the destruction of social and professional lives among both informants and suspected scientists, and the strong necessity for fixed rules in laboratories and departments when raw data are handled.

A recent Swiss case, the Ballart affair,[14] dealt with spectacular studies of the measles virus genome and a recombinant DNA technique for vaccine production, studies which later were shown to be fraudulent. The young scientist committed suicide after it had been discovered that the virus was of a standard type. The results could not be reproduced. The lesson is simple: if a young researcher presents extraordinary results they have to be tested by others in the laboratory before they are released for publication.

THE REACTIONS IN NON-FORMALISED SYSTEMS

There would be no need to consider establishing national investigatory systems if institutions and agencies had tackled known cases of scientific dishonesty in a satisfactory way. With few exceptions the opposite is true. In other words there *is* a need for new structures.

The laboratories and departments where alleged dishonesty has taken place usually react with denial, resentment, and persecution of the whistleblower. Political intervention, usually considered by scientists to be similar to "trolls smelling Christian blood," is necessary and valuable when filling the vacuum that the institutions ought to have filled with vigorous initiatives. Only a few universities have learnt the lesson from the notorious published cases and have established and published guidelines for the prevention and investigation of scientific dishonesty.

REACTIONS AMONG SCIENTISTS

Scientists undoubtedly support the fight against scientific dishonesty. However, those scientists who feel that their own strong norms express a kind of natural law will tend to understate the necessity of educational initiatives for prevention, fixed rules for the filing of raw data, and a formal system for investigation in suspected cases. Their fear of "more bureaucracy" sometimes outweighs the acceptance of plans for more systematic preventive measures. Rarely do they realise how vulnerable scientists are under the present conditions, if accused of scientific dishonesty in the form of rumour campaigns, anonymous letters, etc. In such situations an independent, official investigational system can be invaluable even for the completely honest scientist.

The analytic work of the Danish commission has of course been influenced by the reactions of international research organisations and agencies. The initiatives within the United States, comprising those of the Association of American Universities, the Association of American Medical Colleges, the Public Health Services, and especially the Office of Scientific Integrity have all inspired the commission, sometimes in a positive, sometimes in an opposite direction. Of especial relevance for Denmark are the guidelines on withdrawal of dishonest data published by the International Committee of Medical Journal Editors,[15] and the rules set out by the Royal College of Physicians.[16]

PUBLIC REACTIONS

As a whole, the public and the media in Denmark have not been much interested in the possible existence of scientific fraud in the country. This might be due to a general idea that the scientific community constitutes a "state within the state" and thus will have to deal with its own affairs. Considering that the public nowadays acts as patron of the health sciences this state of non-interference will probably not last. The public reactions to the Danish report, to be mentioned later, seem to support this prediction.

THE PRINCIPLES BEHIND A NEW SYSTEM

The judicial systems of democratic societies have been refined through centuries, based on a clear distribution of roles, general acceptance of a detailed conceptual system, and rules for appeal, etc. The scientific community has no such principles and practices.

THE DANISH SCENE

One of the fundamental principles behind major democratic institutions was that coined by Montesquieu (1689–1755), based on British tradition, that power in society has to be split in three: the legislative, the judicial, and the executive power. This principle was a fundamental starting point in the commission's work on a future Danish investigatory system. The same was true for the contemporary ideas on resocialisation lying behind the sanctions suggested, to be mentioned later, and for the general principle not to do things in a complicated (read: bureaucratic) way, if you can achieve the same result by simpler means.

The Danish proposal

The soil was fit for new ideas to grow, because—as the results of a questionnaire sent to all institutions showed—no Danish universities, ministries, etc had created investigatory structures or had published guidelines dealing with scientific dishonesty.

The commission proposed the following operational principles for a Danish investigatory system:

- It should cover the full spectrum of publicly funded health sciences research, and should be linked primarily to the university sector
- It should be based on agreements between institutions and professional unions, in order to anchor the system in the employment contracts of individual researchers
- It should apply also to cases where researchers and students are wholly or partially paid out of external funds
- It should be extended to include private research institutions through special agreements
- It should be established as two regional committees and one central national committee, termed the National Committee.

Even if a future system of this kind binds only those employed under the new agreement, it is foreseen that it will be generally accepted at the time when it is introduced. This was actually the case when a nationwide system of research ethics committees was established in Denmark during 1979–81.[17]

To secure the system's judicial consistency, Bent Christensen, professor of law at the University of Copenhagen, scrutinised the final version and made several very valuable comments.

THE REGIONAL COMMITTEES

It is proposed that each of the regional committees have three members and three substitutes. One of the members, and one substitute must fulfil the qualifications for being appointed as a judge. The remaining two members and two substitutes must be active researchers. The legal member serves as chairman. The DMRC appoints the scientific members and the legal members after nominations from the presidents of the Danish High Courts. The scientific members are nominated for the regional committee for eastern Denmark by the University of Copenhagen, the Copenhagen university hospitals, hospitals and other government research institutes within the health sciences east of the Great Belt, the Royal Danish School of Pharmacy, the Danish Association of County Councils, the city of Copenhagen, and Frederiksberg municipality. The members of the regional committee for western Denmark, which covers the universities of Odense and Aarhus and hospitals and other government research institutes west of the Great Belt, are appointed on nomination from the universities and the association of county councils. Terms are four years, which may be prolonged once.

The regional committees "function as authorities of first instance and have, when deemed appropriate, power to establish special, professional ad hoc investigatory committees."[1]

THE NATIONAL COMMITTEE

This committee, too, will have a legal chairman and six professional health sciences researchers together with substitutes. The members will be appointed by the DMRC, after nomination by the presidents of the Danish High Courts. The chairman will again have to fulfil the requirements for being appointed a judge in the High Courts. Two of the scientific members will be appointed by the two regional committees, one by the Danish Medical Society, one by the association of city councils, one by the city of Copenhagen and the Frederiksberg municipality, one by the Joint Committee of Directors of Government Research Institutes, and by the Danish University Rectors' Conference, all with substitutes.

WORKING PRINCIPLES AND TASKS

The investigatory system proposed should:
- Be activated on the basis of information/complaint or on the initiative of the committees themselves
- Prepare reports to be forwarded to the employing institution, the informant, and the researcher complained about, with a conclusion as to whether scientific dishonesty has been established, and whether the research work/the publication should be retracted
- Receive feedback from the research institution responsible on the steps taken, including sanctions

- Make a report to the police, if a breach of criminal law is suspected, irrespective of institutional sanctions; further report to the National Board of Health, if breaches of the medical code are suspected
- Publish regularly, with anonymity for all parties, the facts of cases where scientific dishonesty has been proved
- Advise public health sciences research institutions through annual reports
- Ensure that proved fraud is made known to the editors of leading medical journals through indexation in the National Library of Medicine (*Index Medicus*).

The regional committees' work implements these principles in the first line, with the National Committee as point of appeal. The National Committee functions as the first instance in cases concerning Greenland and the Faroe Islands, if their governments wish. The line can be reversed, by the National Committee referring cases for comment, or full treatment, to a regional committee. Both committee levels can establish ad hoc investigatory committees, dealing with individual cases. Such ad hoc committees will have access to laboratories, hospital wards, case records, etc.

Researchers suspected or accused have a right to receive counselling, to be represented or assisted by others, to have access to documents, to be heard, and to receive advice on how to lodge complaints.

A committee report must be sent to the accused scientist with at least one week for objections. Finally the report with additional comments is sent to the scientist's institution. The regional committee starts with an inquiry. The result of this determines whether an investigation shall follow. If not—that is, if there is no reason to suspect scientific dishonesty—this is announced both to informant and researcher complained about.

Anonymity represents a delicate issue. To secure informants' anonymity would probably be unacceptable in Denmark. Yet anonymous accusations cannot always be totally precluded if the content is very serious. Despite the main rule of not accepting anonymous information, a regional committee *can* decide to react with an inquiry, partly to defend the accused person against campaigns of defamation.

A scientist must always be prepared and able to defend the validity of his or her published results. This condition is a sine qua non for editors' acceptance of scientific manuscripts. If a researcher during an investigation for alleged misconduct is unwilling or unable to document the findings, a full investigation by a committee becomes impossible, but still leaves the scientist in a very vulnerable position. A way out would be a willingness to repeat and confirm laboratory results.

Special procedures apply for editors, referees, academic theses, suspicions within the research environment, foreign researchers, and projects in developing countries. Editors, either directly or through the work of referees, when suspecting dishonesty will have to present the problem to the author and ask for clarification and/or statement. If this is unsatisfactory, the editor should proceed by informing the regional committee.[18]

If assessors of academic theses suspect scientific dishonesty, they have a duty to inform the faculty, however late before the public defence the suspicion arises. Again, according to the principles of Montesquieu, assessment and necessary investigation for alleged misconduct must be completely separate. If not solved through the scientist's statement to the faculty, the case must be referred to the official investigatory system.

If Danish research institutions receive information from foreign institutions of alleged misconduct committed by scientists in Danish institutions, the case material will have to be referred to the National Committee. Danish projects in developing countries connected with alleged dishonesty will have to be referred directly to the National Committee, too.

SANCTIONS

Sanctions are integrated in every judicial system. Sanctions in several of the known cases of scientific fraud have varied greatly, ranging from reproof to lifelong exclusions from the scientific community.

Even if the proposed Danish investigatory system is not intended to undertake more than the investigatory phases of a case, and instead leave the possible sanctions to the institutions (except for legal transgressions), it is hoped that the committee system will still influence the resulting sanctions, both their types and their correlation to the different kinds of scientific dishonesty, in order to reduce the case to case variation as much as possible.

In cases in which no base for the alleged dishonesty has been found the researcher complained about will, if she or he wishes, receive an attestation of this fact. Such clearing of unjustly suspected scientists is one of the most important tasks of the investigatory system.

Sanctions may include:

- A warning or reprimand from the research institution
- Transferral to other work or another institution
- Deprivation of public funds, possibly for a specific period of time; in serious cases total or partial repayment
- Removal of the right to academic teaching
- Stripping of academic degrees
- Dismissal or demotion.

The arbitrary handling of previous Danish or foreign cases, especially the lifelong stigmatisation sometimes applied, has not been in keeping with the principle of resocialisation so prevalent in dealing with criminal offenders.

For the same reason the investigatory system will not publish names of confirmed cases.

Good scientific practice and prevention of dishonesty

The most important aim in dealing with scientific dishonesty is not to unmask the transgressors but to use the lessons learnt from the rare and serious cases of scientific fraud to prevent it in future, primarily by teaching good research practice, and its ethical base, during all phases of research education. Such training has already been formalised in Denmark for several years.

The authors of the commission report proposed a set of guidelines for the storage of raw data, etc in research laboratories and departments.[19] The recommendations for preventing scientific misconduct in the publication phase follow the set of guidelines, issued by the International Committee of Medical Journal Editors,[11] again with emphasis on inclusion of these guidelines in all training courses for young researchers in the health sciences.

Reactions and the future

The Danish commission presented its report to the media early in 1992. Most newspapers dealt with the matter in a neutral, informative way. One of the leading newspaper journalists, however, once more showed the gulf that separates journalists and researchers. Where researchers, at least sometimes, work with ideas over several years and ultimately go public without any relation to sensations or scandals-of-the-month, such underlying starting points are sometimes suspected and eagerly sought by journalists.

At a meeting with university rectors and deans the commission agreed to try to establish the investigator system from autumn 1992, but in a less ambitious way, until the magnitude of the problem is known. Establishing the National Committee will be the first step, supplemented by ad hoc investigatory committees. The programmes of prevention, including the teaching of research ethics during the training of young scientists, are already running. They can be further intensified without any additional research policy decisions.

Scientific dishonesty and its counterpart good scientific standards will have to be made much more visible in research education, daily scientific work, the publication process, and in the context of the international scientific network. In this way fundamental values and norms will still be able to balance the seemingly value-free supertechnical equipment of modern biomedical science.

1 Andersen D, Attrup L, Axelsen N, Riis P. *Scientific dishonesty and good scientific practice.* Copenhagen: Danish Medical Research Council, 1992.
2 McBride NB. *Behind the myth.* Crows Nest: Australian Broadcasting Corporation, 1989.
3 Broad W, Wade N. *Betrayers of the truth.* Oxford: Oxford University Press, 1986.
4 Broad WJ. Would-be academician pirates papers. *Science* 1980; **208**: 1438–40.
5 Kohn A. *False prophets.* Oxford, New York: Blackwell, 1986.
6 Hamprecht B, Gullis RJ. Statement. *Nature* 1977; **265**: 764.
7 Buck HM, Koole LH, van Genderen MHP, Smit LS, Geelen JLMC, Jurriaans S, Goutsmit J. Phosphate-methylated DNA aimed at HIV-1 RNA loops and integrated DNA inhibits viral infectivity. *Science* 1990; **248**: 208–12.
8 Maddox J. Dutch cure for AIDS is discredited: faculty synthesis an "honest mistake". Eindhoven chemist at odds. *Nature* 1990; **347**: 411.
9 Eijgengram F. Dutch AIDS researchers feel heat of publicity. *Science* 1991; **251**: 1422–3.
10 Hunt M. A fraud that shook the world of science. *New York Times Magazine* 1981; 1 November, 42–75.
11 International Committee of Medical Journal Editors. Uniform requirements for manuscripts submitted to biomedical journals. *BMJ* 1991; **302**: 338–41.
12 Baltimore D. Baltimore says "sorry". *Nature* 1991; **351**: 94–5.
13 Hamilton DP. NIH misconduct procedures derailed. *Science* 1991; **251**: 152–3.
14 Aldhous P. Tragedy revealed in Zurich. *Nature* 1992; **355**: 577.
15 International Committee of Medical Journal Editors. Retraction of research findings. *Ann Int Med* 1988; **108**: 304.
16 Royal College of Physicians. *Fraud and misconduct in medical research.* London: RCP 1991.
17 Central Scientific-Ethical Committee of Denmark. *Annual report 1991.* Copenhagen: Ministry of Science and Education, 1992.
18 Riis P. What is a proper role of referees and editors of journals in dealing with suspected misconduct in submitted manuscripts or alleged misconduct in published papers? National Institutes of Health: Workshop on Scientific Integrity in Publication for Editors of Biomedical Journals, Bethesda 1–2 November, 1990.

Data audits in investigational drug trials and their implications for detection of misconduct in science

MARTIN F SHAPIRO

Most discussions of scientific misconduct are anchored in fundamental beliefs that colour responses to sporadic, but highly publicised events. Almost none are based on systematic data about the extent and nature of the problem. Indeed, even the idea of collecting such information provokes impassioned responses from members of the scientific community.[1] The idea that someone might look over the scientist's shoulder is seen by some as a form of intrusion that would severely damage the spontaneity and openness of scientific inquiry, chill the atmosphere in the laboratories, and turn thoughtful investigators' energies away from the high sea of ideas and towards the doldrums of documentation.

That of course, is a testable hypothesis. Whether such an endeavour should or should not be attempted (with its acknowledged potential for altering the atmosphere in the laboratory) really depends on whether or not we believe that there is a high enough probability of finding a problem in the way in which scientists go about their business.

There are no perfect sources of information to validate concerns about the integrity of science. The scientific culture varies both by location and by discipline. The more remote the comparison, the more problematic the extrapolation. None the less, it seems obligatory to learn what we can from available sources. Having done so, we must surely be cautious in what we make of them, but it would be injudicious to ignore them altogether.

I have had the opportunity to study the occurrence of misconduct in a very particular form of research: investigational new drug trials conducted in the United States under the authority of the Food and Drug Administration (FDA). These studies certainly are very different from investigations at the laboratory bench. They are, however, quite typical of an important component of clinical research: studies of the efficacy of treatments. There are some distinctions between investigational new drug trials and other studies of therapeutics that will become evident below.

In order to understand scientific misconduct in that setting, it is useful to consider some phenomena beyond the narrow definition of fraud or deceit. A definition that we found useful in our studies is execution of a study in a way that compromises the validity or reliability of the findings, or violation of the rights of individuals who participate in the study.[1,2] This is a functional definition that took account of the need of the consumer of research to know if a study has been conducted ethically and in a way that the result can be believed. It does not include plagiarism or inappropriate authorship, both of which are less relevant to investigational drug trials than to some other kinds of research, but does cover a wide range of problems, ranging from negligence to fraud. It is in the interest of society to prevent whenever possible the conduct of a study in a way in which a reasonable investigator might expect serious problems with validity and reliability, or in which regulations designed specifically to protect subjects are violated by an investigator who has provided assurances that this will not occur. Classification of such behaviours as "scientific misconduct" may draw more attention to the need to prevent their occurrence.

The audit programme of the United States Food and Drug Administration

When we undertook our investigations of scientific misconduct, we felt that the need to identify systematic data was paramount. We turned to the systematic data audit programme of the FDA, principally because it was the only source of such systematic data that we were able to identify. Analyses of the FDA's data enabled us to develop a typology of scientific misconduct, to evaluate the extent of the problem in one kind of research, and to attempt to discern if the measures that the FDA currently is taking are effective.

We used the provisions of the United States Freedom of Information Act to obtain the information described here. We requested information on all data audits from June 1977 to April 1988. We also obtained lists of all investigators who had been disciplined or restricted in their investigative activity from January 1975 to February 1983. We studied in considerable detail the cases of the disciplined and restricted investigators. In addition to FDA data, we obtained demographic and biographical data on them from publicly available sources and on a comparison group of investigators against whom no action was taken. We searched *Index Medicus* and other sources to identify publications by these investigators. We also collected comparison data on a sample of the 16% of investigators who had undergone audits but had been found to be free of deficiencies.

From 1977 to 1988 the FDA conducted 1955 routine data audits, about 180 per year. During the same period there were 395 for-cause audits. It seems that these two programmes had two major effects. Firstly, they increased the rate at which investigators were disciplined (disqualified or restricted) very dramatically. During the 13 years before institution of the audit programme, an average of 1·7 investigators were disciplined per year. In the ensuing six years, the rate was 6·3 per year ($p < 0.01$).

Secondly, they were associated with a decline in the detection of the most serious problems in the research. While minor deficiencies were identified in most audits, in a much smaller proportion were the problems judged to be sufficiently serious to require either a for-cause, more detailed audit or a response in writing about how the problem was being corrected: 11% of audits had deficiencies serious enough to prompt such action (table I). However, over the period during which these audits have been conducted, the proportion in which serious deficiencies were identified has declined significantly, reaching a level of 8% from October 1985 to April 1988. This effect was due entirely to the continuous decline in the proportion of audits for which the problems were judged sufficiently serious to merit a for-cause investigation, from 6% in the first phase of the audit programme to 1% in the most recent period.

While the overall level of seriousness of the problems has declined, the rates of specific deficiencies generally have not. Problems with informed consent actually increased early on, owing to a change in the technical requirements in informed consent forms. Most of the problems in this category are relatively minor technical deficiencies. Drug accountability has improved a great deal since the institution of the programme, from 33% at the initiation of the programme to 15% in the last period examined. Most of the problems in this category are not of the sort that would compromise the validity or reliability of the study findings. Non-adherence to the protocol and inaccurate records continue to be commonplace, each being detected in about one quarter of audits in the most recent period. The unavailability of records has declined, given the better understanding among investigators of the implications of not making their records available for review.

One qualification is necessary as we interpret these findings: the judgments as to the seriousness of the deficiencies identified are those of the FDA investigators. Could their level of scrutiny have changed during the study period? Dr Alan Lisook, the director of the programme, indicated to me that there had been no change at the policy level in how they approach and categorise the reviews. He expressed confidence that a similar standard was being applied in both 1977 and 1988.

Taking that into consideration, it seems that, while there continue to be many problems detected by the FDA's routine data audits, the seriousness of the deficiencies has declined noticeably in the most recent period. It

TABLE I—*Deficiencies detected by the Food and Drug Administration during routine data audits.* Values are percentages*

	Period I: June 1977 to June 1981 (n=549)	Period II: July 1981 to September 1983 (n=415)	Period III: October 1983 to September 1985 (n=422)	Period IV: October 1985 to April 1988 (n=570)	Total (n=1955)
Serious deficiencies found	10	13	13	8†	11
Written response required to show solution to problems	4	9	9	6	7
For-cause investigation launched‡	6	4	4	1†	4
Specific deficiencies:‖					
Problems with patient consent	39	61	58	52	52
Inadequate drug accountability	33	34	22	15†	26
Protocol non-adherence	19	27	31	27	26
Inaccurate records	15	22	23	23	21
Records not available	4	4	2	2	3
Miscellaneous deficiencies	11	22	36	29	24

* From Shapiro and Charrow.[3]
† $p<0.01$, comparing audits in period IV with those in periods I, II, and III.
‡ An additional 321 such investigations were generated outside the routine data audit process.
‖ Some investigators showed more than one deficiency. Percentages in period IV and totals for specific deficiencies are based on 1953 cases with completed analyses.

makes sense that it would have taken several years of a programme to have a deterrent effect. Many of the cases which resulted in disqualification of investigators in the early years reflected research done earlier. It would be expected to take a while for investigators to learn about the new level of scrutiny. Audits often are conducted on work done one or two years earlier. Thus, the audits from 1985 on probably were the first to reflect the work done in the climate of awareness of the federal audit programme.

When we compared 42 investigators penalised from 1975 to 1983 with 63 of 74 investigators with "clean" audits during a subset of the same period, we found that there was no easy way of predicting who was going to engage in scientific misconduct, although there were some differences between the groups (table II). Investigators who were disciplined were somewhat less likely to be board certified (60% against 78%). They were also somewhat less likely to have published a paper in a scientific journal during the year before audit, and were much less likely to be internists and dermatologists. However, no combination of these factors would allow us to predict with confidence that the investigator would fall into one of these two groups. Misconduct occurred in all specialties, and, indeed, the fact that penalised investigators were publishing raises questions about the integrity of the scientific literature, as others have observed previously.[4]

After review of the files of 41 of the 42 penalised investigators, we judged that they all had engaged in substantive misconduct, according to our definition. Fifty nine per cent of those disciplined falsified data, 29% test

TABLE II—*Comparison of characteristics of disciplined investigators and investigators without deficiencies.** *Values are numbers (percentages) of investigators unless stated otherwise*

	Disciplined investigators (n=42)	Investigators without deficiencies (n=63)
Mean (SD) age (years)	49.1 (8.6)	46.1 (8.5)
Mean (SD) time since graduation (years)	22.2 (7.9)	19.6 (8.1)
Academic affiliation	16 (38)	32 (51)
Board certification	25 (60)	49 (78)†
Specialty:		
Internal medicine or dermatology	8 (19)	37 (59)‡
Surgery or obstetrics and gynaecology	12 (29)	10 (16)
Psychiatry	8 (19)	6 (10)
Family practice	11 (26)	6 (10)‖
Other	3 (7)	4 (6)
Papers published in the year before audit	12 (29)	33 (52)‖

* From Shapiro and Charrow.[2] Disciplined investigators were disqualified or restricted in their practice after for-cause investigations; the majority were not originally identified through routine data audits. Investigators without deficiencies had undergone routine data audits in which no problems were found.
† $p<0.05$, ‡ $p<0.001$, ‖ $p<0.03$ comparing disciplined investigators with those without deficiencies.

results, 39% study results; some falsified both (table III). Eighty per cent failed to adhere to protocol, 6% through improper subject selection, 41% through administration of contraindicated concomitant drugs, and 49% by not performing some procedures that were required by the protocol. Forty four per cent failed to obtain informed consent from at least some subjects in their studies; 37% failed to obtain institutional review board approval for their studies, 22% failed to verify that some patients ever received the drugs, and 51% failed to maintain adequate records of drug accountability. Three investigators gave two experimental drugs to subjects at the same time. Two investigators submitted identical case report forms in more than one study. One investigator was not licensed to practise in the state where he was conducting his trial.

Is the problem that we have identified in investigational drug trials unique to research on new drugs? Evidence from clinical cancer trials indicates that studies of other drugs that already have been marketed also have substantial rates of problems detected, when they are audited.[5] Institutions were found to have deviated from treatment protocols for at least some cases 19% of the time, to be deficient in reporting toxicity 10% of the time, and in eligibility of subjects 7% of the time.

A typology of misconduct in investigational drug trials

Four kinds of misconduct were evident in the FDA audits.

DELIBERATE FABRICATION OF RESULTS ("DRYLABBING")

These investigators claimed to have conducted studies on patients when they had not done so. Since these investigators were paid for their "work," it also represents fraud. For example, an obstetrician/gynaecologist was paid by five manufacturers to test analgesics. Audits of his data revealed that he failed to give any of the medications to some patients whom he reported as receiving them. He included incorrect listings of surgical procedures for patients reportedly being treated for postoperative pain. His attorney acknowledged that he did not have accurate data but had filled in the blanks and submitted data to the manufacturers as if the drugs had been administered and then proceeded to get paid for it. The physician also concealed falsified laboratory testing from his practice partners and put the funds that he received for this purpose to his own use and falsified the records of an institutional reveiw committee. In 1983, he was indicted and pleaded guilty to making false statements that he had properly administered medications to over 900 patients. He was declared ineligible to receive investigational drugs.

TABLE III—*Frequency of violations by 41 investigators disciplined for scientific misconduct**

	No of investigators
Failure to maintain adequate and accurate case histories (data report could not be verified)	41
Falsification of data†	24
Tests from which results were reported were not performed	12
Study results were modified or falsified	16
Failure to adhere to protocol‡	33
Certain subjects were included who should have been excluded from the study	19
Patients received concomitant drugs that would have altered study results	17
Some procedures were never performed (or could not be verified as having been performed)	20
Failure to obtain informed consent	18
Failure to maintain adequate informed consent forms	6
Failure to obtain institutional review board approval for study	15
Failure to verify that some patients in study ever received the drug	9
Failure to maintain adequate records of drug accountability	21
Administration of experimental drugs after termination of the study	5
Failure to list coinvestigators; misrepresentation of non-participants as coinvestigators; misrepresentation of the nature of investigator's practice	5
Failure to submit test results to the monitor or sponsor	3
Administration of two experimental drugs to a subject at the same time	3
Submission of case reports in support of one study that had been submitted in another study	2
Administration of experimental drugs before initiation of study (before FDA authorised administration)	2
Other‖	9

* From Shapiro and Charrow.[2]
† Some investigators falsified both test results and study results.
‡ Some investigators violated the protocol in more than one way.
‖ The following violations were ascribed to one investigator: would not permit access to data; not licensed to practise medicine in state where he conducted the study; used an investigational drug without the necessary exemption; had no record of a study design or protocol; denied using the drugs investigationally but published the results and presented them at scientific meetings; study participants received a marketed drug instead of the experimental drug; expanded the study beyond the protocol to include other conditions; failed to ensure that the investigational drug was administered only under the supervision of the investigator; continued to administer drug despite notification that distribution was to cease.
FDA = Food and Drug Administration.

FLAGRANT VIOLATION OF ESTABLISHING REGULATIONS GOVERNING THE RESEARCH

Such regulations are designed to protect the rights of research subjects and to assure an orderly and verifiable process in the research. A remarkable example of violation of these rules is that of an eminent psychopharmacologist, who had introduced an important category of drugs into psychiatric practice. No one ever suggested that he was dishonest. His later research, however, was conducted in ways that clearly were unacceptable: auditors found that he had no controls in a study he had conducted, no structured study design, and no laboratory data in the charts reviewed. He submitted a report indicating that 473 patients had been enrolled in one study, but 20 months later could not identify any of them. He failed to show evidence that he obtained adequate informed consent from any patient in three studies. He eventually acknowledged that he failed to show an adequate plan of study, and that he lacked records that were sufficiently detailed to evaluate the safety and efficacy of drugs. His attorney argued that he was a uniquely valuable researcher whose talents should not be wasted. Eventually he was prevented from continuing to conduct such trials.

MODIFICATION OF DATA TO IMPROVE ITS PUBLISHABILITY OR ACCEPTABILITY ("FUDGING")

These investigators actually collected data, but then manipulated them deliberately to change the results of their studies. For example, one internationally known academic cardiologist was audited for one of the early studies of an unloading agent for congestive heart failure that was published in a leading journal. For eight patients audited, he had completed case reports indicating that radiographs showed venous congestion and cardiac enlargement consistent with congestive heart failure before treatment, even though the radiologist had said there was none. The FDA also audited a study of a beta blocker in angina in which he characterised patients as having up to 14 episodes per week of angina before treatment, when, in reality, they had been having 0 to 1. Thus, in both studies, he manipulated data to enhance the apparent efficacy of the drugs. He finally admitted fudging and falsification of data and voluntarily ceased testing investigational drugs.

FLAGRANT BUT NON-DELIBERATE VIOLATION OF RESEARCH NORMS AND REGULATIONS (INCOMPETENCE)

These investigators were in over their heads. Some of their errors reflected remarkable lack of understanding of basic research principles. Others seemed to suggest that they were not qualified to administer a research enterprise. Sometimes they were found to have engaged in deceit, not to misrepresent the results of studies, but rather to compensate for their disarray. This pattern of misconduct is exacerbated by the lack of any systematic limitation on the number of such studies any physician can take on at any particular time. A telling example is that of an internist who conducted studies simultaneously for three different manufacturers. The FDA found that over four months he submitted reports on several patients to two manufacturers and that he had reported considerable differences in the clinical findings for the same patients on approximately the same dates. Some patients were enrolled simultaneously in trials of more than one drug.

At an informal hearing he told the FDA that it was a problem with his records. "I don't know how to account for it," he said; "there is no doubt that they were given one or the other drug, hopefully not both." He indicated that he might have switched some patients from one drug to another, but could not remember why. It was also found that he had falsified laboratory data. One patient was admitted to the hospital with fulminant hepatic failure and died shortly after the investigator had submitted laboratory data including normal liver function tests. The FDA inspectors could not find these laboratory reports when they examined the records of the laboratory where the tests had purportedly been conducted. The investigator acknowledged the discrepancies; he attributed them to his large practice, and to inadequate monitoring by the drug company. "It was never my intention to submit to the FDA data that was not gone over thoroughly by the drug companies," he said. "If the drug company had come to me and told me this data doesn't gel, it would have been corrected completely. In no way did I intend for the FDA to be misled. The point is that no one audited these studies, no one did anything. I cannot do a study and no one would be able to do a study without being audited." He was disqualified from receiving investigational drugs.

Unquestionably, the FDA audit programme is eliminating some misconductors of research from the performance of drug trials. Are enough people being disciplined? Some investigators whose audits show serious deficiencies never get subjected to for-cause audits, or if they do, ultimately do not get penalised, in some cases because intent cannot be approved. Among the reasons why some people are not being penalised is because their deficiencies are thought not to enhance the apparent safety of the drug.

One example of this is a rheumatologist who was audited for studies of two non-steroidal anti-inflammatory drugs. Serious discrepancies in drug accountability were found between patient diaries and submitted case report forms in all cases reviewed. The investigator contended that informed consent was obtained verbally, but for one of the studies the only documentation of informed consent was handwritten notes in the patients' records, some apparently added retrospectively, stating that the patient had consented. Even this inadequate documentation was lacking in the other study. The investigator failed to transcribe accurately the patients' reports of pain and ability to function, which were critical in evaluating treatment for rheumatic disease. An FDA official indicated in a letter to the investigator, "Your explanation that the information provided on the case report form represents your subjective judgment of what the answers ought to be based on your knowledge of the patient's state of health is understandable, yet posed real questions with regard to the accuracy of such data."

Despite the serious deficiencies in his research, he was not disqualified from using investigational drugs because the FDA found that his errors did not enhance the apparent safety of the drug. Had he systematically falsified to promote the drug further, regulatory action might have ensued. Because the unreliability of his data merely reflected lack of competence in the conduct of the trial, no action was taken. Nevertheless, the manufacturers who had sponsored his research were informed of the outcome of the audit. Fraudulent investigators occasionally could dodge the bullet by promising not to do it again. Recent regulatory changes have closed that loophole, but it still is possible for the other problem to escape penalty—namely, gross error that occurs in a way that does not increase the apparent safety or efficacy of the drug.

Further strategies to reduce misconduct in investigational drug trials

The available data suggest that, while most investigators are honest and effective in their research on drugs, some are not. This has implications for the well being of the public, and for our ability to meet effectively the health needs of the population. The FDA audit programme seems to have diminished misconduct somewhat. It certainly has not eliminated it. Is any level of such misconduct acceptable? Is it adequate to identify it only after the fact? If the answer to these questions is "No," some additional strategies will be needed to reduce further scientific misconduct in drug trials. We have identified five such strategies, all of which have some strengths and weaknesses and none of which can solve the problem alone.[3]

The first of these is the licensing or certification of potential clinical investigators. The idea of this measure is to ensure competence and familiarity with regulations among those proposing to conduct studies of drugs. Because incompetence is an important factor in some cases of misconduct, a standard could be established that would ensure, at the very least, that all investigators took a course on the principles of conducting a clinical trial, including threats to validity, informed consent, and adequacy of documentation. While they were learning about research methods and ethics, they also could be exposed in a formal way to education on the

FDA's regulatory system and potential penalties under it. In these respects, it could act as an opportunity both for education and deterrence. On the other hand, such a programme would cost money to administer. It also would attack only a part of the problem (lack of knowledge) and would do little to diminish fraud or deceit. Finally, some might perceive it as a threat to the freedom of scientific investigation.

A second possible approach would be competitive applications for research contracts. Most federally funded research is open for competitive applications for grants or contracts. A group of the applicant's peers reviews the quality of the proposal and considers, along with scientific merit, the evidence that the investigator is qualified to conduct the research. Introducing such a programme into investigational drug trials would likely enhance the currently rather low prestige associated with such research, particularly if the process were not to be controlled by the manufacturer. This could attract highly qualified academic investigators who currently shy away from doing "drug studies." Such peer review would increase the likelihood that the most qualified investigator would be selected to conduct the study, and not just the one with whom the manufacturer was most comfortable.

There are two potential problems with this approach. First, the response time for the peer review process may be too slow to meet the needs of the manufacturers. In addition, this approach, too, would entail additional expenses.

A third approach would be to limit the investigator's level of participation in clinical trials. This would necessitate keeping track of all such activity on the part of investigators, as some work for several manufacturers at once. They would be allowed to participate in trials of a size that was consistent with their previous experience, their other commitments, and the size of and the resources in their practice for the purposes of the research. The only real potential problem with this approach would arise if there were no one else qualified available to do the work when a particular investigator was limited in participation or excluded from a particular study.

A fourth approach would be to penalise manufacturers for misconduct by their investigators. Such penalties could take the form of either fines or adverse publicity. It should be specified that there would be no penalty if the misconduct were uncovered by the manufacturer. The goal here would be to provide the strongest possible incentive to manufacturers to monitor very closely the quality of the studies that they were sponsoring. The problems with it are twofold. Civil penalties have had little impact on corporations in other settings. The penalty would almost be trivial in comparison with the stakes associated with getting a new product on to the market promptly. Furthermore, the corporations would have an incentive (and certainly the legal resources) to draw out the proceedings as much as possible, thereby straining the resources of the agency and diluting the impact with the passage of time.

A fifth approach to diminishing misconduct would be to suspend investigators pending a hearing. Under this approach, an investigator would be suspended immediately from all investigative activity if an audit revealed substantive misconduct. There would be an opportunity for administrative review, but pending a hearing the investigator would remain suspended. At the hearing, the burden of proof would be on the investigator (as it is in the peer review process when investigators are seeking continued funding for their research).

The advantages of this approach include an incentive for the investigator to move quickly through the administrative review process; cases would be resolved more quickly and at lower cost. The resulting, more rapid, penalty would amplify the deterrent effect of the action. This approach also would increase the likelihood that incompetent and dishonest investigators would be removed quickly from investigative activity. Shifting the burden of proof would decrease the demand on the agency's resources, allowing it to remove more investigators at lower cost. This also would provide a strong incentive to manufacturers to screen potential investigators very carefully, given the potential economic cost to them of having studies terminated prematurely.

The major concern about this approach is that it might be construed as violating the due process provisions of the United States constitution. Does it? In fact, all government action does not need to be preceded by a full, trial-like hearing. Courts weigh the competing interests concerned when judging the appropriateness of a particular action. Predisqualification hearings are required before loss of a professional licence or of employment, but are not required when a delay would jeopardise public safety. A physician can continue to practise medicine even when not allowed to conduct investigational drug trials. Clearly, it is not in the public's interest to allow investigators to continue to conduct studies when there is reason to believe that they have engaged in misconduct, since this can lead to unsafe or ineffective drugs being marketed. For this reason, the courts probably would not judge the right to conduct investigational drug trials as a property right within the meaning of the Fifth Amendment, particularly since it is not guaranteed by medical licensure.[6–10]

Scientific misconduct is common enough in investigational drug trials to be a continuing public concern. The FDA's audit programme has been associated with a decrease in the rate of detection of the most serious deviations from regulatory requirements, possibly through a deterrent effect. There is still a need for further diminution of such activity, and I have outlined several possible approaches, each with strengths and drawbacks. Perhaps some combination of these will be needed to tackle the many kinds of misconduct occurring in drug trials.

Implications of the FDA data audit programme for efforts to minimise scientific misconduct elsewhere

Investigational drug trials are very different from basic laboratory research studies, and even from other kinds of clinical research. Many of the investigators do not have academic appointments. They are not selected to conduct these studies through a peer review process. Many of these studies are never published. We cannot generalise from the experience of misconduct in these studies to any other aspect of science. At the same time, much can be learnt from this experience that may inform decisions elsewhere.

In other aspects of science, the incentive to fabricate data for financial gain generally does not exist. Also, investigators are thought typically to understand the basic principles of research in their subject, so errors of incompetence should be much less common. At the same time, the pressure to fudge data and produce a particular result is at least as great in areas other than drug trials (and probably much greater than any such pressures on non-academicians who are testing investigational drugs). Academicians whose promotions, grants, and publications (the currencies of their professions) depend on producing interesting results are likely to find themselves, at times, in circumstances in which misrepresenting the data could have palpable rewards.

Replication is not a consistent safeguard in investigational drug trials, particularly when measures of outcome are subjective (for example, relief of pain). In basic science, replication is more consistent, but not universal. Particularly, findings of secondary importance (or negative findings), may "enter the literature" quietly with little likelihood of being subjected to replication. In the social sciences, replication is even less helpful. Since no study can exactly duplicate another it is almost impossible to prove that an investigator cheated in, say, a survey or an observational study.

Is a mechanism of after the fact investigation, whistle blowing, and early education sufficient substantially to eliminate misconduct from science? This is unlikely, unless the practice of science is limited to saints. It is important to have access to mechanisms that will identify the unscrupulous investigator. The degree of intrusiveness of the measures to be applied should be proportional to the extent of the problem. The earlier that we obtain information on this subject, the less often will we have to go through those painful reassessments of mechanisms to deal with misconduct which tend to occur while a pall is cast unfairly over all scientific enterprise.

1 Rennie D. Editors and auditors. *JAMA* 1989; **261**: 2543–5.
2 Shapiro MF, Charrow R. Scientific misconduct in investigational drug trials, *N Engl J Med* 1985; **312**: 732–6.

3 Shapiro MF, Charrow RP. The role of data audits in detecting scientific misconduct. *JAMA* 1989; **261**: 2505–11.
4 Stewart WW, Feder N. The integrity of the scientific literature. *Nature*, 1987; **325**: 207–14.
5 Mauer JK, Hoth DF, Macfarlane DK, et al. Site visit monitoring program of the clinical cooperative groups: results of the first 3 years. *Cancer Treatment Reports*, 1985; **69**: 1177–87.
6 Cleveland Board of Education v Loudermill, 105 SCt 1487, 1494 (1985).
7 Arnett v Kennedy, 416 US 134 (1974) (Rehnquist W, Stewart P, Burger W, plurality).
8 Varandani v Bowen, No. 86-2603 (4th Cir 1987).
9 Hall v Bowen, No. 86-2380 (8th Cir 1987).
10 Cassin v Bowen, No. 86-3982 (9th Cir 1987).

Baron Munchausen at the lab bench?

NORMAN SWAN

Next to the United States, Australia has the dubious honour of being the country with the most intense experience of dealing with scientific fraud. The word "intense" is perhaps a curious one to use but it conveys the pain which institutions and even an entire nation can feel when scientists are found to have breached the trust placed in them by the public. The reason for Australia's acquired expertise is not that more fraud occurs Down Under than in other places, it is just that a few very high profile cases have been uncovered in a very public fashion. The benefit has been that, within a decade, Australia has gone from having almost no effective system for preventing and dealing with fraud to a uniform set of procedures which is in place in almost every research institution in the land.

Two of the three most prominent cases in Australia illustrate many of the classic features of scientific fraud—namely, that the whistleblowers often come off worse than the fraudster, that the checks and balances of science do not stop fraud, that institutions may care more about their reputations than the integrity of science, that the medical profession in particular is not good at policing itself, and that when powerful men are concerned, their peers turn into wimps who are prepared to use ad hominem arguments rather than objectivity. The third example shows how hard it can be to investigate fraud and indeed protect future employers on the other side of the world from the fraudster himself.

The case of the disappearing nurses

In 1977 the sleepy, blue collar town of Geelong in southern Victoria was best known for its Australian Rules football team and its élite boarding school, Geelong Grammar, which had educated many of the nation's political and business leaders. But in that year the citizens of Geelong had another reason to be proud. They now had a university, Deakin. One local, a respected paediatrician, Dr Jim Rossiter, was sufficiently enthusiastic to become a member of the university council and later chair of the ethics committee. And when Professor Michael Briggs arrived as foundation dean of science and professor of human biology, with a curriculum vitae which reputedly stretched to 20 pages and apparent international influence in his specialty, the young institution felt it was on the map. Briggs's specialty was the biology and safety profile of oral contraceptives.

Even at that stage he had his supporters and detractors, illustrated by a doubting review of his work for the appointments committee. Briggs was a man with a quick wit, a large ego, and an ability to attract grant money from drug companies. The media liked him because he was a good communicator who rarely equivocated. Despite a long publication list that was short on quality and despite his never having been awarded a competitive, peer reviewed grant, Briggs had considerable influence and was an adviser to the World Health Organisation.

But by the early 1980s there was increasing disquiet about Briggs among a few people at Deakin, chiefly Dr Rossiter and Mark Walqvist, who was then professor of human nutrition. They were sent a copy of a letter which Briggs had written to doctors in the United States from a non-existent laboratory at Deakin, advising them to use an oral contraceptive produced by his largest donor, a major pharmaceutical company. They also discovered that he had presented what seemed to be fabricated research findings to a Spanish conference and published data from tests that had almost certainly never been performed.

In addition, two eminent endocrinological researchers from other Australian institutions began to report disturbing conversations with overseas specialists at conferences. They were asking how Professor Briggs managed to obtain such large numbers for his prolific trials, with unprecedented compliance. The overseas people commented that Australia must be a terrific place to research the "pill" since Michael Briggs managed to do so much so quickly with so few dropouts. One of the two respected Australian researchers so alerted was Professor Henry Burger, who discovered that hormone tests reported to have been performed at the Alfred Hospital in Melbourne could not have been done. Another study, which was supposed to have recruited nurses from the hospital in Geelong, was unknown to Rossiter, who was a consultant there, and in any case it had not been submitted to the ethics committee for approval.

It also transpired that the Deakin appointments committee had not checked on Briggs's qualifications. When Rossiter did his own checking he found that Briggs's PhD from Cornell University did not exist. He had spent only a short time there and gained a master's degree.

To understand what happened next, it is necessary to appreciate the management structure of most Australian universities. The chief executive is the vice chancellor, who is usually a person with a track record as a full professor. The governing body is called either the council or the senate and is appointed by the state government with the chairperson having the title chancellor. Some universities, when there are disputes, are responsible to an archaic institution called the university visitor, who is either the governor of the state or his or her representative.

As chair of Deakin University's ethics committee and a member of the council, Rossiter approached the chancellor, Justice Austin Asche, in late 1983 with this evidence. He suggested to Asche that formal advice should be sought from an external specialist in the subject. Asche disagreed and encouraged Rossiter to write to Briggs, which he did, asking for answers to a list of questions. When no reply came, Rossiter recommended a committee of inquiry be set up. This was refused by Asche but Briggs did reply to a follow up letter. His letter did not answer the substantial allegations and convinced the vice chancellor, Professor Fred Jevons, that an inquiry was indeed merited.

But Briggs, with the assistance of the university staff association, managed to thwart the inquiry by appealing to the university visitor, who quashed it saying it had been improperly created. Jevons, whose academic background was in the history and philosophy of science, went public to claim that this was the first time in history that the legal system had forbidden the investigation of scientific misconduct.

Around this time both Jim Rossiter and Mark Walqvist were suffering in their professional and personal lives. There were threatening phone calls in the middle of the night, and the university was split between those who supported Briggs and those who did not.

In 1985 a second inquiry commenced, but was suspended when Briggs resigned and settled in Marbella on the Spanish Costa del Sol. Under the constitution of most Australian universities and the industrial award of university staff, the resignation of a member of staff means that all investigations have to cease.

To this date only a little of the Briggs affair had leaked into the Australian media. But the lid blew off when the *Sunday Times* in London found Briggs in Spain and drew from him a partial admission of generalising from a small amount of data. But he strenuously defended his reputation and said that no one could question his results, which had been used by drug companies to prove the safety of their preparations. Two months later, Briggs, then aged 51, was dead—reportedly of liver failure. In an ironic concurrence of events, not long beforehand three senior staff members at Deakin, two of them very close to Briggs, had destroyed some of his personal papers at his request because Briggs said that they contained sensitive material.

After the international press coverage the university could no longer avoid the situation, particularly when junior scientists in Briggs's department were facing ruined careers through no fault of their own. An independent scientific investigation of Briggs's work confirmed that much of it was fraudulent but that none of his junior colleagues at Deakin was at fault. The university made efforts to restart the scientists' careers by funding new opportunities for them.

But the wounds were still raw in Geelong. For example, soon after the exposure of Briggs in the *Sunday Times*, some senior executives of the university proposed to council that all the members of the ethics committee be replaced. This had not been discussed with the committee beforehand and was successfully opposed by Dr Rossiter when he discovered the proposal. All the previous members, including Rossiter, were returned.

It was clearly important to examine the institution's internal procedures and recommend changes. This was done by Margery Ramsay, another member of the university council. The Ramsay report was released in early 1989 and went some way to clearing the air by giving the university's official account of the story.

But Fred Jevons, who by that time had moved to Western Australia, felt that, although it set the record straight on some points, there were "significant evasions or suppressions of facts."

According to Professor Jevons, insufficient attention was paid to the role of Justice Austin Asche, with whom he had had a strained relationship. Professor Jevons felt that at times Justice Asche had bent towards Briggs. At one council meeting, the chancellor watered down a resolution supporting the vice chancellor in his actions, after agreeing to stronger wording. At another point, Asche had also unofficially threatened to resign if *he* did not have the support of council. And Fred Jevons, when he was vice chancellor, thought that the university chancellor, Justice Asche, shifted the debate from whether "Briggs was guilty" to "whether Jevons had made errors." But the Ramsay report made it clear that the faults were with the legal advice received by the university.

Justice Asche became a senior judge of the Northern Territory and, commenting on Jevons's reaction to the Ramsay report, said that at all times he had been concerned to affirm Briggs's presumed innocence till proved guilty. Justice Asche's memory was vague on the "quibble" over the motion of support for the vice chancellor but said that Professor Jevons had had council's backing at all times.

The Ramsay report claimed that Deakin could do little other than destroy Briggs's papers according to his instructions even though in retrospect, given the *Sunday Times* article, that may not have been wise. Jevons felt that this meant the committee still didn't set much store by the evidence of fraud available long before the international coverage. Russell Elliot, university secretary and respected by both sides, was one of three who went through Briggs's papers and claimed that there was nothing in the destroyed material which referred to any of Briggs's financial dealings or which could have helped a fraud inquiry.

Professor Jevons also thought that the report glossed over other matters such as the reasons for Briggs receiving overseas study leave when there were fraud inquiries mooted, and the push for a golden handshake by his supporters, retracted only when even the programme for his study leave was shown to be fraudulent.

Dr Jim Rossiter, the person who suffered most from refusing to relent in his formal complaints against Briggs, felt that the Ramsay report probably went as far as it could although some people "got off rather lightly"—not least Briggs, whose qualifications and academic background were overstated in the report, according to Dr Rossiter.

Another missing element for Dr Rossiter was the motivation of Briggs to fabricate his data. Briggs had an opulent lifestyle and wanted for nothing. His grant applications bypassed the university's normal system, and some drug company cheques were made out to Briggs directly instead of to the university. No one knows how much extra money came Briggs's way for studies which were never performed. All Deakin could say was that the money which Briggs gave to it was spent properly.

Many of the major players in this sad tale are still in Geelong, and in a small institution in a small town it is hard for such wounds to heal. What became clear only a year after Briggs's death was that Australian research institutions had not learnt much from Deakin's pain.

The case of the missing rabbits

Australia has few icons but if there was one in the 1960s and '70s, it was Dr William McBride, society gynaecologist and the man who claimed to have been the first to alert the world to the dangers of thalidomide. He played squash with prime ministers, created his own research institution into birth defects (Foundation 41), and was frequently called on by the media to comment on issues from health to parenting. And—until the Medical Board of New South Wales put a halt to it—for a while he even advertised American Express cards.

Phil Vardy was a junior scientist at Foundation 41 in Sydney. One day in mid-1982, while Dr McBride was overseas, Vardy opened an envelope addressed to both of them. Inside were reprints of a paper in the *Australian Journal of Biological Sciences*. The paper's authors were named as McBride, Vardy, and Jill French, another junior staffer in the lab. Even so, Vardy was surprised because he knew nothing about this paper; but on reading through realised that it referred to a small experiment carried out a few months previously. Yet the paper did not seem to reflect his memory of the study, and this suspicion was confirmed when Vardy compared the published methods and results with the original data. It was a study of hysocine, an anticholinergic drug used in travel sickness; a drug related to one of the components of Debendox (Bendectin in the United States). Hyoscine had been given to a small group of pregnant rabbits with insignificant results. The experiment had been done in such a rush that there were not even controls. But in the paper the doses of hysocine were different. There were extra rabbits, there were controls, and it said that the rabbit fetuses had been sectioned, when Vardy still had them in jars intact. All this had the effect of making hyoscine look like a teratogen. Vardy asked Dr McBride's secretary for the file on the paper and found several drafts of the manuscript with progressive changes to the data in Dr McBride's handwriting. What Vardy did not know was that a version of this paper had already been submitted as evidence in a court case in the United States where Dr McBride was appearing as an expert witness for litigants against the manufacturers of Bendectin. So began a saga that would last a decade and receive international attention.

BEYOND THALIDOMIDE

Dr McBride's contribution to the discovery of thalidomide's terrible toxicity to fetuses was an observation of an association in a few babies between unusual limb abnormalities and the use of thalidomide by the mother as an antinausea drug during pregnancy. Although the finding was extraordinarily important, it had not been based on a controlled study and was published in a short letter to the *Lancet* in December 1961. The scientific research was being carried out by others, principally in West Germany.

About 10 years later, Dr McBride received worldwide headlines; the exposer of thalidomide had found another drug which caused birth defects. He had noticed an association in three mothers and babies. This time it was a tricyclic antidepressant called imipramine. Cries went out for the drug to be banned. But a few days later, when the government's drug watch committee managed to interview Dr McBride, they discovered that he could provide no evidence of any deformed babies to justify his public condemnation of the drug.

In the late 1970s Dr McBride turned his attention to Debendox/Bendectin, again with no case control study to back up his belief, often stated by him in the media, that it was a teratogen. He began appearing for plaintiffs suing the manufacturers in the United States and although no suit was ever won, Debendox was eventually taken off the world market because of the cost of defence. Around this time, before a court case and when he was due to give testimony to the US Food and Drug Administration, Dr McBride wanted to test one of the components of Debendox on animals. Unable to obtain the pure preparation, he ordered Vardy and French to test hyoscine, a related compound. Vardy complained that the experiment was poorly conceived, he did not have enough rabbits, and in any case the lab was about to move to other premises. But Dr McBride insisted, and a study which at best could be described as only a pilot went ahead. Vardy wrote up the results, such as they were, and gave them to Dr McBride.

A few months later, when Vardy became certain he was dealing with scientific fraud, he confronted McBride on his return from overseas but got nowhere. He then approached the dean of medicine at the University of New South Wales, who sat on Foundation 41's research advisory committee. Vardy was told to keep his head in since he could not win in this situation. Soon seven other junior scientists at Foundation 41 rallied round once they appreciated the gravity of the evidence and wrote to the committee insisting on an inquiry. This took place some months later and after Vardy had resigned from the foundation. The committee found that McBride could not justify the changes to the paper and insisted that it be retracted. This was never done, and the committee seems not to have followed through on its finding. Instead of a retraction, a small paper was published saying that there had been errors made in the lab with the doses given to the rabbits, so the experiment had been repeated. Vardy and French, who had been waiting for the retraction, were infuriated by the paper and wrote to the *Australian Journal of Biological Sciences* saying that they had not been consulted about the paper and that there were concerns about the data. The response of the editor was to write to Dr McBride saying that in future the journal would direct mail on this subject to him. And there the matter rested till exposed on national radio in 1987.

As for the junior scientists who had supported Vardy and French, the day after the research advisory committee had met, they were asked to gather for a meeting with Dr McBride. He told them that because of funding problems their jobs no longer existed and they would have to reapply for them. The scientists took the foundation to the industrial court and although the notices were never acted on, six of the seven soon left Foundation 41, mostly changing career direction in the process.

In the 1980s Foundation 41 continued to be successful in gaining large charitable donations from the community although Dr McBride had never received a peer reviewed grant. He also continued to appear in Bendectin cases in the United States. Vardy left Sydney (and his PhD thesis) to work in Tasmania, extremely embittered. It eventually broke his marriage.

I knew of the story of fraud but had never been able to lay my hands on the evidence until I came across Vardy by accident and eventually convinced him to give me the drafts of the paper and the original lab books. There was no doubt that this was fraud and I made a radio documentary on the affair, which was broadcast in December 1987. Dr McBride refused to be interviewed for the programme and the response of the rest of the media was dramatic. Dr McBride did not sue for defamation but fought back publicly, claiming his innocence. In the media furore that followed, Dr McBride asserted that the extra rabbits had been dosed at the University of Virginia by Professor Jan Langman, the eminent embryologist. But subsequent inquiries could find no evidence of such a favour and in fact it was likely that Professor Langman was already dead at the time Dr McBride said the experiment had been performed on his behalf.

Dr McBride received support from some prominent media personalities, who asked what were a few rabbits compared with the reputation of a great man and the well being of unborn children. McBride also received backing from the investigative journalist Phillip Knightley, who had extensively covered the thalidomide case.

That week in December also found an Australian scientific community which, with some exceptions, lacked procedures for dealing with accusations of fraud. The National Health and Medical Research Council (NH&MRC) was quietly relieved that Dr McBride's frequent applications for grants had never been good enough to be funded. This meant that the council did not have an obligation to investigate. Some members of the Australian Academy of Science knew that the nation's scientific reputation was at stake and wanted the academy to do something. But they were stopped by fears of litigation, a lack of powers, and a request from Foundation 41 later in the year not for an inquiry but for advice on how best to repeat the fraudulent experiment.

The Australian Vice-Chancellors' Committee called for a policy paper on dealing with scientific fraud then, under pressure from one or two of its members, dropped it for fear of generating even more publicity on the issue. It was taken up again later with more success.

The board of Foundation 41 supported Dr McBride for six months before relenting and calling an independent inquiry—headed by the former Chief Justice of Australia, Sir Harry Gibbs—which included two senior and respected scientists, Professor Roger Short, a reproductive biologist, and Professor Robert Porter, then head of the John Curtin School of Medical Research at the Australian National University.

The Gibbs inquiry found that Dr McBride had indeed committed scientific fraud. McBride resigned from Foundation 41 only to be reinstated as a director later after a coup which replaced the foundation's board.

He then had to face disciplinary proceedings before the Medical Tribunal of New South Wales. This was under the Medical Practitioners' Act, which requires doctors to be of good character. The health department brought 15 complaints against him, nine of which related to his clinical practice and six to allegations of scientific misconduct. This hearing became the longest against a doctor in history, costing both sides millions of dollars, and at the time of writing had still not handed down its findings. One of the most dramatic moments during the hearing came in May 1991 when Dr McBride admitted to publishing false and misleading data. He said that he consciously changed them "in the long term interests of humanity." He said that his belief in the danger of the drug was so great that it had allowed him to depart from "proper scientific principles" in the public interest. But, going to the heart of the case, he maintained that this did not detract from his good character. In the four years since the broadcast he had considered the issues carefully and concluded that this philosophy was wrong.

The case of the disappearing schizophrenia

In April 1987, a consultant psychiatrist working part time at the Mental Health Research Institute in Melbourne went to the institute's biostatistician with data that he said he had collected on the month of birth of 8000 people with schizophrenia. The psychiatrist, Dr Ashoka Prasad, claimed that he had found a remarkable relationship with seasonality.

The biostatistician thought the data looked a bit peculiar and asked for clarification. Six weeks later Prasad delivered further material, but the statistician was still worried and reported his concerns to his superiors. They did not delay and interviewed Prasad to find out how he had gathered the information.

To have obtained these data, Prasad would have had to look through as many as 16 000 records on at least two occasions. Yet he had only ever been seen in medical records once and in the particular location where Prasad had said he had worked, there were only 2000–3000 records. It is possible that he could have collected information at night, but night staff had not seen him around either.

In addition, the summaries from which Prasad said he had noted the patient information did not actually contain it all. After this, Prasad's story began to change frequently and he included another hospital and an anonymous collaborator. On being asked to find his primary data, he could only come up with a few sheets of paper, some of them crumpled.

When the biostatistician did his own analysis of the figures from the two hospitals, there was a shortfall of several thousand cases and unlike Prasad's data these showed no significant seasonal variation in the birth dates of people with schizophrenia.

An independent investigation was called but almost stalled at the beginning. Prasad had hired a prestigious and expensive corporate law firm to represent him. The lawyers wrote to each member of the committee a strongly worded letter threatening defamation proceedings in the Supreme Court unless the case was withdrawn. Nothing was withdrawn, and the committee eventually found that Prasad had indeed committed scientific fraud, that the PhD he said he had was fictitious, as was his supposed DSc from a non-existent Swiss university in Zug. Neither had he won the prestigious Anna Monika Award for psychiatric research as he had said. Because of continued worries about defamation, the report of the investigating committee instead of being released in the usual way was tabled in state parliament under privilege.

Prasad then resigned, but the story did not finish there because he kept on turning up around the world. He presented research at overseas conferences which he claimed he had carried out in Melbourne on aboriginal women but which in fact had never been done. He edited a book on neurotic disorders and next to his name were both his fictitious degrees and the title of head of psychopharmacology section at the Mental Health Research Institute when not only had he left in disgrace but also it did not have a psychopharmacology section at that time. And that was despite the institute having been assured by the publishers that they would cease that credit.

The story became even more extraordinary. In December 1988, the editor of the *British Medical Journal*, Dr Stephen Lock, published a paper on scientific fraud in which he mentioned the Prasad affair. Prasad wrote to the *BMJ* and had a letter published in which he tried to exonerate himself. This letter was followed by one from Professor John Funder, who had chaired the investigating committee. Funder refuted Prasad's assertions.

Then in July 1989 the *BMJ* received a letter from a Professor Charles Royane of Dalhousie University in Canada. (Prasad was in Nova Scotia at that time.) The letter said that they had obtained papers from Melbourne and constituted an inquiry of their own into "Professor" Ashoka Prasad and essentially had cleared him, having found that the Melbourne inquiry had not been carried out properly. This letter was never published by the *BMJ* because it was discovered that no papers had been requested from Melbourne and indeed a professor with a similar name to Royane had died six months before the date on the letter.

There were more examples of Prasad's continuing activities, including his having obtained membership of the World Psychiatric Association and chaired a session at one of its congresses. He also turned up in British Columbia receiving press coverage for the extraordinary claim that he had been nominated for the Nobel peace prize. His career there ended with his being struck off the medical register in that province.

The issues

The Briggs and McBride cases illustrated many of the traditional problems that arise with scientific fraud when a famous or powerful person is accused in an institution with no system in place to prevent or deal with scientific misconduct. That has now changed in Australia. In November 1990 the National Health and Medical Research Council, the country's equivalent of the National Institutes of Health or the Medical Research Council, passed a set of guidelines and procedures on scientific practice which had to be in place by early 1992 in all institutions applying for grants. This document included several of the clauses used in the United States but also some of its own, learnt as the result of the Australian experience (see appendix C).

There is a strong case for extending traditional checks in this way so that it is easier and safer to be scrupulous. There are really two classical defences against fraud: peer review and replication of experiments; and there has often been complacency about both.

The problem with peer review is that it varies in its robustness according to the institution. It did not exist at Foundation 41 or at Deakin University. Professor Briggs avoided attempts to have his work on oral contraceptives opened to scrutiny—although it has to be said that when Briggs and McBride were exposed to rigorous peer review, such as in trying to obtain grants, they always failed.

But peer review cannot be legislated for and it often falls apart when misconduct is alleged. People are scared to challenge their colleagues or superiors when crookedness is suspected rather than faulty thinking. The determined fraudster can also elude peer review by presenting internally consistent data which do not look peculiar. And referees for scientific journals who examine submitted papers are often overloaded and miss inconsistencies when they do occur.

Replication of experiments by others is also held up as the great test of science. But replication will find only incorrect results, not fraud. It is hard to obtain funding for replication studies, and journals are loth to publish negative results. Plus fraudsters often do not take risks and simply extend existing findings, making replication unappealing.

Thus university departments and research institutions need to introduce processes to prevent misconduct and deal with allegations. This latter procedure is the most difficult of all. Many whistleblowers seem to have been so mauled by the experience that they recommend not complaining about a colleague because it is so bad for one's career. It is as important to protect the accuser as it is to assume the innocence of the accused till proved otherwise.

The tragedy of the McBride, Briggs, and several American cases is manifest in several ways: it took exposure in the media for the institutions concerned to take remedial actions; the accused is often protected while the accuser suffers and scientists are made to look as though they cannot regulate themselves.

There is also fear about litigation when inquiries are undertaken. According to one lawyer who has studied this, legal action is most likely to succeed in institutions which have not formulated proper procedures. Due process for fraud should be part of the terms and conditions of employment.

Institutions can only minimise the chances of fraud taking place, since it will never be eliminated. If banks cannot secure themselves against fraud with the billions they spend on security then research, which has to be based on trust, cannot be expected to do better. But there are basic preventive measures which help.

It is vital that there be proper record keeping of experiments in bound and page-numbered lab books to which are attached machine printouts or references to them. The chief of one prominent Australian molecular biology unit spends two hours a week with each researcher and even photocopies their data every Friday. All original data from experiments should be retained. Determined fraudsters can tamper with original data too, but it is hard to imagine where else an audit or investigation can begin.

Only those people who have contributed significantly to the work should have their names on the paper and ought to sign a declaration to that effect. "Gift authorship" whereby lab chiefs have their names on papers on which they have done nothing breeds cynicism and contempt among juniors. This was one of the reported difficulties with Dr McBride at Foundation 41. At the first Fenner conference at the Australian National University, Professors Sir Gustav Nossal and Gordon Ada both remarked on how seldom they had shared authorship with Nobel laureate Sir MacFarlane Burnet despite having worked under him for years. "Mac" encouraged his juniors to shine.

Authorship lines are often crucial to fraud. Famous names on otherwise mediocre papers can lend them credibility and American fraudsters such as John Darsee at Harvard and Emory Universities and Robert Slutsky of the University of California, San Diego, regularly gave gifts of authorship to people who had not contributed significantly to the work. Some of Slutsky's coauthors had never even been asked whether they wanted their names on papers.

Scientific departments should review their own work before it goes out to a scientific journal, and empires must never expand to the extent that good supervision of research becomes impossible.

Institutions should remove the need for researchers to have long publication lists, the so called "publish or perish" phenomenon. Harvard Medical School has suggested that applicants for positions or promotions should nominate only their five or 10 best papers depending on the level of the appointment.

Just as institutions must have ethics committees before they can apply for peer reviewed grants, so they ought to have fixed fraud investigating procedures which protect both the accuser and the accused. There has to be a safe and independent person, perhaps a lawyer, to whom a worried staffer can go in absolute confidence with his or her concerns. The lawyer (or whoever) would then have two or three weeks to decide if there is a prima facie case. If so, then the organisation would be obliged to set up a group of external and unimpeachable scientists, perhaps also with a lawyer, to investigate the allegations meticulously. The integrity of scientific knowledge must be respected in that an inquiry cannot be averted by the resignation of the accused.

An unresolved issue in Australia and several other countries is what to do about places like Foundation 41, which have no external review and are stand-alone institutes with no peer reviewed funding.

Fraud can never be stopped totally but there are ways of deterring all but the most dishonest people. The International Committee of Medical Journal Editors has resolved that journals will publish findings of fraud. The committee also says that one example of fraud calls into question all the perpetrator's previous work since he or she has been shown capable of abusing the trust of science.

As for the Prasad case, which was handled promptly, several other issues arise. For instance, the affair has taken and continues to take up an inordinate amount of the time of busy people at the Mental Health Research Institute in an effort to keep track of the man. And what are the limits and legal safety of the institute's responsibility to inform people around the world? Should there be an international register of such people? Or, as a group of reasonable people, does the scientific community believe that one can be rehabilitated after committing scientific fraud? The view of the Slutsky committee at the University of California, San Diego, was that although a scientist is innocent till proved guilty, once guilty, his or her entire work is under a cloud.

What about the personality of fraudsters—is there, for example, a type? The history of attaching personality types to problems is fraught with pitfalls and there is unlikely to be one type for scientific misconduct. But one condition in the psychiatric literature may illuminate some cases. It is known as Pseudologia fantastica. Pathological lying would be an oversimplified definition but it is certainly a condition in which the person has difficulties distinguishing truth from falsehood. Pseudologia fantastica may be the primary problem which can lead in some people to Munchausen's syndrome, that extraordinary situation where a person creates a fictitious world based on invented diseases. As Professor John Funder has asked, is scientific fraud just another form of Munchausen's?

But the damage from scientific fraud and being loose with data goes far deeper than the image of science or the fate of a single drug. The most astounding feature of Dr William McBride's eventual admission that he had published false and misleading data was the excuse he gave: that the ends justified the means. There are, of course, many questions that arise from Dr McBride's testimony before the Medical Tribunal of New South Wales, such as why, if this was the reason for his misconduct, it had taken him nine years, the careers of several junior scientists, and millions of dollars in legal expenses to make this admission. But more importantly, you have to ask what hope the public has of assessing health risks rationally if a prominent doctor who was taking charity for a scientific institution could not see the value in scientific evaluation.

Several years ago I coined terms for two quite widespread phenomena in the health and sickness industry when it comes to exploiting our fears and exhorting us or governments to give money. They are the "Russian roulette phenomenon" and the "Schmaltz lobby." Both were used to the hilt by Foundation 41 and neither assists personal or policy decisions about our health.

The Russian roulette phenomenon is the terror of the spinning revolver chamber of life. The next pull of the trigger might be your or your loved ones' last. Your baby might be the one who needs an exotic expensive treatment, you might be the one in a million to come down with cancer because of high tension power lines or the pesticides in your food. The Russian roulette phenomenon is extremely potent. It brings tiny or invisible risks to the foreground and plays on our fear of situations outside our control. The thinking goes this way: "It's all very well to say that crossing the road is thousands of times more dangerous than most risks from chemicals in the environment, but at least I can decide whether to walk against the traffic lights. There's no choice about what is in my food or what a drug company tells me about its latest pill."

Fair enough, if it wasn't for the Schmaltz lobby, which lives off Russian roulette. Schmaltz lobbyists are the ones who trot out the cute babies or the stories of human tragedy to tell you that we must have this marvellous piece of technology or fund a given line of work. They imply that the next bullet could well be for you. The Schmaltz lobbyists do not like statistics much; they rarely show you the trade-offs, the commoner and more serious problems that won't be looked after if the money goes on their pet project. They also hardly ever explain the basis for their assertions and the relative risks. The trouble is that being scientific is hard work.

In the case of Dr McBride, his campaign against the antimorning sickness drug Debendox began with a straw poll of a group of mothers of children with limb abnormalities. It was the late 1970s and they had come along to a meeting to hear the doctor speak. He asked them how many had taken Debendox in pregnancy. A high percentage put up their hands, and he jumped to the conclusion that there was trouble with Debendox.

Dr McBride then proceeded in what superficially seemed like a scientific fashion. He dressed up in a white coat, walked into a laboratory, and started to give pregnant animals Debendox and related drugs to see what happened. But that was not science although it had all the trappings. He had missed the first and vital step, which should have been to test his original assumption that women who had children with limb abnormalities were more likely to have swallowed Debendox in pregnancy. You do not do that by running off to the lab with a couple of rabbits but by comparing these women carefully with similar women who have had normal babies. When that was eventually done by other researchers, they found that Dr McBride's impression was false. The women took Debendox at the same rate as those with normal babies. In addition, an examination of the published papers would have shown Debendox to be one of the most studied drugs in history. But it was too late. By 1983 the manufacturers had taken Debendox off the market, not because any government told them to, but for the commercial reason that it was cheaper than continuing to defend court cases successfully.

Dr McBride should have learnt from the time in 1971 when he condemned imipramine. This was a risky claim given that antidepressants save lives by preventing suicide. The media ran his statements uncritically, and when the Australian government investigated it found that Dr McBride did not have the evidence. At best thousands of women would have been needlessly terrified and at worst some of them could have come to harm, not because of the drug but because of unscientific statements.

Some may argue that occasionally the situation is so clear that it is silly to wait on formal scientific proof. That is sometimes true when, for example, a universally fatal disease becomes curable when a new drug is tried. But you cannot blame the public for not perceiving the lack of science in Dr McBride's claims over the years. Surveys in Australia and the United Kingdom have shown that, while there is enormous public interest in science and health, people do not have a good knowledge of scientific principles. In an age when we have correctly become obsessed with the ethics of medical research, it often seems to be forgotten that in most circumstances it is unethical to change medical care without good evidence or properly testing the new treatment.

Professor John Paulos, a mathematician at Temple University in Philadelphia, argues that, in order to have more critical media and a more critical community, it is essential to have more practical mathematics tuition in schools. Paulos thinks that we do not easily appreciate very large or very small numbers. To say, for instance that smoking kills 18 000 Australians each year is dramatic but conceptually fairly meaningless. Few of us can imagine what a group of 18 000 people looks like. If you translate the figure into the equivalent of a jumbo jet crash every eight or nine days, then it starts to make sense.

In terms closer to Debendox, it is harder to give people an appreciation of coincidence. Quite unusual situations occur by chance much more commonly than you might imagine. For a 50% likelihood of two people in a room sharing the same birthday you only need 23 people to be present. Two Americans meeting at random have a one in 100 chance of having an acquaintance in common and 99 chances in 100 of being linked by two intermediaries.

Much of the expenditure and effort in scientific research goes into rising above this "noise" of chance in order to discover whether the phenomenon is just coincidence or truly related to the drug or chemical in question. It means studying large numbers of people who have been meticulously selected and eliminating or taking into account every possible nook and cranny of chance occurrence.

But how is the public to know that a piece of research has been carried out in this way? The answer is that we can all know a little of what we should be looking for and retain a good deal of scepticism unless the relevant information is present. It is also the responsibility of media organisations to ensure that their specialist reporters are equipped to make the judgment on behalf of the audience or readers. The media made Dr McBride and broke him. Perhaps we should have been more critical in the first place. But it is vital that an atmosphere of antifraud hysteria does not take over, averting scientists from taking risks with their work. As Sir Peter Medawar once said, science, if it is to be any good, has to take the risk of being wrong. We just have to ensure that it is straight.

Bibliography

Ben-Yehuda N. Deviance in science. *British Journal of Criminology* 1986; **26**: 1–27.
Engler RL, Covell JW, Friedman PJ, Kitcher PS, Peters RM. Misrepresentation and responsibility in medical research. *N Engl J Med* 1987; **317**: 1383–9.
Harvard Medical School. *Guidelines for investigators in scientific research*. Cambridge, Mass: Office of the Dean for Academic Affairs, 1988.
International Committee of Medical Journal Editors. Retraction of research findings. *Med J Aust* 1988; **148**: 194.
King BH, Ford CV. Pseudologia fantastica. *Acta Psychiatr Scand* 1988; **77**: 1–6.
Lock S. Fraud in medicine. *BMJ* 1988; **296**: 376–7.
Lock S. Misconduct in medical research: does it exist in Britain? *BMJ* 1988; **297**: 1531–5.
Medawar P. *Memoir of a thinking radish*. Oxford: Oxford University Press, 1986: 109–10.
Parliament of Victoria. *Report to the minister. A summary of the resolutions of the committee of enquiry examining research practices employed by Dr Ashoka Prasad in relation to the research project entitled "Seasonality Study"*. Melbourne: Government Printer, 1988.
Paulos JA. *Innumeracy: mathematical illiteracy and its consequences*. New York: Hill and Wang, 1989.
Prasad AJ, ed. *Biological basis and therapy of neuroses*. Florida: CRC Press, 1988.
Rossiter EJR. Reflections of a whistleblower. *Nature* 1992; **357**: 434–6.
Ramsay M. *Deakin University and the inquiry into the case of Professor Briggs*. Geelong: Deakin University, 1988.
Stewart WW, Feder N. The integrity of the scientific literature. *Nature* 1987; **325**: 207–14.
Swan N. Preventing and dealing with scientific fraud in Australia. *Med J Aust* 1989; **150**: 169–70.
Woolf PK. Ensuring integrity in biomedical publication. *JAMA* **1987**; **258**: 3424–7.

Fraud and the editor

STEPHEN LOCK

Given the pivotal position of publication in many, if not most, instances of research fraud, what is the journal editor's role—in dealing with established cases or raising suspicions about submitted work? Clearly editors can rarely do the actual investigations: that is the job of the department where the fraud may have occurred (in the much misunderstood words of a former editor of the *Journal of Clinical Investigation*, "we are the *JCI*, not the FBI").[1] Nevertheless, an editor can do a lot: pressurise the authorities until the investigations on a suspected case have been completed, publicise the results of an investigation, and set the record straight with statements of retraction (or vindication). Even more important, I believe, is the editor's role in prevention, by setting and enforcing good standards over all aspects of the publishing process. In this chapter I will describe what some of these are and how they can be used to try to cut down what is almost certainly a small but important blemish on the face of research.

The evolution of scientific journals

Scientific journals started in 1665 with the publication of two that are still extant: the *Journal de Sçavans* and the *Philosophical Transactions of the Royal Society*.[2] Interestingly enough, right from the beginning, two of the themes consistently put forward in favour of publishing journals were establishing priority of discovery and protection from piracy or plagiarism (the "philosophicall robbery" of Robert Boyle). The standards of both the first and other early journals were variable, but from the outset several relied on peer review of the original papers submitted for publication, though this became routine only after the second world war. Nevertheless, by the middle of the nineteenth century both the contents of the journal and the structure of the scientific article had come to resemble their present day counterparts.[3] Journals were aiming at doing what a later celebrated editor of the *Lancet*, Sir Theodore Fox, said they should: "Inform, interpret, criticise, integrate, reform, and even perhaps amuse."[4] Though original articles did not consistently have the IMRAD structure (Introduction, Methods, Results, and Discussion), the narrative was logical and supported by data in tables or illustrations, or both, together with references to past work.[3] The real revolution in the treatment of scientific data, however, came about in the late 1940s with the introduction of the randomised controlled trial and statistical analysis.

Another major development in the nineteenth century was the rise of the specialty journal, so that by its second half several of today's major journals had been started (including the *American Journal of Obstetrics, Brain, Annals of Surgery*, and the *Journal of Pathology*). During the earlier part of the present century not only did other geographical areas (such as Britain and the Nordic countries) start similar specialty journals of their own where these did not exist already, but other new journals were developed everywhere to serve the new specialties as they arose. Moreover, the journals themselves started to hive off subspecialty and subsubspecialty journals, the most recent having evolved as far as those devoted to single organs, such as *Pancreas* and *Breast*. As I write, the journal that everybody has been predicting will happen is just about to appear; this is the new electronic publication, the *Online Journal of Clinical Trials*, by which submitted articles will be peer reviewed and "published" on line, without any hard copy version being printed.

The physicist and philosopher of the history of science Derek de Solla Price was the first to perceive a pattern behind all this.[5] For over 300 years, he showed, publications have grown steadily by 6–7% a year. A scientist who publishes one article every year can absorb the contents of more than one other paper per month, but less than one a day. This leads to a few hundred people keeping each other in business—the so called "invisible colleges," which are the same size as the early scientific societies. Disciplines tend to split every 10 years or so and the new subdisciplines do not necessarily correspond with the existing organisational and professional structures; for this reason, the new specialty usually needs a new journal, for which initially at least the authorship and the readership are identical. Authors, de Solla Price concludes, write for a small readership of peers and count themselves successful if the latter read these articles and build on them.

If such a model is valid for the development of scientific journals, then as in any "biological" system (such as bacteria in a culture flask), growth should eventually start to slow down. For the developed world there is some evidence that the pace of the introduction of new journals has diminished;[6] but in the developing world it has probably not (though we have few data on precise numbers). Nevertheless, apart from a concern with the total number of scientific journals (currently perhaps about 100 000, 25 000 of these being biomedical), and the scattering of references to a topic among many more journals than a generation ago, another major worry has emerged. Many think that the purpose of publication has been hijacked. No longer are scientists following Faraday's injunction,

"Work, think, publish" with its implication of making a serious contribution to science, exposing this to critical comment by the scientist's peers. Instead, publication is being used for demonstrating academic activity by individuals or departments—aiming their lists of articles at grant giving bodies whose evaluation is now based as much on quantity as quality. As a result, today a single piece of work is often split into several different articles ("salami" publication of the smallest publishable unit), often bearing the name of several "honorary" or "gift" authors. The same article may also appear in several different journals (specialist and general, national and international), often without the authors informing the editor of the duplication or cross referring within the article to the others. And if any confirmation was needed that all was not well with scientific publication several workers have now shown the poor quality and utility of many of the articles. Many articles are neither read nor cited; indeed, many articles are demonstrably poor, and their contents are rarely relevant to the real world of the patient at the bedside.[7]

The editorial process

All these concerns formed the backdrop to the revelations in the late 1970s and early '80s of frauds in scientific research. Many individual cases are described elsewhere in this book, so that I will concentrate on whether some might have come to light during the editorial process. It has to be emphasised, however, that most cases have been disclosed by whistleblowers and even the most stringent editorial scrutiny would not have detected them. And to approach any article primarily with fraud in mind is to threaten the mutual trust on which science has always depended: as a former editor of the *New England Journal of Medicine*, Arnold Relman, has said, science is "intensely sceptical about the possibility of error but totally trusting about the possibility of fraud".[8] Even so, misconduct in research can be viewed as a continuum, which begins with faults that all of us have committed—producing erroneous data, misinterpretation, and bias—but then goes down a slippery slope through gift authorship and conflict of interest to piracy, plagiarism, and forgery of data (see figure). So not only should any tightening of standards also lead to better science (and papers); it should also shift any such progression towards fraud "to the left." This is the concept behind several of the recommendations on preventing fraud, such as close supervision of research students and the ready availability and prolonged retention of data.

FINANCIAL INTERESTS

The first stage of the editorial process occurs when the paper is submitted to a journal. It is registered in the editorial office, which checks

Good Faith	"Trimming and Cooking"	Fraud
Wrong observations	Manipulating data	Piracy
Wrong analysis	Suppressing	Plagarism
Wrong references	inconvenient facts	Forgery
Bias		
Self delusion		
	Gift authorship	
	Duplicate publication	Undeclared interest
	Salami publication	

FIGURE — *Some elements in poor science. ("Trimming" and "cooking" were terms introduced by Charles Babbage* (Reflections on the Decline of Science in England. New York: Kelly, 1976))

whether it fulfils the requirements in the instructions to authors. Most of these are concerned with minor detail—the correct number of copies, spacing, reference format, and so on—but at least two have been recognised to have a potential role in preventing or detecting fraud. The first is a declaration of any financial interests the authors may have in relation to the manuscript, such as a paid consultancy to a pharmaceutical company concerned in the work, or holding its stock. At least if the editor and referee know about this, they will be better placed to assess any claims made in their proper context—and concealed interests certainly featured in at least one furore over some hyped initial claims for the efficacy of a vitamin A enriched ophthalmic ointment which was subsequently shown to be little better than placebo.[9]

AUTHORSHIP

The second statement that authors are required to make concerns authorship and has recently been expanded in detail. For some time several journals have asked all the authors to sign their consent to publication of a paper before they submit the paper. The editor can then query an apparently inordinate number of authors. For example, I have been concerned with one particular suspect who has produced papers reporting multidisciplinary work—including statistical analysis—that was too complex to have been done or be reported by a single author; more usual, however, is the paper that is not fraudulent but contains a dozen "authors" putting their name, say, to an apparently simple case report. The "signing off" policy may also have another role: gift authors themselves may come to realise the existence of the paper (and even the work) for the first time, and, given that they cannot take intellectual responsibility for its content, withdraw their names from it. And in a few instances of fraud where the work actually had not been done at all a policy of signing off might have brought the fraud to light much earlier—for example, if anyone familiar with the equipment and materials available in the particular laboratory might realise that the work described could not have been carried out.

Requiring signatures from all authors will not deter all outright fraudsters, several of whom have forged coauthors' names, but it may be an important deterrent to gift or honorary authorship, particularly given the number of past instances of fraudulent articles where this is featured. More importantly, several journals have now made the authorship statement much more specific than it used to be. In the statement of "authorship responsibility" used by the *Journal of the American Medical Association* all authors have to confirm that they have participated in the study sufficiently to vouch for its validity and to be able to take public responsibility for its contents; that they have reviewed and approved the final version of the manuscript; that they confirm that the work has neither been published previously nor is currently being considered by any other journal; and that they will produce the data on which the manuscript is based if requested to do so by the editor.[10]

DUPLICATE PUBLICATION

Another aspect that several journals specifically mention in their instructions to authors concerns possible duplicate publication. The *Uniform Requirements* prepared by the International Committee of Medical Journal Editors state that: "When submitting a paper an author should always make a full statement to the editor about all submissions and previous reports that might be regarded as prior or duplicate publication of the same or very similar work. Copies of such material should be included with the submitted paper to help the editor decide how to deal with the matter."

In my experience authors rarely raise this possibility in the letter accompanying the submission of the paper, and are surprised when the editor or the referee points to closely similar work which they have already published elsewhere. But duplicate publication might be disclosed more often if journal offices were to routinely search the databases. At one time searches through the reference books would have been both lengthy and laborious, but with the ready availability of on line and CD systems such a check should be both quick and easy. It would not, of course, disclose simultaneous submissions of the paper, publication in minor journals not listed in the database, or articles the title of which had been completely changed between one version and the next (as happened with several of Darsee's abstracts).[11] Perhaps a more important role of such a check would be to highlight an author who was publishing papers so frequently, and on such a diversity of topics, that questions should be asked. At one stage, for instance, Slutsky was publishing an article every 10 days, while his total bibliography comprised 147 manuscripts, 137 of which had been published.[12] (Even so, it could be argued—and indeed has been—that an excessive number of research projects should also be of concern at an earlier stage: that of approval by a research ethics committee (institutional review board).)

DATA CHECKS

A far more radical and contentious suggestion for checking manuscripts early in the editorial process was made in 1989 by Drummond Rennie, deputy editor of the *Journal of the American Medical Association*.[13] He based his proposal on two premises. Firstly, that even the most cursory audit would have detected what peer review had not: the fabrication of whole collections of patients and experiments by Soman, Darsee, Slutsky, and Breuning (see p 9 *et seq*). Secondly, the follow up to the Shapiro study (p 128) had shown that Food and Drug Administration surveillance system of routine audit might be having a deterrent effect on the incidence of serious deficiencies in drug studies.

In Rennie's scheme editors would set up the rules for good laboratory and clinical practices—and, after a period of notice, advise authors that their papers would be considered only if they agreed to be audited. Papers would be chosen at random and audited not by the editors, but by those with recent experience of research—such as retired faculty members—who would visit the institutions and assess simple matters such as the relationship between the data in patient records and submitted manuscripts, and whether the studies had any basis in reality. Being experimental and confidential, the audit results would not affect the subsequent publication of any manuscript. Nevertheless, they would be published, without identifying the authors or the institutions, the aim being not to police the system but to establish the prevalence of sloppy, or shady, science, as a basis for making institutional and journal policy.

There are several benefits of such a scheme, in Rennie's view:

- It might deter the fraudulent and detect some outright fraud
- It should reveal gross errors and omissions
- It would spruce up the sloppy
- It would go some way to satisfying governments and the public that the scientific establishment was taking its responsibilities seriously.

But most important, I believe, is his final claim: that at last the community would get an idea of the extent of the problem, an aspect about which there are few data but many theories—with estimates varying from one in 1000 papers being tainted[14] to 99·9999% of reports being accurate and truthful.[15]

I have devoted considerable space to describing Rennie's proposals because they have not had the serious discussion they deserve. For they were received mostly with scepticism, particularly concerning the detail, such as the bureaucracy needed to put them into practice. Nevertheless, his arguments are cogent, and, as with peer review, another key aspect of scientific communication about which we had few data until recently, probably the nay sayers will come round to accepting his call for research. Perhaps there is a good case for waiting for a couple of years, say, while all the proposals and guidelines for preventing and managing research fraud are put into universal practice—but about how many other important aspects of science do we still have so few basic facts?

Peer review

Rennie's proposals had in fact been anticipated by similar ones made a few years earlier in the conclusion to an analysis of the 18 full length original articles published by John Darsee and his colleagues.[16] This claimed that all but two articles contained errors or discrepancies that could have been recognised simply by examining them carefully. Given that most of these articles were atypical, however, the authors—the "fraudbusters" Walter Stewart and Ned Feder of the National Institutes of Health—suggested auditing a random series of published articles to find out the size of the problem; such an audit could either be external (looking at the article itself for errors) or internal (looking at the data on which the article was based).

In fact, external audit is surely what editorial peer review is all about (or should be). Given peer review's three objectives—to prevent the publication of bad work, improve the scholarship (to see that the relevant literature is cited and discussed in relation to the new findings), and improve the language and presentation of data[17]—we have to ask why the various referees (or the journal editors and technical staff preparing Darsee's articles for the press) did not recognise some of the more egregious errors. For, although many errors were minor, others were egregious indeed, being in the words of Stewart and Feder, "so glaring as to offend common sense."

Part of the problem comes from the lack of time. Peer review is a largely unpaid chore additional to other tasks which confer more visibility, kudos, and appreciation. Good reviewers are likely to be rewarded only by getting more papers to assess, from more than one journal (not to mention other projects such as book manuscripts and grant proposals to adjudicate on). So few referees can spend more than two or three hours in assessing a paper.[18] To be sure, in biomedicine, they are not expected to work out examples in detail (as are referees in some other disciplines, such as mathematics), but their lack of meticulous scrutiny is shown in other ways—for example, that in many articles a quarter of the references cited do not say what the authors claim they do.[19]

Another reason for indifferent peer review has been the editors' failure to spell out what features they want advice on and to give the reviewers feedback on the outcome. Many referees see their main role merely as deciding whether the paper should be published or not. But this is not their job; it is the editor's, undertaken with all sorts of other factors in mind (including the pressure on space, the acceptance of other—and possibly better—articles on the same topic, and the opinion of other referees, often on specialist aspects of the work such as statistics). What editors need, on the other hand, is expert advice about the following: the importance of the question and originality of the work; the appropriateness of the approach or experimental design; the soundness of the conclusions; the relevance of the discussion; and the clarity of the writing and the soundness of the organisation of the paper.[20]

Next, referees are more likely to take trouble, I believe, if they feel involved in the whole process. They should be sent copies of any other assessor's report and told specifically in a personal letter if and why the editor did not follow their advice. Ideally, also, it would be a good thing to tell them where their advice fell short of what was needed, but I suspect that such a policy would lose more friends than it gained. Even so, if every few years the most active and faithful could be invited to a gathering where they could discuss their problems with the editor and one another, everybody would gain (though self evidently this would be feasible only in a smallish country and with a prospering journal).

Few of us would expect reviewers to come out with a clear statement that a paper is probably reporting fraudulent work. Rather they are likely to say that they cannot believe or understand the results, possibly suggesting that the author should supply the raw data. At this stage, having confirmed the referee's suspicion (alone or together with another referee or the editorial committee, or both), the editor is committed to a course which he (or she) must pursue until the case has been fully investigated. Either he and his adviser have to be persuaded that the work is above board, or, if doubts remain, he must take his suspicions to the responsible authority, such as the head of the department or the dean of the medical school. Not only that: he must not be fobbed off and should make himself a nuisance until the matter has been settled; only with distant countries without Western standards of research values may he give up. All this is to place an editor in a different position vis-à-vis fraud from where he was five years ago, but this new and essential role cannot be shirked.

Before we can conclude, however, that reviewers are all slapdash, or return to the principle that it is not the task of peer review to be on the lookout for fraud, let us remember that we have no idea of how often it is detected before publication. In this I would draw an analogy with the early days of the ethics of human research experimentation. I was a junior member of the *British Medical Journal* staff in the era before these aspects were highlighted as a concern of publication. Those (few) papers in which the ethical aspects were dubious (to put it mildly, with hindsight) tended to be rejected on general grounds, largely because the main concerns were uncodified. Later, once guidelines had been promulgated, the *BMJ* would referee papers specifically to an ethicist and take up any points with the authors, rejecting on overt grounds of poor ethics, if necessary. Similarly I can remember a decade later, when a referee had suggested that the data were too good to be true, rejecting articles again on general grounds. Today the attitude would be much less complaisant and most editors would follow through any suspicions until the problem had been settled.

Though we have no data on how often fraud is suspected before publication, one study concluded that peer review in its widest sense (lab seminars, public professional meetings, reading a paper to friends, and assessing it for grant support) had been one of the most effective methods for detecting fraud—highlighting it in at least six out of 41 cases (three of them through editorial peer review) (P Woolf, personal communication). And in one famous case—of Robert A Slutsky—major frauds were brought to light when a percipient referee spotted inexplicable statistical discrepancies between two articles submitted in an application for promotion.[12]

The main talking point about peer review in connection with fraud, however, has been entirely different: the possibility that reviewers may abuse their trust and steal the original work. Such a suspicion is often voiced but until 15 years ago was little documented. Now we know of at least two major instances (Alsabti[21] and Soman[22]) where fraudsters purloined material in a paper refereed to a colleague. Little can be done about a really determined fraudster provided with such an opportunity, but the possibility that seems to worry authors is that referees will be much more covert in using the new findings reported for their own purposes. In a well documented case, discussed by Marcel LaFollette,[11] a special National Institutes of Health panel found that C David Bridges, a referee for the *Proceedings of the National Academy of Science*, had patterned "his experiments after those detected in a manuscript sent to him for review, using the information to publish his own work and falsifying his records. [There was] clear abuse of the peer review system with the clear intention of gaining personal aggrandizement." Though Bridges maintained his innocence, his debarment from serving as a referee for the NIH or receiving its funds was not reversed on appeal.

Codes of refereeing

The major guidelines on refereeing spell out the assessors' ethical responsibilities unequivocably: "The unpublished manuscript," the Council of Biology Editors' guidelines state, "is a privileged document. Please protect it from any form of exploitation. Reviewers are expected not to cite a manuscript or refer to the work it describes before it has been published, and to refrain from using the information it contains for the advancement of their own research."[20]

The guidelines also attempt to deal with other fears—that referees might damn work unfairly by giving an unjustifiably adverse report, or delaying this for several months:

A reviewer should consciously adopt a positive, impartial attitude towards the manuscript under review. Your position should be that of the author's ally, with the aim of promoting effective and accurate scientific communication.

If you believe that you cannot judge a given article impartially please return the manuscript immediately to the editor with that explanation [some editors' letters to the referee now specifically mention conflicts of interest].

Reviews should be completed expeditiously, within [state here the time you consider reasonable, for example, two weeks]. If you know that you cannot finish the review within the time specified, please telephone the editor (collect) to determine what action should be taken.

One way editors can help in preventing such abuses is not only to remind assessors of the code governing peer review (which is repeated in every letter the *BMJ* sends to its referees), but also to publicise instances when they occur. The paucity of such accounts might suggest that such instances are rare, but I suspect that the reality today is similar to the cases of fraud that were brushed under the carpet before the revelations of the late 1970s and the codes that were brought in to prevent or deal with future cases. Laboratory gossip is, after all, full of such talk, and I suggest that what usually happens when referees abuse their position is a combination of circumstances: authors are often junior and feel powerless and at risk if they complain, instances are often not clear cut or are poorly documented, and/or the editor is reluctant to get involved (as has happened with printing statements of retraction; see below).

Commentators often suggest that one way of overcoming such abuses would be open reviewing, in which assessors sign their reports. The dinosaur reaction to this, which I have supported, is either that referee reports would become bland, or that referees would refuse to do the review. Possibly with the general trend towards openness (as seen in journals where there are now signed editorials, book reviews, and news paragraphs) the anonymity of the assessor will disappear—though will senior scientists tolerate harsh criticism, however justified and unemotionally expressed, from junior referees, who may be untenured? Far better, in my view, at least initially, would be to try blind review, where the referee does not know the authors' identities. Again, documented fact is at variance with tittle-tattle: the former maintains that most prejudice arises out of different research attitudes,[23] the latter that it is personal.[24] And the dinosaurs have again had something to say: blinding the referee can't work. In fact it does, as shown by some research at the University of North Carolina.[25]

In a randomised trial McNutt and his colleagues sent each of 127 consecutive manuscripts submitted to the *Journal of General Medicine* and reporting original research to two reviewers. One of these was randomly chosen to receive the manuscript with the name of the author and the institution removed; the other received it unaltered. Blinding took an average of only 15 minutes to complete in the journal office (by the end of the study the time had fallen to five minutes) and was successful in 73% of cases. Moreover, on a five-point scale editors graded the quality of blinded reviews as significantly better than those of the non-blinded ones. Referees were also asked, but not required, to sign their reviews. There was no difference in the proportion of referees who signed in the two groups, but the editors rated the signers as more constructive and courteous and authors rated signers as more fair. (So much for my own belief that signing referees' reports may not work.)

The authors comment that, given that their study was done in a small general journal, their findings may not necessarily apply to larger journals or to those in other disciplines. Nevertheless, considering their clearcut results, I believe that editors now have to prove that blinding will not work for their own journals—in particular, they can no longer ignore the issue by pretending that blinding is not feasible. As I write, in fact, a large-scale collaborative study of blind peer review is about to be launched by general and specialist journals on both sides of the Atlantic.

Retraction of research findings

Once an investigating team has determined that reported work is fraudulent, its duties then have to extend to determining the validity of previous work by the same author(s). Such exemplary zeal was first shown in the Slutsky case.[12] After an ad hoc committee had found evidence of fraud in at least three recent manuscripts, a second committee was set up to examine all his publications (during which time Slutsky's attorney retracted 15 articles from eight journals). This second committee, containing 10 faculty members, looked at 137 articles, correlating statements in these with laboratory records and interviews with laboratory personnel, postdoctoral trainees, and coauthors. They classified articles as *fraudulent* if there was documentation or testimony from coauthors that the publication did not reflect what had been done, *questionable* if no coauthor could produce the original data or had participated in the research and writing the paper, and *valid* if a coauthor had participated in the latter stages. Of 135 articles, 12, 48, and 75, respectively, fell into these categories.

Nevertheless, the investigative process does not stop there; the findings have to be made public and the authorities informed—including the institution where the work was done, the grant giving bodies, the disciplinary authorities, and the editors of the journals in which the work was published. Clearly work cannot be wiped out of the literature: it is published and will remain on the printed page. Nevertheless, the record can, and should, be put straight in a formal retraction of research findings (or a statement of validation). Such a policy was introduced by the International Committee of Medical Journal Editors (the "Vancouver group"), which in its statement distinguished between honest error (possibly major enough to require publication of an erratum or a correction) and scientific fraud. "If a fraudulent paper has been published," the statement by the Vancouver group stated unequivocally, "the journal *must* print a retraction" (my italics). It went on to specify that the retraction should be labelled as such, appear in a prominent section of the journal, be listed on the contents page, and include in its heading the title of the original article; ideally, but not necessarily, the first author should be the same as in the original article, and the text of the retraction should explain the reason for it and give a bibliographic reference.[26]

In practice, things have not been so easy. The San Diego team investigating Slutsky wrote to 30 journals with its conclusions in 1986 (the year before the recommendations by the Vancouver group), requesting them to publish a general statement together with a specific statement about the classification of articles published in that journal. Journals responded only slowly; half of the journals needed additional letters over the next two years to produce a reply. Of the 30 journals, 18 published some statement of retraction or validation covering 64 articles; of 13 journals publishing only valid articles, eight did not publish a statement; of 17 journals publishing any non-valid articles, only nine published retractions covering all of these; of the seven journals publishing the 12 articles specifically regarded as fraudulent, two published nothing. Moreover, the wording used in the headings of published notices varied—retraction, notice, validation of a study, publication investigation, addendum, and statement—as did their locations and identifiability in the journal.[12]

Concluding his account of correcting the literature (on which my account above relies heavily), Paul Friedman, a member of the San Diego committee, comments that, given that validation statements were a new concept, it is hard to fault the journals' reluctance to publish them. On the other hand, journals that declined to publish statements about fraudulent or questionable articles (as did two unless the request were to be initiated by the coauthors) failed in their duty to science and to their readers.

Journals surely had an obligation to develop written policies and procedures for responding to allegations of improper research.

Fortunately the National Library of Medicine has recognised the need for action, developing a new rubric of "retraction." This will be used for a statement relating to an article published in the same journal as the retraction and written by the editor of the journal, a coauthor of the retracted publication, the publisher, or an authorised agent of the author. Despite all this, however, there will still be confusion. Currently the National Library of Medicine will not label anything as a retraction unless the journal calls it that. If any passage does not mention the term retraction (even though in effect that is what the passage is about) then the library will index it under errata or comment. My personal hope is that it will be possible to separate honest error from fraud before too long, though editors will have the primary role in advising how this can best be done (meaning that they will first have to agree among themselves to call a spade a spade). Given that there is still disagreement about whether the retracted literature still continues to be used—one group found that retraction reduced citations by only 35%,[27] another that it "purged" the literature[28]—clearly the sooner it is done the better.

Conclusions

There is, I believe, hope on the horizon. For as I write there have been two recent developments. The first is that in at least three disciplines—paediatrics, dermatology, and radiology—the editors of the principal specialty journals have come together to agree that if they detect duplicate publication within their own group of journals both publications will issue prominent statements to this effect. Secondly, if the new all online journal the *Online Journal of Clinical Trials* has the success it deserves, it will be copied in all disciplines. Authorship will no longer have its spuriously high visibility and there should be sufficient electronic space for authors to spread themselves a little more. Will anybody read this new type of journal? (the answer is that they often do not read the present ones—and who can blame them?). In any case, in John Hunter's famous words, "Why not try the experiment?"—remembering, of course that increasing the traditional emphasis on scientific rigour will still probably have the major role in discouraging and detecting research fraud.

So I come to two personal conclusions about how improving the ethics of publication might help to diminish the amount of research misconduct. Firstly, editorial attitudes need to change. Editors (and I have been as guilty as any) have done too much to encourage articles that are short rather than long enough to be able to report and discuss all the findings in a single paper. They have also done too much to discourage articles confirming important results or reporting negative results. Hence I would suggest a new philosophy of encouraging the longer and better article at the expense of the shorter and meretricious one.

Secondly, we must end this ludicrous emphasis on authorship as a goal in itself, the obsession with having one's name on as many articles as possible. Often denied at the formal level, this occurrence is readily admitted to in informal conversation—there is, for instance, the story of the four senior registrars who agreed at the start of their jobs to multiply their output by putting each other's names on all papers they wrote, with a rotating first authorship, or that of an informant ringing up a specialised unit asking for some tests and their costs. "£60 for the tests; £30 if you put my name on the paper as coauthor," was the reply. Surely the time has come for all academic units to develop, and enforce, a sensible authorship policy—with appointment committees restricting the number of articles that may be cited in a curriculum vitae. And editors must remember that it is part of their job to be difficult and ask awkward questions if the number or character of the authors of a paper seems inappropriate for its contents. As a distinguished Victorian editor of the *BMJ*, Ernest Hart, told an American audience in 1893, "An editor needs and must have enemies; he cannot do without them. Woe be unto the journalist of whom all men say good things."[29]

A few passages in this account have appeared either in *A Difficult Balance*[20] or *The Future of Medical Journals*.[29]

1 Majerus P. Fraud in medical research. *J Clin Invest* 1982; **70**: 213–7.
2 Zuckerman H, Merton RK. Patterns of evaluation in science. *Minerva* 1971; **9**: 66–100.
3 Paton A. A toast to the *BMJ*. BMJ 1990; **301**: 741–3, 755.
4 Fox TF. *Crisis in communication*. London: Athlone Press, 1965.
5 Price D de S. The development and structure of the biomedical literature. In Warren KS, ed. *Coping with the biomedical literature*. New York: Praeger, 1981; 3–16.
6 Pendlebury D. Science's go-go growth: has it started to slow? *The Scientist* 1986; 7 August: 14, 16.
7 Haynes RB. How clinical journals could serve readers better. In Lock S, ed. *The future of medical journals*. London: BMJ, 1991; 116–266.
8 Relman A. Comments at the colloquium on scientific authorship: rights and responsibilities. *FASEB J* 1989; **3**: 209–17.
9 Booth W. Conflict of interest eyed at Harvard. *Science* 1988; **242**: 1497–9.
10 Lundberg GD, Flanagin A. New requirements for authors. *JAMA* 1989; **262**: 2003–4.
11 La Follette M. *Stealing into print*. Berkley: University of California Press, 1992; 130.
12 Friedman PJ. Correcting the literature following fraudulent publication. *JAMA* 1990; **263**: 1416–19.
13 Rennie D. Editors and auditors. *JAMA* 1989; **266**: 2543–5.
14 Broad W, Wade N. *Betrayers of the truth*. New York: Simon and Schuster, 1982; 94–5.
15 Koshland D. Fraud in science. *Science* 1987; **235**: 41.
16 Stewart WW, Feder N. The integrity of the scientific literature. *Nature* 1987; **325**: 207–14.
17 Waksman BH. Information overload in immunology. *J Immunol* 1980; **124**: 1009–15.
18 Lock S, Smith J. What do peer reviewers do? *JAMA* 1990; **263**: 1341–3.
19 Yankauer A. The accuracy of medical journal references. *CBE Views* 1990; **13**: 38–42.
20 Lock S. *A difficult balance*. London: BMJ, 1991; 110.

21 Anonymous. Must plagiarism thrive? *BMJ* 1980; **281**: 41–2.
22 Broad W. Imbroglio at Yale (1): emergence of a fraud. *Science* 1980; **210**: 38–41.
23 Crane D. The gatekeepers of science. *American Sociologist* 1967; **2**: 195–201.
24 Colman AM. Manuscript evaluation by journal referees and editors. *Behavioural and Brain Sciences* 1982; **5**: 205–6.
25 McNutt RA, Evans AT, Fletcher RH, Fletcher SW. The effects of blinding on the quality of peer review. *JAMA* 1990; **263**: 1371–6.
26 International Committee of Medical Journal Editors. Retraction of research findings. *BMJ* 1988; **296**: 400.
27 Pfeifer MP, Snodgrass GL. The continued use of retracted invalid scientific literature. *JAMA* 1990; **263**: 1420–3.
28 Garfield E, Welljams-Dorof A. The impact of fraudulent research on the scientific literature. *JAMA* 1990; **263**: 1424–6.
29 Bartrip P. The *BMJ*: a retrospect. In Bynum WF, Lock S, Porter R, eds. *Medical journals and medical knowledge*. London: Routledge, 1991.

A head of department's view

IAIN E GILLESPIE

Although I was vaguely aware that one or two notorious acts of scientific fraud had been well publicised at infrequent intervals over many years, I had the naive belief that these misdeeds were all in the long distant past, and of course in other lands—or at least in other centres. It was only when for the first time I came, even indirectly, in contact with a suspected serious example on my home patch—and even more so, directly involved as a senior officer of the faculty—that I realised the full impact of the problem. Throughout earlier training years, learning from and working under greatly respected leaders in my chosen fields of research, I never thought for a moment of the remote possibility of any irregularity, sins of omission or commission in experimental work. Clearly all members of the scientific, particularly medical scientific, world—that brotherhood united in the powerful motive to conquer disease and ignorance—were above all such suspicion. Then, relatively late in my academic career, reality dawned.

Of course, it was blind and rather arrogant to think that this population of scientific investigators was, in human terms, any different in its basic ingredients from any other sector of our community, and not to realise that, given the various opportunities, inducements, and pressures of one sort and another, a small proportion would submit to the temptation to cheat.

Before becoming directly concerned in the Royal College of Physicians working party on fraud, I believed myself to be aware of the problem in general, and indeed had had limited exposure to one or two specific cases. However, participation in the working party focused my mind on a wider range of possible types of fraud, and gave an even greater degree of alertness to the problem. The discussions made me think back over a number of instances where there just might have been some deliberate irregularities in the conduct of work, which may have slipped by unnoticed at the time. Were papers for refereeing perhaps held back a little so that the referee's own lab's results could catch up or overtake? Was correspondence between one worker and a collaborator delayed—again for similar purposes? Did that series of remarkably similar results really include absolutely every result? Were some of the figures in this or that table rounded up—and if so, perhaps too much? There was a real danger of becoming over suspicious.

The next thought, arising from this increasing list of questions and suspicions, was, "Are there different degrees of seriousness of such misdemeanours?" Are some merely examples of undue competitiveness and ambition and perhaps more readily condoned than frank falsification of experimental results? This soon seemed a dangerous path to follow, otherwise we might end up with a sliding scale of sins from one to 10. Rightly or wrongly, I came to the view that, in the exacting and responsible professional scientific community—to which it is a privilege to belong—an equally serious view must be taken of all transgressions, and that quantifying them for severity was not appropriate or helpful.

Although of course there could be no proof to back up the conclusion, it seems entirely likely that someone who got away with what was initially regarded as a relatively minor transgression might later be tempted to perpetrate a more major fraud. Thus my simple conclusion came to be that, "A cheat is a cheat, is a cheat"—and that all suspected acts should merit the same degree of attention.

It was next helpful to go over the long list of motives and pressures that had been recognised as triggers to acts of fraud, and review to what extent they might be active on individual members of the department.

Motives and pressures

PERSONAL AMBITION

Of course all the members of an academic department are ambitious, and that is one of the main reasons we appointed them in the first place. We want them to acquire new skills and become productive so that they can add to the lustre of the department, and they in turn want to earn their own reputations and secure, in good time, promotion to more senior positions. There is also the very human desire to please the boss—and if he is difficult to please then this may require an unreasonable amount of results of very high quality. The personal ambition is also sharpened by looking sideways at the rate of progress of one's contemporaries. It is only natural to feel resentful at a colleague's apparently much more rapid progress, and short cuts in trying to overtake may be tempting.

There is one factor commonly encountered in research projects which may at times frustrate the ambitious and somewhat impatient worker, and thereby raise the temptation to cheat. After the first few results of an exciting new project have been obtained and they tend to agree, there is a great risk of jumping to the conclusion that the hypothesis you have set out to test is proved, and incidentally that your preconceived notion is of course correct. It is heady stuff. The next one or more results go quite another, unexpected way—and it is uncomfortable. The project must continue along precisely the planned lines till all results are available for proper analysis. The good scientist will worry away with reviewing all the details of each experimental run, double check the techniques used, and seek as many alternative explanations for the rogue results as possible. He or she may have to accept that additional series of experiments must be undertaken. Often this will be rewarded by the appearance of new, and equally interesting, questions. However, there can be a temptation to manipulate the results so that the precious preconceived notion seems to be confirmed.

NEED TO PUBLISH

It is a legitimate expectation that anyone engaging seriously in scientific investigation should publish the results of his or her work, preferably in refereed journals in the first instance. Apart from the personal satisfaction of receiving printed recognition and therefore credit for producing the papers, it is a proper way of submitting the work for public scrutiny throughout the wider scientific world. All staff seeking promotion and appointments to more senior posts in the open market know that an impressive list of publications in prestigious journals greatly increases chances of being shortlisted, and ultimate success in obtaining the appointment. Although in recent years the opinion has been increasingly voiced that it is quality rather than quantity that matters, I do not think this is fully accepted by applying candidates, and appointments committees still put considerable emphasis on total numbers. Here the danger is that potential candidates produce duplicate papers on virtually the same material, but with only the slightest change in accent and presentation. Discouraging this practice is surely among the responsibilities of the head of department.

This responsibility is now being to some extent sabotaged by the increasingly detailed attempts to categorise and quantify virtually every action of every member of every funded unit and group—including an enumeration of all printed output of every academic staff member. Clearly total numbers will have direct funding implications for the departments concerned. Yes, there are statements that some categories of publication will earn more "brownie" points than others, but the simple fact that total numbers are being requested makes it difficult to believe that they will be ignored. So the pressure to publish more and more papers remains, and indeed increases as far as the individual is concerned. Two further pressures are brought to bear.

First is the approach of deadlines, which have previously been accepted and agreed as the projects got under way. Then, as often happens, snags arise, some experimental runs have to be abandoned, specimens go astray, a key person falls ill etc, etc, and inexorably the deadline for presentation of a paper, a poster, or a publication looms up. None of us likes to admit failure to deliver, and this pressure is a hard one, particularly if the work is part of a collaborative, or multicentre programme. The second pressure concerns obtaining or renewing research grants to support one's work. In the first place most grant giving bodies look for evidence of a track record, even a limited one, in the particular investigative area before awarding initial funds, and if renewal or extension is being sought there is a demand to see presented or published evidence of real progress with the first part of the studies. This sounds not unreasonable, but deadlines are very inflexible things and panic regarding continued survival in the academic scene if the grant is not obtained or renewed can be experienced. There are very real pressures.

FINANCIAL PRESSURES

These seem to be less obtrusive in hospital based research, especially in a surgical discipline. They mainly raise their heads in the case of drug trials sponsored by pharmaceutical companies, when a payment is offered for each subject introduced into the trial, and for whom a completed protocol of results has been returned. I frankly discourage participation in studies planned on this basis, and if the drug is of particular interest to the department prefer to reach some other arrangements. The inducement to ensure that a complete set of values is entered on every return, and to use imagination to fill any occasional blanks, is one which some people will find hard to resist.

HEALTH PROBLEMS

These are predominantly psychological or psychiatric, and often they will take some time to come to notice, and I suspect some have passed unobserved. Although there must be a large spectrum of behaviour patterns that may eventually culminate in acts of scientific fraud, from my own happily limited knowledge, I might perhaps, in an oversimplifying manner, separate them into two broad categories.

In the first the act of fraud may be a symptom, and possibly the first one to come to light, of a personality disorder—in which case, the investigator may be completely unaware that the deed or more likely repeated deeds were fraudulent, and may even defend them as quite commendable. In such a case known to me a senior colleague simply became suspicious that the results, part way through a study of subjects' answers and reactions to certain events and situations were just "not quite right." He simply had a hunch that all was not well with the study. It took several sessions of patient discussion, persuasion, and search through what could be retrieved of the initial raw data to uncover the finding that some responses had been excluded, or even destroyed, because it was felt that they might cause displeasure or offence to the participants, or the ultimate readers. The lack of insight into the unacceptability of such an action in a scientific study was part of a symptom complex of a disorder for which appropriate treatment was sought.

In quite a different second category I would put the occasional succumbing to the, perhaps one-off, temptation to fake a figure or so just for the excitement of doing it. I would liken this to the childhood playing of "chicken," the young motorcyclist's dash up the fast lane, and the compulsion to shoplift. There's a chance to do it: it is only this once, who is to notice? Does this go on? I think it probably does. Often? Almost certainly not. If it was a repeated occurrence with any one individual it would likely come eventually to notice because of the very repetitive pattern of results. Does it matter much? In principle, yes; as far as likelihood of significant effect on the main conclusions of major scientific work, I doubt it.

Having looked in detail at the estimated size of the problem, and then the various pressures pushing investigators towards the temptation to fraud, let me turn next to what, as head of an academic department, I then felt I should do about the problem. It seems that I have three responsibilities, and much can be done under each of these to reduce or contain the disease, or when it occurs treat it effectively. These are prevention, detection, and action.

Prevention

In view of the factors encouraging acts of scientific fraud there is clearly a duty to reduce the opportunities for it to occur, and reduce as far as possible the pressures, or the effects of them on members of staff. Some of the steps are disarmingly simple. So far I have discussed only matters relating to postgraduate members of staff. However, our responsibility also extends to the undergraduate students attending on our units, and the degree examinations. An interesting example of cheating, the blame for which falls primarily on our own oversight of simple practical detail, came to light during the marking of some papers. It was noted that a silly answer to one of the questions was repeated on several papers. It was only then realised that, on this occasion, the papers had been answered in a tiered lecture room not normally used for examinations—and of course it is difficult not to see clearly at least part of the paper in the row in front. I believe that in these circumstances few if any people could avoid an occasional word from the row ahead registering on the retina. All that is needed is the future use of properly spaced tables in a level hall.

As far as the pressures on staff are concerned, I see the first duty of the head of department being to ensure that reasonable time and facilities are available for staff members to achieve a realistic amount of work. Some, of course, work faster than others, some have more demanding technical requirements, and others need considerable backup support. Whatever the requirements for a project are, it is important to make a reasonable judgment of both the staff member's ability to undertake the work and the resources needed. Provided these are properly matched then one set of pressures will be avoided.

The next main step should really be regarded as a basic requirement for good practice in any academic department or group, and that is to ensure that there is an established practice of each research worker having a personal more senior supervisor, either the head of department or the most senior person in charge of the particular research activity concerned. Also each investigator should regularly present progress reports to all the other members of the unit, and wider audiences, so that all can offer suggestions, exchange views, ask detailed questions. Such a practice has, of course, many benefits to the whole team, but it does expose the individual and his or her results to perhaps the very closest and most critical scrutiny of all—that of one's immediate coworkers. It is at such sessions that the first inkling that some irregularity might be occurring is most likely to arise. If so then it will arise within the enclosed small grouping of peers and is probably able to be nipped in the bud. Further, the knowledge that such presentations, with raw data accessible to challenge and the likelihood of sharp questions from one's immediate colleagues, are soon to be required must be a very strong disincentive to cheat.

Whether or not the specific project comes within the expertise of the head of department, it is important that he or she keeps an interested eye on the progress of all research workers under his or her administrative care. This applies for example in the case of someone working primarily under the day to day direction of a senior lecturer or similar member, in a more specialised area of interest than that of the general unit. As well as reassuring the investigator of the personal human interest in his or her contribution and welfare, this also gives the head of department opportunity to assess how well and effectively the supervision and guidance are progressing.

Extending this practice to studies requiring collaboration from others in different departments, and multicentre trials and joint projects, it is every bit as important to arrange repeated joint meetings, with all concerned present, to make full, open presentation and discussion of all results up to date. The head of the department should make every effort to be present at these sessions.

Detection

It is trite to say that the earlier any act of fraud is detected the better for all concerned; as in the early diagnosis of important disease, a high index of suspicion is an advantage. Certainly my first contact, albeit distant, with a specific case of such misconduct notably increased my alertness to the possibility of similar occurrences arising nearer to home, and participation in the working party still further re-enforced this awareness.

When one is reviewing the number of different signals which could point to possible cheating or other misconduct, the list became daunting, and if not careful one could end up going around the department like one of Agatha Christie's sleuths. It is also of great importance that members of the department do not regard the boss as a policeman hovering around and suspicious of every move. After all, we are members together of an academic community in which respect and trust are cornerstones, and we are considering a matter, which, although very serious, remains very rare.

What, then, are the main signals that have been recognised in the past, and for which the alert head of department should be on the lookout? These can be classified into sins of omission or commission.

The principal omission is the deletion of results which do not seem to fit in with the rest. Everyone who has any research experience is fully aware that there is always a rogue result, a technical hiccup, a stray wandering outside the 95% confidence intervals, an "off-day," or whatever. Indeed the presence of such vagaries is almost the label of authenticity of the work. It is the absence of any such deviation from the norm of a table or figure of results, the too neat coming together of all the data, which may raise the first query. This should call for a prompt return to the original records and scrutiny of the raw data. The temptation to exclude figures which spoil an otherwise nice correlation or reduce an otherwise impressive p value on the statistical analysis, is real—but to be firmly quashed. Keeping results of experiments in old fashioned, bound notebooks with numbered pages has much to commend it for reducing the opportunity to commit this offence and to have it remain undetected. This is also much less likely to arise if there is a frequent review of the work by the supervisor, and/or head of the department.

To turn to sins of commission, the first and most flagrant misdemeanour is the deliberate invention or falsification of data. One of the main occasions when this is most likely to come up is when deadlines are approaching faster than the real results are emerging. Here again, regular frequent contact with the researcher's supervisor should strongly discourage taking the wrong path. However, the clues are usually somewhat subtle—the experienced reader of the data getting a "feel" that there is something not ringing quite true about them. It may be the frequent repetition of the same value in a table in which a more random spread might be expected. The writing on the tables and other lists of data may look just too neat and tidy and regular, giving the impression that they were not entered as the experimental run took place and results were recorded. There may be a group of entries which seem to have been inserted together en bloc but at a different time from the others. With us all there are tiny but perceptible differences in handwriting when we make written entries at different times, and a series of identically constructed figures or letters can be a telltale sign that they were written at a later time than the other ones. There may well be a simple acceptable reason for this, but it is right to draw attention to the observation and seek that explanation. It is perfectly possible to make this search for the answer in the spirit of scientific inquiry after the interesting truth, rather than in any accusing or condemnatory fashion: and conveying the impression that the "old man" is just not quick enough to grasp the significance of the data and needs to be patiently taken through it all not only allays suspicion but also adds a touch of flattery to the researcher.

Let me turn now to an aspect of misconduct not so far considered in this chapter but of much concern and which, when it comes to light, is as likely as not to do so to a head of department. I refer to plagiarism. As heads of departments are most likely to be concerned with marking examination papers, refereeing papers submitted for publication, and assessing theses, they are most often in the best position to detect copying of other workers' material and passing it off as that of the candidate or aspiring author. For this reason it is the duty of those assessing work claimed to be original to check at least a proportion of the quoted references, if they are not already thoroughly familiar, to ensure that the reference is correctly quoted, and that large segments of the original have not simply been lifted and included in the text. This consideration also applies to editors of journals or multiauthor books. In this situation experience of the contributor's usual style of presentation, mannerisms, and general approach may draw to one's attention any gross departures from usual. One contributor whose correspondence over a lengthy period was usually quite difficult to unravel, presented a chapter for a book which was a joy to read, with an easy flowing style that was so unlike any previous writing that alarm bells rang at once in the editor's mind.

It is very difficult to detect all acts of plagiarism, and doubtless some are overlooked. Given the millions of published articles in thousands of journals of all degrees of special interest and sizes of circulation, it is entirely possible for some blatant transgressions to escape detection. All one can do is be as vigilant as possible, perhaps most of all when dealing with material submitted in a relatively small specialty, with limited readership. Detection can be entirely a matter of chance. A good example of this arose when a senior investigator learnt that a thesis on a subject within his specialist sphere had been accepted by and lodged in the library of a university. On going to that library to consult that thesis he recognised large portions of it as direct plagiarism from his own work previously published in slightly esoteric journals. Prompt action was taken and the degree withdrawn. Once again, as far as this form of fraud is concerned the main lesson for heads of departments and people in similar positions of responsibility is the need for thorough evaluation, checking, and cross checking of all material under the claim of original work. It is time consuming and often entails seeking out large amounts of previously published material, but it is important to do it.

Action

Dealing with a suspected or alleged case of any of the acts under the heading of fraud or misconduct is always a difficult and delicate matter, which carries great risk of damage to the reputation, possible end to a career, poor reflection on innocent bystanders, and personal animosity and disappointment. There are also of course possible legal implications. For these and many other reasons it seems to me essential that there should be a clearly established machinery for dealing with such occurrences and it is vitally important that not only are the correct steps taken, but also that they are taken with absolutely minimal delay. It is in no one's interests to have a protracted exercise. To my relief the procedure for handling such matters in my own university is simple and straightforward, conforms to the suggested three-stage guidelines produced by the Royal College of Physicians working party—and, as I know, works.

The three levels of action seem to me very important and most incidents should be satisfactorily dealt with at either the first or second level of the process. This severely limits the number of people involved and allows a rapid return to normal activity in the department. A complete or at least very high degree of confidentiality is maintained.

Any allegation of any of the practices which could be construed under the heading of fraud or misconduct has to be taken seriously by the head of department, and my first caution to the person making the allegation is to make it to absolutely no one else, until there has been a chance to check on the substance of the complaint. One has, of course, to be aware of the occasional mischievous complaint made from personal or personality differences or grievances. These should be fairly easy to diagnose and immediately quashed, with firm advice to the complainant not to repeat such a misdeed.

If, however, there seems on preliminary investigation to be some substance to the allegation, or it comes directly to the attention of the head of department, then it is a matter to inform to the dean of the faculty, who in turn will call together an inquiry team of three people, usually himself plus two other senior scientists from outside the faculty. Their task is to evaluate the written evidence available and reach a decision on whether it is necessary to invite the person accused of the misconduct to explain matters privately. Up till this point discussion and correspondence have been completely confidential to the head of department, the dean, and the two selected scientists. If the accused person is called to interview it is again emphasised to him or her that matters are still confidential to this small number of people. Again, if this group is satisfied that there is no ground for pursuing the case further, it is dropped and both parties have this confirmed in writing, again under completely confidential cover.

Should concern about misconduct persist after this stage, then the registrar of the university will appoint a disciplinary committee on behalf of the senate and council of the university to take what evidence it sees as appropriate, make a judgment, and recommend a course of action. The council has the final authority in these, as in all other matters, but it would be highly exceptional for it not to accept the recommendation once that had been endorsed by the senate.

It is comforting, as head of a department, to know that this machinery is there to help if one is ever faced again with a suspicion of any irregularity in behaviour in the clinics or laboratories. One needs to act quickly and decisively, and not have to ask around, wonder what to do, dither, and perhaps, with the best will in the world, do the wrong thing. This is a minefield, and people can be permanently scarred or killed professionally if the correct action is not taken, based on true facts, properly substantiated.

I like to think that in the past, a few words here and there in the laboratory, sitting down with an investigator and commiserating with him or her over that stray result which looked as if it might spoil an otherwise watertight hypothesis, suggesting a few additional observations when appropriate, reassuring that life will still go on successfully even if the experiments go wrong, etc may have prevented even one or two researchers from yielding to temptation. For most, however, I am as sure as I was before I joined the working party, such thoughts never do enter their minds.

This line of thought brings me back to getting the matter truly in proportion. Yes, its occurrence is pretty rare. There is such a huge amount of research work going on that, as far as the major advances in scientific/medical knowledge are concerned, it is not likely to hold things back. I would counter this viewpoint by reminding ourselves that the practice of medicine remains primarily a matter of trust between an individual patient and his or her doctor. My fear is that anyone who succumbed to the temptation to cheat, even a little, in the experimental laboratory might also be tempted to take a short cut in clinical practice, where the opportunities present with at least the same frequency. I feel, therefore, that it is our responsibility to take this matter seriously.

Appendices

Appendix A

Standard operating procedure for the handling of suspected fraud

1. OBJECTIVE

The objective of this SOP is to set out the procedures and responsibilities for the investigation and management of cases of suspected fraud occurring in clinical research.

An outline of the procedures adopted by the Association of the British Pharmaceutical Industry and the General Medical Council, following company notification, are also covered.

2. SCOPE

This SOP covers all cases of suspected fraud occurring in clinical research from Phases I–IV regardless of the type of study. The SOP is also applicable to Medical Research Division studies.

3. APPLICABLE TO:

ACTIVITY	RESPONSIBILITY
Detection of suspected fraud	Anyone who handles clinical data or has contact with investigators
Chairing of the initial assessment meeting following discussion of the original person detecting the fraud with their line manager	Quality Assurance Manager
The quarantining of data and adverse drug reactions	Clinical Data Manager
The decision to withold payments	Medical Adviser/Medical Director
Initiating the site audit	Quality Assurance Manager
Presentation of positive audit data to Managing Director, Chief Executive Officer and Legal Affairs.	Medical Director
Production of the Statutory Declaration	Medical Director, Association of the British Pharmaceutical Industry
Liaison with the General Medical Council and formal hearing	Medical Director, Association of the British Pharmaceutical Industry

APPENDIX A

4. POLICY

4.1 It is a requirement of continued employment with this Company that all employees suspecting fraud report them, as outlined in this SOP.

4.2 It is the policy of this Company that all cases of suspected fraud confirmed by site audit will be prosecuted.

4.3 The method of prosecution will be through a Statutory Declaration made jointly between the Medical Director of the Company and the Association of the British Pharmaceutical Industry Medical Director.

4.4 Cases of suspected fraud will *normally* be pursued through the ABPI procedure and not through the civil courts.

4.5 Cases of suspected fraud not positively confirmed by audit, but where a high index of suspicion remained, will be dealt with at the discretion of the Medical Director/Medical Adviser.

5. PROCEDURE

5.1 Cases of suspected fraud, whoever detects them, will be reported to the line manager of the person concerned.

5.2 If the line manager agrees that a prima facie case for fraud exists he/she will notify the Clinical Quality Assurance manager.

5.3 If the line manager does not concur with the reporting person's suspicion there exists the right for the reporting person to communicate directly with the QA Manager to avoid collusion.

5.4 The data will be reviewed at a meeting of the Data Manager, the Quality Assurance Manager, the Project Manager/Medical Adviser and the reporting person under the chairmanship of the Quality Assurance Manager.

5.5 If this meeting does not believe there is a prima facie case for fraud a report is issued by the Quality Assurance Manager to the line manager of the reporting person and the reporting person summarising their reasons for not proceeding. [This process may take five days.]

5.6 If a prima facie case exists the following activities are initiated:

  5.6.1 The Data Manager is responsible for quarantining the data and adverse drug reactions.

  5.6.2 The Medical Adviser/Medical Director will review the feasibility of withholding payments and notify the Management Information Systems administrator of their decision.

  5.6.3 Data verification audit will be initiated by the Quality Assurance Manager.

  The type of audit may vary according to the study in question. It should ideally consist of the Quality Assurance Manager together with the Trial Monitor, Medical Director or Medical Adviser. It may, in the case of post marketing surveillance be only the Trial Monitor responsible for that area.

5.7 A formal report of the data verification audit is issued. The following activities may then be initiated:

  5.7.1 If fraud is not confirmed at audit any further action is at the discretion of the Medical Director/Medical Adviser.

APPENDIX A

    5.7.2   If clinical fraud is confirmed at audit a formal report is issued to the Medical Director.

5.8 On receipt of this report the Medical Director will set up a meeting with the Managing Director, the Chief Executive Officer, and a representative of Legal Affairs and will brief them on the case to date.

This whole procedure, from the first suspicion of fraud to the briefing of the Chief Executive Officer will take no more than 25 working days.

5.9 Following the briefing of the senior executives meeting and assuming a decision to proceed it is the responsibility of the Medical Director to communicate with the Medical Director of the Association of the British Pharmaceutical Industry to prepare a Statutory Declaration.

5.10 Procedures adopted by the Association of the British Pharmaceutical Industry. Upon receipt of the Statutory Declaration signed jointly by the Medical Director of the Association of the British Pharmaceutical Industry and the Medical Director of the Company, the Association of the British Pharmaceutical Industry will forward the declaration to the General Medical Council for their consideration.

    5.10.1   If the *preliminary assessor* at the General Medical Council believes that there is a sufficient case to proceed, he will brief the Legal Department of the General Medical Council and forward the case to the full committee of the General Medical Council for their consideration.

          If either the Medical Director of the Association of the British Pharmaceutical Industry or the *preliminary assessor* at the General Medical Council decide that there is insufficient grounds to proceed then a report will be issued and communicated to the senior executives of the Company, the Data Manager, Quality Assurance Manager, Project Manager/Medical Adviser, the person reporting the initial suspected case and their line manager. Any further action will be dependent on the decision of the Medical Adviser/Medical Director in conjunction with the Legal Affairs Department.

Appendix B

A model statutory declaration

The President
General Medical Council
44 Hallam Street
LONDON
W1M 6AE

Sir

We, the undersigned, Dr ... [position occupied], of the Association of the British Pharmaceutical Industry, of 12 Whitehall, London SW1A 2DY, and Dr ... [positioned occupied], of ... [company] Limited, of ... [company address] do solemnly and sincerely declare as follows:

That Dr ... [name], general practitioner [or professional status], of ... [address of doctor] has acted in a manner which has brought the medical profession into disrepute. Having considered details of the case which are summarised in the report, a copy of which is attached to this formal declaration and forms part of it, we allege that a question of serious professional misconduct is raised by ... [brief statement of the irregularities] ....

We make this Declaration conscientiously believing the same to be true by virtue of the Statutory Declaration Act 1835.

Signed (a) ....(b) ....
Declared at: [address where declared]...
On: [date of declaration] ....
Before me:..

(Justice of the Peace or Solicitor)

(Justice of the Peace)

Appendix C
[Australian] National Health & Medical Research Council statement on scientific practice

This statement was prepared after extensive consultation with the Australian Vice-Chancellors' Committee (AVCC). This Statement and the AVCC'S document on the same topic ("Guidelines on Responsible Practices in Research and Problems of Research Misconduct") have most sections in common. As the NH&MRC provide research support for many institutions, not only higher education institutions, it is essential that the NH&MRC formulates its own guidelines. Adherence to the NH&MRC Guidelines is essential for all institutions applying for and receiving funds from the NH&MRC. To assist readers of *this* document, sections which differ from, or are additional to, guidelines in the AVCC document of November 1990 are shown in italics.

PREAMBLE

The broad principles that guide scientific research have been long established. Central to these are the maintenance of high ethical standards, and validity and accuracy in the collection and reporting of data. The responsibility of the scientific community to the public and to itself is acknowledged. *This responsibility is particularly important in the areas of medical and health research.*

The processes of scientific research protect the truth. Communication between collaborators; maintenance and reference to scientific records; presentation and discussion of work at scientific meetings; publication of results, including the important element of peer refereeing; and the possibility that investigations will be repeated or extended by other scientists, all contribute to the intrinsically self-correcting nature of science.

Competition in research can have a strong and positive influence, enhancing the quality and immediacy of the work produced. However, competitive pressures can act to distort sound research practice, if they encourage too-hasty preparation and submission of papers, the division of reports on substantial bodies of work into multiple small reports to enhance the 'publication count' of the author(s), or an undue emphasis on "logical-next-step" research at the expense of more creative and more innovative lines of study. Accordingly each institution should give due emphasis to quality and originality of research, as well as to quantity of research output, and set up codes of conduct which are seen as a framework for sound research procedures and for the protection of individual research workers from possible misunderstandings.

The NH&MRC, the principal Commonwealth funding agency for health-related research, has long insisted on high standards of integrity in the research it supports and has provided for termination of a grant ". . . . the research for which is not being carried out with competence, diligence, and scientific honesty and integrity." (Conditions of Award, 16 i)

The purpose of the present statement is to set forth a series of guidelines for sound scientific practice, and for the protection of this. Institutions applying for or receiving research funds from the NH&MRC will be required to certify that they have established administrative processes for assuring sound scientific practice. These processes must address all of the issues raised in this statement. It is emphasized that it is a matter for the grantee institutions to establish their own programs for the promotion of good research practices, and their own procedures for prompt investigation of allegations and apparent instances of scientific misconduct.

APPENDIX C

GENERAL CONSIDERATIONS

(a) It is basic assumption of institutions conducting research that their staff members are committed to high standards of professional conduct. Research workers have a duty to ensure that their work enhances the good name of their institution and the profession to which they belong.

(b) Research workers should only participate in work which conforms to accepted ethical standards and which they are competent to perform. When in doubt they should seek assistance with their research from colleagues or peers. Debate on, and criticism of, research work are essential parts of the research process.

(c) Institutions and research workers have a responsibility to ensure the safety of all those associated with the research. It is also essential that the design of projects takes account of any relevant ethical guidelines.

(d) If data of a confidential nature are obtained, for example from individual patient records or from certain questionnaires, confidentiality must be observed and research workers must not use use information for their own personal advantage or that of a third party. In general, however, research results and methods should be open to scrutiny by colleagues within the institution and, through appropriate publication, by the profession at large.

(e) Secrecy may also be necessary for a limited period in the case of contracted research.

SPECIFIC MATTERS

1. Data gathering, storage and retention

(i) Data must be recorded in a durable, and appropriately referenced form.

(ii) Sound research procedures entail the discussion of data and research methods with colleagues. Discussions may also occur well after the research is complete, often because of interest following publication. If at all possible, it is in the interests of all research workers to ensure that original data are safely held for periods of at least five years.

(iii) Wherever possible, original data should be retained in the department or research unit in which they were generated. In some cases, such as when data are obtained from limited-access data bases, or in a contracted project, it may not be possible to hold them in this way. In such cases, a written indication of the location of the original data, or key information regarding the limited-access data base from which it was extracted, must be kept in the department or research unit. Individual researchers should be able to hold copies of the data for their own use. Retention solely by the individual research worker provides little protection to the research worker or the institution in the event of an allegation of falsification of data.

2. Publication and authorship

(i) Where there is more than one author of a publication, one author (by agreement among the authors) should formally accept overall responsibility for the entire publication. Such formal acceptance must be in writing, and kept on file in the department or unit of that author, together with names and signatures of all other authors.

(ii) The criteria for authorship of a publication must be determined and announced by each research unit or department. Minimum requirement for authorship would be participation in conceiving and/or executing and/or interpreting at least that part of the publication in a co-author's field of expertise, sufficient for him/her to take public responsibility for it. Each co-author must acknowledge his/her co-authorship in these terms, in writing, and that this must be kept on file in the department or unit of the responsible or executive author. This requirement must be met, at a minimum, by all authors signing a statement that they are "authors" of a specified publication in the terms defined by the research unit or department. Such statement must include an indication that there are no other "authors" of the publication, according to this definition. If, for any reason, one or more co-authors are unavailable or otherwise unable to sign the statement of authorship, the head of the research unit or department may sign on their behalf, noting the reason for their unavailability.

(iii) 'Honorary authorship' occurs when a person is listed as an author of a publication when he/she has not participated in a substantial way in conceiving and/or executing and/or interpreting at least part of the work described in the publication. 'Honorary authorship' is an unacceptable practice.

(iv) Due recognition of all participants is a part of a proper research process. Authors should ensure that the work of non-authors, including research assistants and technical officers is properly acknowledged.

(v) Publication of multiple papers based on the same set(s) or subset(s) of data is improper unless full cross-referencing occurs within the papers (for example, by reference to a preliminary publication at the time of publication of the complete work which grew from it). Simultaneous submission of papers based on the same set(s) or subsets(s) of data to more than one journal or publisher should be disclosed to each journal or publisher at the time of submission.

3. Student research trainee supervision

(i) Supervision of each research student/trainee investigator (including honours, masters, doctoral and junior postdoctoral research workers) should be assigned to a specific, responsible and appropriately qualified senior research worker in each research unit or department.

(ii) The ratio of students/trainees to supervisors should be small enough to assure effective scientific interaction, as well as effective supervision of the research at all stages.

(iii) Research supervisors should advise each trainee of applicable government and institutional guidelines for the conduct of research, including those covering ethical requirements for studies on human or animal subjects, and requirements for studies involving potentially hazardous agents.

APPENDIX C

(iv) Research supervisors should be primary sources of guidance to research students/trainees in the matters of sound scientific practice.

(v) As far as possible, research supervisors should ensure that the work submitted by research students/trainees is their own and that, where there are data, they are valid.

4. Disclosure of potential conflicts of interest

Institutions must have clearly formulated policies regarding potential conflicts of interest, because these may be detrimental to sound scientific practice, especially if undisclosed. Disclosures of such potential conflicts is therefore essential.

(i) Procedures regarding disclosure of affiliation with, or financial involvement in, any organization or entity with a direct interest in the subject matter or materials of research workers must be formulated and advertised within institutions. These procedures must cover the full range of interests. These would include those involving benefits in kind such as the provision of materials or facilities for the research, and support of individuals through provision of benefits (eg travel and accommodation expenses to attend conferences). The procedures should include guidelines on confidentiality of disclosures, and any limits on this. They should address the matter of disclosure of such interests to the editors of journals to which papers are submitted for consideration for publication (some editors require such disclosure now before consideration can commence), to the readers of published work, and to external bodies from which funds are sought.

(ii) The NH&MRC will require disclosure of all affiliations with, or financial involvement in, any organization or entity with a direct commercial interest in any research it supports, from 1991.

5. Procedures where serious departures from sound scientific practice may have occurred.

Scientific practice may fall short of desirably high standards in a variety of ways. At one end of the spectrum would be honest errors and various manifestations of carelessness, including poor record-keeping, or errors in the reading or calculation of data. At the other end of the spectrum would be scientific misconduct and fraud. Institutions may have in place provisions for dealing with a range of possible forms of misconduct. This document is concerned with misconduct that may undermine the credibility of research. Provisions for dealing with such misconduct may well be incorporated in the general framework of an Institution for dealing with misconduct, but some features of scientific misconduct requires special attention.

This NH&MRC Statement, and the closely related AVCC document on 'Guidelines on Responsible Practices in Research', aim to ensure a research environment that minimises the incidence of misconduct in research. It is inevitable, however that there will be some allegations of misconduct. It is essential that procedures for dealing with such allegations should be in place before the event.

Definitions:

"Misconduct" or "Scientific misconduct" is taken here to mean fabrication, falsification, plagiarism, or other practices that seriously deviate from those that are commonly accepted within the scientific community for proposing, conducting, or reporting research. It includes misleading ascription of authorship including the listing of authors

APPENDIX C

without their permission, attributing work to others who have not in fact contributed to the research, and the lack of appropriate acknowledgement of work primarily produced by a research student/trainee or associate. It does not include honest errors or honest differences in interpretation or judgements of data.

[What follows is a section which is common to this Statement, and the corresponding Section of the AVCC 'Guidelines', except where additions in <u>this</u> Statement occur, and these are in italics. It must be noted that this section of the NH&MRC and AVCC documents are compatible with clause 9 of the Australian Universities Academic Staff (Conditions of Employment) Award (Appendix A)].

The NH&MRC notes that the Academic Staff Award places great responsibility on the Chief Executive Officer of an Institution, and allows that person considerable discretion, especially regarding judgements about whether journals, funding organizations, and other possibly affected parties are advised about findings of preliminary and formal investigations. There is a potential conflict of interest here for a Chief Executive Officer, as he/she is likely to be conscious of possible adverse publicity for his/her Institution if misconduct is alleged or proven. Some cases of misconduct overseas have been dealt with unsatisfactorily because of failure of Institutions to advise funding agencies and journals of instances of misconduct. The NH&MRC would prefer that the Chief Executive Officer was not given the central role provided for in the Australian Universities Academic Staff Award. For institutions not covered by that Award, the NH&MRC prefers the following guidelines to read "an independent person, nominated and announced by the Chief Executive Officer", wherever the Chief Executive Officer is specified.

PROCEDURES

Protection of interested parties

Allegations of research misconduct require very careful handling. When an allegation is made, the protection of all interested parties is essential.

Interested parties may include:

- The person bringing the allegation.
- The staff member against whom a complaint is made.
- Research students and staff working with the staff member concerned.
- Journals in which allegedly fraudulent papers have been or are about to be published.
- Funding bodies which have contributed to the research.
- In some cases the public — for example if a drug is involved.

Adequate protection of the complainant and the accused demands absolute confidentiality and reasonable speed in the early stages of investigation. On the other hand, the protection of other parties may involve some disclosure. Such judgements should be made by the Chief Executive Officer.

5.1 The receipt of complaints

Allegations of misconduct in research may originate inside the institutions, from other institutions, in learned journals or in the press. Allegations from outside the institution should be dealt with directly by the Chief Executive Officer. Inside the

APPENDIX C

institution, allegations may come from other members of staff or from research students. The latter may feel themselves to be in a difficult situation because of their degree and their future career can depend on interaction with a supervisor.

(a)   Advisers on integrity in research

Institutions should nominate several persons to be advisers on integrity in research who are familiar with the literature and guidelines on research misconduct. Their task should be to give confidential advice to staff and students about what constitutes misconduct in research, and the rights and responsibilities of a potential complainant, and the procedures for dealing with allegations or research misconduct within the institution.

(b)   Designated people to receive formal complaints

There should be a small number of designated people to whom allegations are to be made. These should be senior academics experienced in research and preferably from different discipline areas and should be a mix of males and females. It is important that the Chief Executive Officer should be informed immediately a complaint is received and be kept informed as the case progresses.

A designated person should consider the material provided by the complainant and should decide whether the allegation should be dismissed or investigated further. If a preliminary investigation is to proceed, it must be authorised by the Chief Executive Officer.

5.2   The preliminary investigation

If there is the possibility of a charge of misconduct, the Chief Executive Officer must organise a preliminary investigation and then take action in accordance with the provisions of subclause 9(c) of the Australian Universities Academic Staff (Conditions of Employment) Award 1988.

ACTION WITH STAFF MEMBER CONCERNED

(a)   As good practice, if there is to be a preliminary investigation of the allegation under subclause 9(c) of the Award, the staff member concerned should be informed in writing and given an opportunity to respond in writing. The name of the complainant should not be released.

(b)   The Chief Executive Officer may require the staff member to produce experimental data files or other material to be kept secure, but not disclosed during the preliminary investigation.

FORM OF THE INVESTIGATION

(a)   The form of the preliminary investigation will depend on the case and must be decided by the Chief Executive Officer. The Chief Executive Officer must have the power to conduct the preliminary investigation in person if that is appropriate. In some cases, there will need to be a small committee from inside the institution from areas not affected by the research in question. In other cases, it may be necessary to seek expert help from outside the institution.

(b)   The Preliminary investigation should be limited to determining whether a sufficient case exists for formal charges of misconduct to be laid.

APPENDIX C

ACTION ON COMPLETION OF THE PRELIMINARY INVESTIGATION

(a) No case exists

 (i) If no case is found to exist, the staff member concerned should be informed that there will be no further action taken and the conclusion should be recorded on his or her file, as far as possible, in a form satisfactory to the staff member.

 (ii) If it is considered that the complainant has brought charges improperly, the complainant should be disciplined. If the charges were reasonably brought but incorrect, the case should cease.

 (iii) The Chief Executive Officer will need to exercise judgement at this point to determine whether there are individuals or organisations that need to be informed. This will depend on the degree of confidentiality that has been achieved.

(b) A case is seen to exist

If the preliminary investigation finds cause for further investigation this should be commenced as soon as possible. The first step is the provision of particulars to the staff member in writing. The staff member has thirty days to respond, also in writing. The Chief Executive Officer will need to consider whether the staff member should be suspended from all or part of his or her duties at the point when particulars are supplied. If further investigation leads to the staff member being cleared of charges, the same considerations arise as if no case had existed requiring further investigation (see above).

If the staff member is in receipt of a grant from an external funding agency, the Chief Executive Officer will advise the Secretary of that agency, in confidence, that a case is being formally investigated, on the understanding that the funding agency will not terminate a grant until the outcome of the formal investigation is known, although it may choose to suspend funds in the meantime.

5.3 The formal investigation

AWARD PROCEDURES

Formal procedures for dealing with misconduct are governed by clause 9 of the Australian Universities Academic Staff (Conditions of Employment) Award 1988 (Appendix A). Subclauses 9(e) to (q) set out the legal requirements.

SPECIAL REQUIREMENTS

There are other matters which need to be considered in setting up adequate procedures for dealing with a formal investigation into research fraud or misconduct.

(a) Section 9(i) of the Award provides for a three person Committee including a nominee of the Chief Executive Officer, a nominee of the President of the local branch of the union and senior member of the legal profession or a person with appropriate experience in industrial relations appointed by agreement between the Chief Executive Officer and President.

(b) The Committee should have access to legal advice and expert advice on the research subject. The institution should pay for this advice and ensure that the committee members are indemnified.

(c) While confidentiality remains important during a formal investigation, other matters may take precedence.

    (i) It is important to protect the accused. If the charges are dismissed, he or she will need to be reinstated with a clean record. A charge of misconduct could damage a person's future prospects and defamation action could result unless procedures laid down are carefully followed.

    (ii) It is important to protect the complainant. There is a possibility of victimisation which could seriously affect their career.

    (iii) There may in some circumstances be a reason to inform the publishers of a journal that the authenticity of a paper or papers is in doubt. A false paper may be dangerous to the community.

It is not possible in advance to state what should happen. The adjudicating body in the formal investigation must determine what should be made public and when, bearing in mind the interests of all concerned.

(d) If allegations are made which appear to cast doubt on the validity of one or more research publications produced by a staff member, it may be necessary to investigate the person's past research as well as that covered by the allegations.

(e) If the claim of research misconduct has been substantiated, it is important that the position of research students and staff working with the accused be clarified. In some cases, if there has been misconduct, it may be necessary to provide compensation to innocent people who have been affected.

Action following the formal investigation

(a) If a person is found guilty, the institution should take disciplinary action quickly. Relevant publishers and sponsoring agencies should be notified.

(b) If a person is found to be innocent, action may be needed to redress any damage resulting from the allegations.

(c) (i) If an external funding body was advised of a formal investigation made under Section 5.2 'Action on completion of the preliminary investigation' (b) above and the staff member has been exonerated, then the external funding body will be advised accordingly.

    (ii) If the staff member has been found guilty and is in receipt of a grant from an external funding body or bodies, currently, or was so when the alleged misconduct occurred, or is currently an applicant for a grant from an external body or bodies, then the Chief Executive Officer of the institution must provide the Secretary(ies) the external funding or body or bodies with a full written report of the formal investigation.

Action if the accused resigns

Subclause 9(q) of the Academic Staff Award states that if a staff member charged with serious misconduct resigns, procedures should cease. The institution cannot take any further action against the staff member.

It is not necessarily satisfactory for an enquiry into scientific misconduct to be abandoned if a resignation is received. Almost always others will have been affected or will be affected perhaps very seriously, unless the facts are determined. It should therefore be part of an institution's procedures that, in the event of resignation, an enquiry is convened to report on the status of the research and on any remedial action needed to protect affected people and the public. Those who need to be considered are listed in this document under section 5, 'Procedures, Protection of Interested Parties'. External funding bodies that supported the research or the research worker concerned must receive the report on the status of the research and the remedial action recommended.

[Passed by Council November 1990]

Index

Abbs, James 22
Accountability 2
Action, three levels 181–2
Ada, Gordon 153
Aiding and abetting 101–2
Alsabti, E A K 7–8, 119, 166
Ambition 174–5
American Association for the Advancement of Science 19
Anonymity 124, 167
Antisocial conduct, and law 101
Aronow, William 11
Asche, Austin 145
Association of American Medical Colleges 19
Association of American Universities 19
Assocation of the British Pharmaceutical Industry 29, 48, 58
  policies 89–90
  role 75, 77, 78
Astra Clinical Research Unit 88
Attitudes
  editorial 170
  Europe versus United States 53–4
  France 108
  public 121, 156
  scientists 82, 118, 121, 173
Audit 6, 55, 109
  in academic institutions 111–12
  data 6, 38–40, 61, 163–4
  drug trials 128–41
  external 164
  for-cause 6, 57, 130
  trial materials 36
Australia 6–7, 142–57
Australian Academy of Science 149
Australian Vice-Chancellors' Committee 149
Authorship 14, 161–2, 170, 171
  coauthors 19
  gift authorship 12, 19, 153, 162
  multiauthorship 2

Bak, Martin 15
Ballart, Isidro 16, 120
Baltimore, David 13, 18, 120
Berger, Philip A 14
Blind review 167–8
Bonnes Pratiques Cliniques 112, 113
Bonnes Pratiques de Fabrication 112, 113
Borer, Jeffrey S 18
Boyle, Robert 158
Braunwald, Eugene 10, 11
Breach of contract 104–5
Breuning, Stephen 13–14, 163
Bridges, C David 14, 166
Briggs, Michael 6, 143–6
British Medical Association 48
British Medical Journal 151, 166
Buck and Goulsmit 120
Burger, Henry 143
Burnet, Sir MacFarlane 153
Burt, Sir Cyril 5

Case record forms 38–9
Cases of misconduct 7–16, 28–9, 33–4, 36–8, 39, 45–6, 81–9, 142–51
Causes 2
  See also Motives
Cheating, student 177
Christensen, Bent 122
Civil prosecution 80
Clinical research, detecting fraud in 31–40, 54–8
Clinical trials
  audit of materials 36
  control of 100
  detecting fraud 54–8
  pharmaceutical companies 25, 30
Coauthors 19
Codes of practice 3
Coincidence 156
Commission, acts of 43–4, 179
Committee on Safety of Medicines 44

197

INDEX

Communication, and legal process 96–7
Confidentiality 48
Conflict of interest 10
Conolly, Art 8
Contract, breach of 104–5
Contract research organisations 44, 50–60
Contracts
 competition for 138
 contract research organisations 59–60
 terms 104, 105
Cook's distance 70
Cort, Joseph 10
Costing 60
Crabb, Barbara 22
Criminal fraud 14, 42, 100–2

Danish Medical Research Council, initiative 177–22
Darsee, John 10, 17, 153, 162, 163, 164
Data
 checking 38–9, 61, 163–4
  graphical methods 66, 68, 72
  statistical methods 65–6, 66–8, 68–72
 different meanings from 2
 falsification 179
 feel for 34
 fraudulent 61–2, 64–5
 genuine 62–4
 invented 64–5
 manipulated 54–5, 64
 modifications 135
 monitoring 34–5
 raw 66
 statistical analysis 159
 time sequence 72
 unreliability 137
 variability 63, 64, 67
 verification 39–40, 48, 92
Data Analysis and Research Limited 86
Data massage 119
Debendox/Bendectin 147, 155–6
Deceit, claiming damages for 104
Defamation 92–5
Defences against fraud 152
Demedluk, Paul P 15
Denmark 116–27

Detection 31–40, 166, 178–81
 in clinical reseearch 54–8
 statistical aspects 61–74
 versus prevention 30–1
Digit preference 63
Dingell, John 13, 20
Disciplining 182
Disclosure 6
 official 109
 pharmaceutical companies 50–1, 53, 57, 76
Drug trials
 penalty for misconduct 138
 See also Pharmaceutical industry
Drylabbing 133
Due process 19, 22, 139, 152
Duplicate publication 111, 160, 162–3

Eagan, George E 16
Editorial process 160–4
Editors
 and retraction 167
 role 158–72
 statistical hints for 72–4
Edsall report 19
Eisen, Herman 13, 18
Elliot, Russell 145
Empires, of scientific departments 153
Error 55
 prevention 46–7
 versus fraud 43
Ethics committees 100
 role 40
European Commission 47
 guidelines 75, 76, 99–100
Evidence 55

Facts, verification 92
False negatives 74
False positives 74
Fast recruiters 53
Feder, Ned 13, 164
Felig, Philip 9
Financial aspects 3, 60, 104–5, 161, 175, 176
Fisons 86
Flier, Jeffery 10
Food and Drug Administration 47, 54, 163
 audit programme 129–32, 136

drug trials   128
powers   58
Foundation 41   146, 148, 149
Fox, Sir Theodore   158
France   108–14
Francis, Kollunnar   8, 85–6
Fraud
  classic features   11, 12, 14, 142
  continuum   54, 120
  definition   118, 129
  giveaway signs   32, 35
  range   1
Fraudsters, personality   16–17, 154, 176
Frazier, Shervert   14
French, Jill   146, 148
Friedman, Paul   19, 169
Fudging   135, 140
Funder, John   151, 154

Gallo case   120
General Medical Council   6, 29, 42, 48, 58
  disciplinary procedures   78–80, 105–6
  preliminary proceedings committee   79
  professional conduct committee   79–80
  referral to   105
General practice, research in   42–3
Gibbs, Sir Harry   149
Gift authorship   12, 19, 153, 162
Glaxo Pharmaceuticals   82, 85
Glueck, Charles   12
Gonsai, R B   9, 86–9
Good, Robert   9
Good clinical practice   43
  and ethics committees   100
  main tenets   54
Gottlieb, Jeffrey   8
Greed   16, 26–7
Green, Harold   18
Greenberg, Daniel   20
Guidelines   19–20, 48
  Association of the British Pharmaceutical Industry   75, 76
  Australia   151–2, 187–95
  European Commission   54, 75, 76, 99–100
  France   108, 112
  good clinical practice, European Commission   54

pharmaceutical industry   40–1
refereeing   167
Royal College of Physicians   20
universities   121
See also Policies, Protocols
Gullis, Robert   7, 120
Gupta, Viswa   5

Hadley, Suzanne   21
Hallum, Jules   21
Hart, Ernest   171
Harvard Medical School   153

Identification of fraud,
  France   108–11
Imalas technique   119
Imanishi-Kari, Theresa   13, 120
Imipramine   147, 156
Inaction *See* Disclosure
Incompetence   135–7, 137
  See also Error, Omission
Influence, statistical   70
Initiation visits   32
Inliers   71
Intent   118, 136
International Committee of Medical Journal Editors   20, 154, 162
  statement   169
Intervention, political   121
Investigation
  Danish system   122–5
  procedures   96–7
  See also Audit, Data checking
Investigator agreement   30–1
Investigators, clinical
  See Researchers
Invisible colleges   159

Jevons, Fred   144, 145
Journals
  France   111
  on line   159, 170
  scientific, evolution   158–60
  specialty   159, 170
Junior staff   31, 32, 33
  as authors   167
  supervision   12, 177
Justice, principles of   95–6

Knightly, Phillip   149
Knowhow, absence of   110
Kumar, Sheo   9

INDEX

La Revue Prescrire 111
LaFollette, Marcel 11, 18, 166
Langman, Jan 148
Latta, David 9, 88–9
Legal aspects
  England and Wales 91–107
  France 113
Legal process 80
  civil law 102–5
  criminal law 100–2
Leverage 70
Libel 93–4
Lisook, Alan 11, 130
Litigation 102–5, 152
  funding 104–5
Lock, Stephen 151
Long, John 10
Longitudal review 35

McBride, William 7, 119, 146–50, 154, 155–6
Mahalanobis distance 71
Malice 94
Malpractice 17
  France 112
  See also Fraud, Misconduct
Management style, negative effects 120
Medawar, Sir Peter 9, 17
Media
  responsibility 157
  role of 144, 152
Medical Act 1983 78
Medical and Clinical Research Consultants 82, 85
Medical inspectors 114
Medical Practitioners' Act 149
Medical records 48
Medicines Control Agency 98
Medicines Regulations 1971 98
Mendel, genetic experiments 72
Milanese, Claudio 12–13
Misconduct
  continuum 160, 161
  reducing 137–9
Misinformation 1
Misrepresentation, and civil action 103
Misrepresentation Act (1967) 104
Mistakes *See* Errors
Mitchell, Lonnie 15
Model, statistical 69

Monitoring 55
  check list 58–9
  pointers in 55–6
Monitors, duties under European Commission guidelines 99
Montesquieu 122, 125
Motives 16–17, 26–7, 44, 62, 174–7
Multiauthorship 2
Multiple publication 2
Munchausen's syndrome 154

Naito, Herbert K 15
National Health and Medical Research Council 149, 151
National Library of Medicine 124, 170
National Science Foundation 22
Nelson, Douglas 14–15
Nossal, Sir Gustav 153

Office of Scientific Integrity 21–2
Office of Scientific Integrity Review 21
Omission, acts of 43, 179
Online Journal of Clinical Trials 159, 170
Open reviewing 167
O'Toole, Margot 13, 18
Outliers 66, 70

Pandit, Lakshmi 9, 83–5
Patients, implication for 14
Paulos, John 156
Peckham initiative 3
Peer pressure 26
Peer review 10, 152, 158, 164–6
  blind 167–8
  France 111, 114
  open 167
  See also Referees
Performance indicators 2
Personality disorders 176
Pharmaceutical industry, United Kingdom
  clinical research in 25, 30
  disclosure of fraud 50–1, 53, 57, 109
  inaction, reasons for 76
  information sharing 77
  payments 176
  relation with doctors 27–9, 44, 50
  research fraud 25–41

INDEX

short cuts   26
United Kingdom, response   75–90
Piltdown man   5
Plagiarism   1, 180
Police   101
Policies
  Association of the British
    Pharmaceutical Industry   89–90
  Office of Scientific Integrity   22
  pharmaceutical companies   75
  See also Guidelines, Protocols
Porter, Robert   149
Prasad, Ashoka 7, 150–1,   154
Pressure   174–7
Prestige   11
Prevention   47–9, 126, 153–4, 177–8
  versus detection   30–1
Privilege
  legal professional   97
  qualified   94, 96–100
Procedures
  investigative   153
  National Science Foundation   22
  Office of Scientific Integrity   21, 22
  written   96
Productivity   12
Proof, standards of   4
Prosecution   77–81, 95
  civil   80
Protocols   46–7
Pseudologia fantastica   154
Public, scientific knowledge   156
Public arena   20–3
Publication
  France   114
  policy   110–11
  pressure   3, 175
  publish or perish   153
  purpose   159–60
  quality versus quantity   2
Publication bias   62
Purves, Michael   8

Quality
  in contract research
    organisations   53
  versus quantity   2, 3
Quality control, France   114

Ramsay, Margery   145
Range, statistical   65, 67
Record keeping   153

Referees   3
  anonymity   167
  codes for   166–8
  fraudulent behaviour   166
  role   165
  statistical hints for   72–4
  See also Peer review
Regulatory law, obligations under   97–100
Rehabilitation   154
Relman, Arnold   160
Replication   140, 152
Research
  in general practice   3
  in pharmaceutical companies   25
  See also Clinical trials, Drug trials
Researchers
  career structure   2, 3
  duties under EC guidelines   99
  good clinical practice   113–14
  health problems   176–7
  job description   31
  legal protection   91
  licensing   137
  principal   32, 46
  reaction   17–23
  recruitment   58
  suspension   139
  training   3, 137–8
Residuals   70, 72
Responses, institutional   19
Retraction   168–70
Rewards   3, 17
Rigour, scientific   170, 174
Rincover, Arnold   15
Rosner, Mitchell   16
Rossiter, Jim   142–4, 146
Royal College of Physicians   1, 20, 76
Royane, Charles   151
Russian roulette phenomenon   155

Safety information reporting   97–9
Salami technique   119
Sample size   68
Samples, preparation   108, 109, 112–13
Sanctions, Denmark   125–6
Santo, Russell P   16
Scatter plots   72
Schmaltz lobby   155
Scientists   *See* Researchers
Sedgwick, J P   7

Serious professional
  misconduct 79–80
Shimokawa, Hiroaki 15
Short, Roger 149
Siddiqui, V A 6, 8, 81–2
Significance, statistical 4, 62
Singhal, Rakesh 16
Slander 93, 94–5
Slutsky, Robert 11–12, 19, 153, 163, 166, 168–9
Snow, C P 18
Social sciences, and medicine 2
Soman, Vijay 9–10, 120, 163, 166
Source documents, verification 54, 55
Spector, Mark 10, 17
Stahl, Stephen 14
Standard operating procedure 31, 183–5
  in contracts 60
Statistical aspects 61–74
Statutory declaration 186
Stem and leaf plots 66, 67
Stewart, Walter 13, 164
Straus, Marc J 9
Summerlin, William 5, 9, 17–18
Sunday Times 144
Supervisors 177
Supply of Goods and Services Act 1982 104
Suspected fraud, action on 57–8

Terry, L Cass 15
Thalidomide 147
Trials, clinical 25, 30, 36, 54–8, 100, 113–14
  conduct of, France 113–14
Trust, climate of 11

United Kingdom 58
  fraud in general practice 42–9
  known or suspected misconduct 7–9
  pharmaceutical industry response 75–90
  university system 2
United States
  initiatives 121
  known or suspected misconduct 9–16
  public hearings 20
Universities, Australia 143

Validation statements 169
Van Thiel, David H 15
Vancouver group *See* International Committee of Medical Journal Editors
Vardy, Phil 146–7, 148
Verification 120
  facts 92
  source documents 54, 55
Visits 32, 34

Wachslicht-Rodbard, Helena 10
Walqvist, Mark 143, 144
Wells, Frank 6, 54
Wheelock, E F 8
Whistleblowers 18, 152, 160
Wierda, Daniel 8
Wild, Ronald 7